CW00665914

The
Empowered
Empath

OWNING, EMBRACING AND

MANAGING YOUR SPECIAL GIFTS

Rose Rosetree

Women's Intuition Worldwide
Sterling, Virginia

The Empowered Empath
OWNING, EMBRACING AND MANAGING YOUR GIFTS

PUBLISHER'S CATALOGING-IN-PUBLICATION

Rosetree, Rose.

Empowered empath : owning, embracing and managing your gifts / Rose Rosetree.

322 pages ; 14 x 21.59 centimeters cm. — (An Empath Empowerment® Books series ; book 2)

Issued also as an ebook and in a "Quick & Easy" abridged edition.

Includes bibliographical references and index in an online supplement.

ISBN-13: 978-1-935214-32-8

ISBN-10: 1-935214-32-2

1. Empathy. 2. Intuition. 3. Sensitivity (Personality trait) 4. Self-actualization (Psychology) 5. Aura. 6. Self-help techniques. 7. Consciousness. I. Adaptation of (work) Rosetree, Rose. Empowered by empathy, 25 ways to fly in spirit. II. Title.

BF575.E55 R67 2014   158/.2

ISBN: 978-1-935214-32-8

LCCN: 2014939379

Please direct all correspondence and inquiries to

Women's Intuition Worldwide, LLC
116 Hillsdale Drive, Sterling, VA 20164-1201
rights@rose-rosetree.com
703-450-9514

Visit our website: www.rose-rosetree.com

Dedication

Drip. Drip. Drip. In the apartment where you live, the faucet leaks. It always has.

That kitchen sink overflows, making puddles, causing a mess.

Shoes get wet a lot. Fine, you can cope with that. But mysterious problems happen too, like how your bedroom slippers sometimes get wet.

Really the answer is simple. Certain nights you get up for a midnight snack and you're thinking "Food" not "Puddles." Slippers get wet from that totally forgettable trip to the kitchen. Later you notice how your bedroom slippers have developed patches of wetness. It creeps you out.

Strange new problems come up all the time. You complain to your best friend, "There's a horrible smell of mold in my apartment. And I can't stop that leaky kitchen faucet from dripping."

"Just turn it off. That's what I do." says your friend.

This advice doesn't help one bit. What are you supposed to do now? You cope on your own, that's what.

So you place fans in certain strategic places. You figure out how to use hairdryers for a quick fix. Certain skin lotions help better than others for dealing with all your rashes from all the dampness.

In the back of your mind, you are constantly monitoring all that dampness.

Look, this faucet analogy is not about some hypothetical person and a hopeless problem. It's about you.

You may have a fairly common problem that afflicts 1 in 20 people. That problem is being born as an empath.

Your lifelong talent can be so special, helpful, delightful, embrace-able... provided that you learn how to use it with skill. Being born with empath *talent* is different from having *skill*. All empaths are born talented. Skills must be learned. That's what you can learn here. You'll be able to learn just fine.

Really, it's a privilege, having the equivalent of an extra faucet in your kitchen sink. I will help you learn how to work that faucet.

As a result, you will stop having certain problems. You certainly won't have to work so hard at coping. If you have been blaming yourself, soon you'll stop. Every empath's faucet is installed dripping. That's just how they're made.

Guess what else? The liquid from your special empath's faucet is magnificent. Think fine wine. Think a really superb kind of vino that you could use for personal entertaining and even decant at work, gaining ever-greater prestige and success.

You see, what you have is the equivalent of an *extra* faucet in your home. Your empath talent is precious. I'm going to help you to own this very human talent of yours, then embrace it and manage it... to support every other good thing about your life.

Table of Contents

Online Supplement at www.rose-rosetree.com

Glossary — Recommended Reading — Index

Table of Empath Gifts

Techniques Designed for Empath Empowerment®

PART ONE

Owning Your Empath Gifts

An EMPATH is someone with at least one significant gift for directly experiencing what it is like to be another person. Many different empath gifts are possible, but the process of developing empath skill is identical whether you were born with one empath gift or many.

Whichever of these 15 special empath gifts you have, it was installed on the day you were born. Installed fully switched ON.

Don't just cope with that special talent. Make it work for you. I can teach you how, and it won't take much effort.

In fact, a skilled empath works way less hard than somebody who never learned this skill set.

Most unskilled empaths work very hard indeed. Maybe that includes you.

- Some empaths create their own workarounds, like using hairdryers in the dripping faucet analogy.
- Some empaths have created support groups, or found help online where they share tips and tricks to help them cope.
- Some empaths have studied with experts who don't prevent problems but, instead, help empaths adjust to the problems that come from being unskilled.
- All this can keep an empath busy and hopeful. Very busy, yet still unskilled.

Skill! Have you noticed how I keep using that word SKILL?

What kind of skill matters for an empath?

Not psychological boundary work or anything about behavior.

Not energy work to clean up the mess from being an unskilled empath.

Not avoiding energies of negative or overwhelming people. (With appropriate skill, an empath can go anywhere while remaining energetically protected.)

Which kind of skill do empaths need? It comes from using your AWARENESS, a gentle way of being awake inside. Ever since you were born, all your waking hours, you have had awareness. That subtle yet dependable awareness is there for you every single day of your life, available as soon as you wake up and think something like, "Hello, earth. Here I go again."

Thanks to awareness, you know whatever you know. You see whatever you see. You feel whatever you feel.

What, you already know about awareness?

Some of you empaths may have spent years actively exploring awareness (a.k.a. consciousness). Maybe you learned about it through yoga or meditation or prayer. All that experience can make it extra easy to learn empath skills.

Alternatively, you might have learned about awareness through studying energy. Maybe you learned Reiki. Or studied intuitive development. Or you work religiously with your angels. Or you work religiously at an Official Religion. Or you get along just fine with your own brand of disorganized religion.

With all due respect, none of that is expressly designed to help empaths, so put it aside for now. Prepare for success by bringing BEGINNER'S MIND, exploring as if for the first time. Trust your regular, everyday awareness. It is an amazing resource, ever fresh.

What if you are a beginner at anything about awareness?

No worries. You're starting clean and I'll teach you clean.

Being born as an empath doesn't mean that you have to like far-out New Age anything. So far you may have resisted Energy Talk with all your might. Well, becoming a skilled empath doesn't have to change that, not much.

What will I give you? Practical knowledge about energy. That will have to include some technical terms, used precisely, because I think like an engineer in this field. Rest assured, techie terms that will be introduced to you are no weirder than the word "Internet."

What won't I give you? Unnecessary extras. No radically changing your lifestyle or asking you to wear crystals or start channeling a ghost who claims to be a big deal from back in Atlantis.

Empath skills are simply skills. Like learning to tie your shoelaces or use a mobile phone.

Comfortable Pacing

Expect that. I'll aim for that.

First I will coach you to own your gifts, then how to embrace them, then how to manage them.

To pace this book for your needs, Q&A sections will be included, drawn from my experience teaching empath students worldwide: Beginner questions, fancy questions, heartfelt questions, the kind of ironic questions that come naturally if you are Gen X, Gen Y, a Millennial, or otherwise gifted with sarcasm.

Of course, the first thing is to wrap your mind around what it means — really means — to be an empath. The first thing and also our first official chapter!

CHAPTER 1

Different Empath Gifts, Different Problems

MALLED is one word for it, that strangely mutilated psychic state that some of us suffer after a trip to the mall. Emily always gets malled. Returning home after a shopping trip, she feels like an emotional basket case. No wonder she usually stays home instead.

"How can kids hang out at the malls just for fun?" Emily sighs.

(Note: Quotations throughout this book come from memory. Anecdotes are true, just not reported with court transcript accuracy. Also, first names used here are fictitious unless paired with last names. The dialogues in upcoming Q&A sections will be either reconstructed or fictitious, based on my experience teaching Empath Empowerment.)

Back at Emily, it isn't so much that she's curious how kids handle the malls. More like she's trying to divert attention. "How can kids hang out at the malls just for fun?"

It's hard for Emily not to blame herself. Millions of people — most people so far as she knows — don't find shopping a major ordeal. So what's wrong with her?

Talent as an empath is the problem, talent that Emily hasn't yet learned to use on purpose. Many unskilled empaths interpret their talent negatively, inappropriately calling themselves names like "Over-sensitive," "Neurotic," or "Co-dependent."

Ridiculous, Brave Empath! You have a gift. It's tricky but, with skill, you can purposely use that gift to fly in spirit.

BRAVE EMPATH, that is what I will be calling you in this book as I coach you in empath skills.

You are brave. Otherwise you wouldn't have been attracted to this system for helping empaths. Plenty of other books exist to console empaths who feel like victims. It takes uncommon courage to embrace who you are, to pursue skills that can abolish empath-related suffering, and to claim the leadership role that is rightfully yours.

Yes, leadership role. Of all the skill sets I teach, Empath Empowerment is my very favorite because that leadership is so important. Granted, before you gain skills as an empath, you may not feel much like a leader at all. You might feel more like John.

A Second Example of Being an Unskilled Empath

John first discovered his talent as an empath one lovely spring morning in 1994. He woke up feeling suicidal. "Don't get me wrong," John told me afterwards. "I have my ups and downs like everyone else. But this feeling was different.

"For years Greg has been my hero at the newspaper where we work. You could call him my mentor. That morning, a friend of ours called me to say that Greg was in bad shape. The day before, I wasn't at work. Greg was. And apparently the pressure got to him.

"He walked into the newsroom and lost control. You know those things that you can say to people, the things that are true but unforgivable? Well, he said them all.

"The morning after, Greg didn't know how to go on. So those suicidal feelings I was noticing? They belonged to him, not me. "Eventually Greg managed to pull himself together. The feelings passed for us both. But I'll never forget that episode because it served as a kind of initiation. Ever since, I have known that I had empath talent. Every day I connect to other people's pain. I have learned to accept this. Only I sure wish I could use my empath talent for happy things, too."

That's where empath skills make such a difference. You don't have to pick up other people's pain. You don't have to accept this as a necessary consequence of being sensitive.

Brave Empath, skills can make the difference. With skills of EMPATH EMPOWERMENT®, it will become a habit to keep your empath gifts turned OFF. That's right, skills expressly designed to help empaths will allow you to break the drip-drip-drip habit of having empath gifts perpetually turned ON.

Afterwards I can teach you dedicated techniques to turn your empath gifts ON — at will — with Skilled Empath Merge. That use of your gifts can take you deeper and bigger and clearer than ever before. This is a skill when you purposely fly in spirit. Technically you know what you're doing. And how to do it. Who chooses when to turn that experience OFF or ON? You alone.

My name for that kind of experience, turning empath gifts ON, is SKILLED EMPATH MERGE. Which sure is a contrast to what unskilled empaths do (including me back in the day).

Not only are an unskilled empath's gifts habitually turned ON. Innumerable times each day, that talented empath slips into unskilled empath merge. Most of these are subconscious, super-quick travels in consciousness; you'll be learning about the various types.

Various types? Yes, you read that right. Moreover, each unskilled empath merge adds up to that drip-drip-drip kind of helplessness you may know all too well. Soon you will learn about different types of unskilled empath merge and, especially, you will learn how to prevent them. So fear not. Your life is about to become so much easier.

⁓ I will show you how to stop those unskilled empath merges.

- Later I can help you learn to do the safe, skilled kind.
- Afterwards some lifestyle suggestions can be useful.

Note the order, Brave Empath. Because it is much more common for empaths to be offered lifestyle suggestions only. In my opinion, that puts the cart before the horse. Actually, there isn't any horse. How useful is it, attempting lifestyle changes before you get basic empath skills? That doesn't work very well, except for providing an interesting hobby. Do you really need a never-ending form of psychological busywork?

Ha, I thought not. By contrast, effective skills will require relatively little time and take zero effort.

A Third Example of Being an Unskilled Empath

Back at examples of real-life empath students, let's turn to William. He suffered from problems related to a different form of empath talent than Emily's or John's. Until recently, William blamed himself for being a hypochondriac.

"I would go into a business meeting and come out with weird ailments. For years I thought I was making this up. Eventually I realized the aches and pains were real, only they belonged to other people, not me.

"A woman where I work suffers from migraines. When they start to hit, this woman, Ellen, is in such denial about her body, she has no clue. By the time she notices anything wrong, her headache has become a full-blown migraine and so she has to go to the emergency room.

"Finally I connected all this with me. When we're together at work and her symptoms start, who else gets a headache? Me. It's her headache but I'm sharing it.

"Sound crazy? Then get what we do now: At *my* first sign of a headache, I call Ellen and say, '*You* have a headache. Go take your medicine.' Now it never gets to the point where she has to go to the hospital.

"Great, I'm glad to help Ellen. But she never pays me to be her doctor or headache wearer. How can I stop taking on people's physical symptoms when I don't want to?"

Many so-called "hypochondriacs" are really volunteers who connect empathically with other people's health problems. Having a gift for receiving this kind of information becomes far more enjoyable when you learn to use the on-and-off switch.

Altogether, wishing to have control over your empath talent is healthy. Just because you have a gift doesn't mean you must be a slave to it, perpetually on call. The solution is to use empath talent in a way that empowers you.

Most empaths don't have experiences as extreme as those of William, John, or Emily. On the other hand, you may be misinterpreting pesky problems in your life due to unskilled empath talent. Undoubtedly you're underestimating the joys of using your empath gifts on purpose.

Curious about Empowerment?

Whatever makes you curious about being an empath, there's one thing you have in common with my other students: Talent that deserves to be nurtured.

There is no one talent or type of problem that all empaths have. So maybe you're wondering:

1. How can I tell for sure if I am an empath?
2. What are the different empath gifts, and which do I have?
3. How can I learn to switch my empath gifts OFF for most of the time?
4. How can different techniques switch my empath gifts ON most strongly?

5. How can I best protect myself as an empath?

6. I sense that living as an empath could be the basis for important kinds of spiritual service. Is that true? How can I do that more? How can I do that *safely*?

I'll help you to answer these questions and more with this Empath Empowerment Series. *The Empowered Empath* will help you to answer Questions 1, 2, 3, and 5. *The Master Empath* will provide juicy answers to the two remaining questions, information that must come later. This sequence for learning will make sense to you if you agree with sayings like "You've got to walk before you can run."

One thing's for sure. If you're reading this book, it's a little late to choose whether or not you would like to *be* an empath. Assuming that you're reading of your own free will, chances are that you qualify — although probably not yet as a *skilled* empath.

I'm glad to help. Systematically I will help you to develop Empath Empowerment, skills that have helped thousands of empaths before you, with results that have ranged from merely satisfying to downright transformational.

CHAPTER 2

Owning, Not Moaning

Grant is a skilled empath today. Unfortunately it took him a while to find this Program for Empath Empowerment.

Before then, he signed up for a series of teleclasses for empaths. Participants recounted their sad tales. Since there was no video, Grant couldn't tell for sure. Probably, though, he was the only one not crying. The teacher included.

Every meeting, class discussion focused on being an empath as if it were some kind of disability.

Those "Poor, sensitive empaths" were taught to console themselves by taking baths and monitoring the wretched state of their auras. They were coached to use crystals for clean-up, fixing themselves energetically — again and again and again.

As you prepare to own your empath gifts, it might be time for some lifestyle decluttering. In case you're wondering, how much time will you need for daily aura rehab as an Empowered Empath?

Usually none. Occasionally you might use *"Empath's First Aid."* With experience as a skilled empath, even that quick-and-easy technique won't be used very often.

Skills make the difference. Effective skills as an empath will prevent random energies from other people knocking your aura out of balance.

Instead of perpetual cleanup, let's start something proactive... learning.

Introduction to Empath Skills 101

Personally, I wish Empath Skills 101 had been part of my formal education along with reading, writing, and arithmetic. Today's elementary school children aren't taught about empath talent yet, although many today are told about empathy.

As you can read in Daniel Goleman's *Emotional Intelligence*, being taught that Dick and Jane have feelings, "just like mine," can produce feelings of empathy. Sure, Goleman's EMOTIONAL INTELLIGENCE is a good kind of training in itself. Of course it is socially useful, learning how to name your emotions correctly. Also useful? Finding out how to stick the correct emotional label onto other people's behavior.

Emotional intelligence and empathy can improve manners, which is nothing to sneeze at (especially without covering your mouth). However, becoming skilled as an empath is totally different from learning either of these social skills.

EMPATH TALENT, as discussed here, involves shifts of consciousness, not mere social niceties. Empath talent, real empath talent, can bring an experience of OTHERNESS.

Otherness means transpersonal knowing, transcending your usual sense of self to explore someone else's completely different way of being. When you activate empath talent by using a technique for Skilled Empath Merge, your gifts can pull you out of the box of your personality, pour you into another person's reality, then plonk you safely back home to your everyday energy presence.

This is a far cry from mouthing schoolroom ideas about consideration for others. Mind you, trying to be a "nice" person is fine as far as it goes; it just doesn't go very far. Or deep.

Soon I will introduce you to numerous gifts that empaths can have. Depending on what's in your personal set, empath talent can lead you to experiences that are either spiritual, intellectual, physical, or emotional in nature; plus some additional empath gifts are even more far out.

Emotional forms of empath talent are the easiest to confuse with relatively superficial ideas like social sensitivity. By contrast, each empath gift can introduce you to a world of deeper knowing.

Every empath gift you have could be considered the call of your soul's deep striving, a motivation that no schoolteacher can magically bring into being. Either your soul invites you to empath talent or it doesn't. Empaths are hardwired that way for life.

And, sooner or later, the souls of us who are natural empaths will cry out for training. Eventually an inner discomfort prompts this realization: *Having* a gift doesn't mean the same thing as possessing skill for *using* that gift.

Look, that's what teachers are for. Probably you needed help learning to read. That was no reflection on your ability. Teachers save us time and vexation. Well, for those of us who need the knowledge, Empath Skills 101 is as essential as reading, writing, and arithmetic.

In a way it's more essential. As millions of illiterates can attest, it's frustrating not to know how to read. Also inconvenient, limiting; even humiliating at times. Situations come up where you wish you could read but the skill simply can't be found. Unskilled empath talent, by contrast, is always switched ON.

That's right, Brave Empath, your talent comes plugged in and switched on. Apparently the only way God can give it to us is for empaths to have their gifts installed from Day One. As I'll explain in more detail later, empath talent could be compared to Christmas presents. That wondrous machine your kid finds under the tree requires that Santa (or someone you, personally, know) can figure out how to read the operating instructions, assemble the toy, and push in the batteries. Skills!

Maybe you have already noticed: If you don't know how to use empath skills to direct your talent, that empath talent is going to use *you*.

When you can switch a gift OFF or ON at will, that could be called having CONTROL as an empath. However, I'm not crazy about using that word in conjunction with empath talent. Control has two connotations, doesn't it? One is skill, which applies very nicely to an empath's training. But the other connotation is exerting your will over people, which definitely doesn't apply.

A more useful understanding, I think, involves FREEDOM. When you can choose to fly into another person's mind or heart — whether to give a gift of service or to learn something outrageously new — control would be a burden to bring along. Far better to travel light, with innocence.

Just as empath skills help you to use your free will, one requirement for those skills is that you respect the free will of others. Freedom all around!

Freedom also describes the relief you will feel when you learn to switch off your inner Tickle Me, Elmo© or whatever else you name the empathic toy within that keeps on mechanically doing its thing (even when you feel like it's driving you nuts).

Sure, you can gain freedom and skill and control as an empath. Even if you have felt just the opposite. I sure have lived both sides of that story. Coming up next.

CHAPTER 3

Aha! for One Empath

Unskilled empaths suffer. It's that simple. Ironically, these days you can graduate from high school and learn more about computers than about your own psychic and spiritual software. Knowledge of empath talent sure wasn't taught to me. Even on the college level, there was no elective on Empath Skills 101.

At my college, Brandeis University, favorite classes initiated me into the wonders of literature, motivation and social psychology, even secrets of nonverbal communication. I'll be forever grateful. Yet for the purpose of gaining empath skills, it was no better than preschool.

After my B.A., I did graduate study in education and social work. These academic pursuits were interspersed with years of training as a meditation teacher, plus impassioned study of many religions and techniques for personal development. Unfortunately all this taught me the exact same amount about becoming a skilled empath. Zilch.

In fact, my first class in Empath Skills started quite by accident and didn't even take place until I was 45 years old.

Picture the scene. It's a Christmas party at the home of Steve and Birdie Pieczenick, where I have been hired as a party entertainer to do professional work with my system of Face Reading Secrets®.

At first I think this gig is going to be pretty routine. Stationed at a table, I'm giving guests personal readings about the talents and tribulations that show in their facial characteristics.

Although my work here is typical, the party host is not. For the entire time I do my readings, Steve observes me and my subjects with rapt attention. Guests may come and guests may go but this attentive observer goes on forever. After the first two hours, the gig is extended for another couple of hours. All the while my host Steve keeps observing, quiet except for occasional exclamations of "That's exactly right!"

When the party is over Steve Pieczenik tells me why he finds my work so interesting. (By the way, don't let his tongue-twister of a last name make your eyes glaze over. Just pronounce it *pih-CHEH-nik*.) Dr. Pieczenik is a best-selling novelist, sometimes co-authoring with Tom Clancy, other times on his own. Pieczenik's thrillers make use of his rare background as a Harvard-trained psychiatrist, a Ph.D. in International Relations, even four assignments as Deputy Assistant Secretary of State.

What does Dr. Pieczenik do professionally when not writing? He psychs out international leaders, helping security advisors and politicians to handle them, especially the weirdly dangerous ones like Saddam Hussein or Muammar Gadhafi.

Here's how I remember our conversation:

"Your sensitivity amazes me," Steve says.

"Thanks. But it's no big deal. I just know face reading."

"Listen," he says. "My work is to deal with people at the highest levels of national security. It's my responsibility to know about people. I'm telling you that your gifts are really extraordinary. How do you manage to hold it together?"

"Huh?"

"Being that ultra-sensitive, how do you keep yourself in balance? It must be very difficult."

Being a Highly, Highly Sensitive Person Can Be Hard

What an awakening! In the first place, never before had I considered myself particularly sensitive, let alone ultra-empath-anything. I had no clue.

Thank you forever, Steve Pieczenik, for calling this undefined thing about me a gift! I hope to do unto others as you have done to me.

Especially surprising for me was the discussion that followed with Dr. Pieczenik. Not only was I a highly, highly sensitive person. According to him, difficulties came automatically. Problems not just for me. Problems for anyone wired that way.

Steve Pieczenik told me, "The more sensitive you are, the harder that is to handle."

Gee, the very idea made me want to cry. For years I had denied this sensitive aspect of myself. Whenever it showed up, I considered this my personal weakness and called myself names like *neurotic, unstable, weird, embarrassing, fussy, moody,* and *weak.*

After every social situation where I reacted in ways that seemed different from others, I blamed myself.

Not once had I framed my personal pain in terms of what it means for everyone with extreme sensitivity.

Could this chronic condition really be a talent? Wow!

For months following this conversation, I started thinking in new ways about sensitivity.

This happened six years before Dr. Elaine Aron would publish her groundbreaking book, *The Highly Sensitive Person.* Besides, I was thinking about something that went beyond being an HSP.

The effortless knowing at depth about Steve Pieczenik's friends, the degree of accuracy that Steve found uncanny, what was that exactly?

Empath talent was its rightful name, I realized. For there are many ways of being sensitive that don't necessarily involve deep knowing about what it is like to be other people.

By now, it has been 20 years since Dr. Pieczenik complimented me on how well I was "holding it together." Which was the gentle equivalent of a Zen master's whack on the head.

Within months, I signed up for Empath Skills 101 (self-taught) and began to explore my gifts. The system that developed was co-created with Divine downloads. Over the years, Empath Empowerment® has been refined and verified through skills of energetic literacy.

By teaching this method, I can spare you having to re-invent the wheel. Actually, I can spare you something much harder. Physical wheels lie outside your mind-body-spirit system. Experimenting on your internal self? That can be much more difficult.

Even *recognizing* your empath gifts can be tricky. Until you find a teacher, self-discovery for an empath can resemble the game called "Pin the Tail on the Donkey."

Brave Empath, remember that childhood game? Not entirely pleasant! The picture of a donkey hangs on a wall in front of you. You're holding the paper tail that belongs to it, eager to pin it down right.

Seemingly that's simple, except what happens before you can try? You are blindfolded and spun around until you're dizzy. Then you lurch forward. Or sideways. And usually miss the mark.

That's life for an unskilled empath here at Earth School. All of us born as empaths must learn to recognize what would be spiritually obvious if only we weren't too blind and dizzy to tell.

Empath talent, for us, is like the tail that belongs to that donkey. How satisfying to put it in place!

For the kind of perspective you'll need as an empath, let's start here: Do you think that being an empath might be different from being a Highly Sensitive Person?

CHAPTER 4

Empath or HSP?

Could you be both?

Is an empath automatically both?

Hold on. What does these two terms mean in the first place?

EMPATHS are driven to constantly seek more spiritual truth. We're fascinated by those aspects of life that are the least obvious, the most secret, sacred, and tender. Our search is helped by sensitivity, yet not defined by it.

SENSITIVITY means a way of being neurophysiologically wired from birth to be extra-responsive, as described in Dr. Elaine Aron's groundbreaking book *Highly Sensitive Persons*. Her research has shown that 1 person in 5 can qualify as a HIGHLY SENSITIVE PERSON (HSP).

If you're an HSP, things bother you that don't bother others. You notice more, both consciously and physiologically. Over-stimulation happens. Hurt feelings happen. So do exceptional abilities — if you aren't too exhausted to notice. Nevertheless, as noted by Dr. Aron, American society, on the whole, is prejudiced against those who are sensitive.

Empaths are a special group within the HSP category. Only 1 out of every 4 HSPs — or 1 out of 20 people overall — is an empath.

When it comes to social problems, we empaths get a double whammy:

- ‿ Problems related to being sensitive
- ‿ Plus problems related to empath talent

Ironically, Brave Empath, you may be the last one to know you're either an empath or an HSP. Why? Even the world's bravest empaths aren't sensitive to absolutely everything.

Remember how Thoreau wrote about some people marching to the beat of a different drummer? Whatever kind of information you specialize in receiving, your empath talent causes you to tune out other kinds of information. This doesn't make you insensitive, although sometimes it may seem so.

An extreme example of specialized sensitivity is Alex Mont. He isn't an empath but a high-functioning autistic nine-year-old who also happens to be a math genius. In minutes he masters the same concepts that his father's students at Cornell University would take days to comprehend.

But Alex forgets the non-mathematical rules. A profile in *The Washington Post* illustrated how inconvenient this might be. Shopping for clothes at J.C. Penney, for instance, his dad pulled some pants off the rack and asked Alex to try them on. Oops, Alex started to take off his clothes right in the Children's Department.

"Alex!" exclaimed Mr. Mont. "You need to go to the dressing room."

"Oh, I forgot," Alex apologized. "You're not supposed to take your pants off in public. I forgot that rule."

Yes, there could be reasons aplenty for not being sensitive to absolutely everything. And, definitely, empaths are not autistic. However, I like Alex's story because it is such a great example of abundant sensitivity (of a highly unusual kind) along with zero sensitivity (of a socially common kind).

When I first read Dr. Aron's book, what shocked me most was her finding that 42% of the people she questioned said "They were not sensitive at all." Apparently they weren't ashamed to admit it, either.

At first I just couldn't compute this. How could someone not feel shattered, saddened, at least *reluctant* to admit not being sensitive?

America's cultural bias against sensitivity — even among psychologists, Aron points out — makes this easier to understand.

Alex Mont's talents are probably more lopsided than yours. And they move in the opposite direction. His numerical sensitivity can be measured on tests, while your empath's sensitivity cannot.

Alex tops out on the national Math Olympiad. What intellectual or psychological test can rate how you score empathically?

So far, none.

With the high incidence of autism today, diagnostic tests and specialists are available to make it easier to identify. Autism is a significant mental health problem. Being an empath is not a mental health problem, not a disability. No wonder there is no scientific test yet.

Socially we empaths can function normally enough. Our suffering is subtler. Similarly, our vast potential for superb discovery is also subtle. (You might consider it your private treasure trove.)

On the surface of society, labels and hype abound for just about every kind of gift that exists, anything from success at Math Olympics to mud wrestling. Be it a skill or a hobby, that label can rate tests, competitions, awards. Often there are songs or demonstrations or parades or conventions or celebrities. Undoubtedly there is some kind of support group.

So what? Empath Empowerment does not come from songs or support groups, nor from coping skills or friendly tips from people who aim to be helpful. The real deal? It comes from learning effective skills, especially how to turn your empath gifts OFF as an effortless habit.

Brave Empath, don't expect social groups to bestow empath skills upon you. This can only be accomplished through developing a certain easy-breezy, yet precise, skill set for using your consciousness.

What will come next? Figuring out whether or not you really are this special kind of person, an empath.

Empath Quiz 1

Could I be an empath?

It's a fair question, especially since 95 people out of 100 aren't. Remember, 5% is my ballpark estimate for the number of adults, living now, who are naturally gifted as empaths. But you don't need to know statistics, not nearly so much as you need to know about you.

Here come a few quizzes to satisfy your healthy curiosity, one quiz per chapter.

Take each quiz before reading the answers. Following that, you will find questions from your fellow students in our virtual classroom.

Empath Quiz #1.
THE QUICK QUESTIONNAIRE

Empaths can fly... in consciousness. Many times each day an unskilled empath will shift into another person's way of experiencing life, whether physically, mentally, emotionally, or spiritually. Do you have talent as an empath? Here's a quick aptitude test.

Answer **TRUE** or **FALSE**.

7.	When I'm with people who interest me, I wish I knew what it was like to be them.	T F
8.	It annoys (or amuses) me when people put on a show of being very tuned into others and I can tell that they're really not.	T F

9. I'm thin-skinned about other people, not just myself.   T   F

10. One of the best parts of falling in love, for me, is seeing the world through my lover's eyes. Everything becomes different and new.   T   F

11. Of all the compliments I have received, some of my favorites are variations on, "You really answer my questions." and "You understand me better than others do."   T   F

12. When with different friends, I don't just talk to them. My whole wavelength shifts. For example, when I'm with an artist, colors look brighter than usual; when with a musician, I'm more aware of sounds; when with an athlete, I feel more physically vibrant.   T   F

13. If I have to give the same speech to three different strangers, it comes out differently each time. Somehow I sense information that causes me to adjust the words automatically. With a highly educated listener, for instance, I find myself using longer words — even if nobody has told me that this person is highly educated.   T   F

14. When in the presence of somebody who is ill, it takes no effort for me to experience some of what that person is going through. In fact, if I were to let myself go, my experience of that person's illness could be overwhelming.   T   F

15. In certain situations (e.g., Talking or dancing or teaching), I get right on another person's wavelength — how he or she thinks. This kind of sharing is very special to me.   T   F

16. I don't just talk to my plants. I feel like they talk back to me.   T   F

17. Energetically it is freeing for me to be outdoors, and
more than a change of scene. The way I think and
feel changes, as though I pick up on different kinds
of consciousness expressed in animals and plants, or
the landscape itself.   T   F

18. During times of closeness with my pet, I enter my
pet's world. For me, that's the truly fascinating part
of having a pet.   T   F

19. Looking in the mirror shocks me. "That's supposed
to be me?" Truth is, I identify with being a (non-
physical) energy presence more than identifying
with this one particular face and body.   T   F

20. Friendship, for me, goes far beyond sharing
common interests. I enjoy that my friends show me
different ways to be.   T   F

21. I have a longing to connect with other people who
are seeking a deeper dimension to life. Whenever I
encounter these kindred spirits, I feel a kind of relief.
Even if our paths cross only long enough to make
quick eye contact, that chance meeting can lighten
my spirit for hours.   T   F

Empath Quiz #1. ANSWERS

Brave Empath, if you answered yes to even one of these questions,
you are probably a *natural* empath. And you will love how your
life changes when you become a *skilled* empath.

Consider yourself well prepared for our survey of empath gifts
in future chapters. That will help you tell for sure if you are an
empath and, specifically, which empath gift(s) you have. Before
then, we have two more quizzes in store.

Empath Quiz #1. Q&A

Q. *I feel so validated already. What a relief to know I'm an empath. Isn't this all I need, really?*

A. If all you care about is a label for yourself, sure stop here. But this Program for Empath Empowerment can actually change your life.

Consider that you have just tasted a tiny sample of the benefits to come.

Q. *How come folks don't usually talk about this? My favorite part of having a pet and all that. Usually if I tried to explain this kind of thing, I'd get tongue-tied.*

A. Understandably so. The *essence* of being an empath is to move in and out of deep experiences of consciousness. Yet everyday experiences, and problems, for an empath are very human. In developing this Empath Quiz, I sought ways to put a human face on those abstract, deep experiences.

Q. *Why expect a skeptic like me to be persuaded by such a general questionnaire?*

A. A better goal for yourself might be self-recognition, rather than persuasion.

Remember, an empath is someone with at least one significant gift for directly experiencing what it is like to be another person. Just one gift is enough to make you an empath. If you happen to be an empath, this Program for Empath Empowerment can greatly improve your life.

What is the purpose of this quiz or any quiz provided here? Motivating you to explore this program, to discover the benefits.

If you have not related to any of the questions in Empath Quiz #1, all the more reason to proceed to Empath Quiz #2, coming right up.

Empath Quiz #2. Who, Indeed?

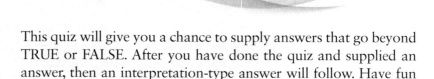

This quiz will give you a chance to supply answers that go beyond TRUE or FALSE. After you have done the quiz and supplied an answer, then an interpretation-type answer will follow. Have fun with this one!

Empath Quiz #2. WHO, INDEED?

Find a quiet place and five minutes to do some inner detective work. Because your eyes will be closed most of this time, you will need to read through the following instructions in advance. When you do go through these steps, open your eyes and take a quick peek as needed, until done.

1. Sit comfortably. Close your eyes and take a few deep breaths.

2. Ask this question mentally: "Who am I?"

3. Take some more deep breaths. Then just sit there, confident that your question will be answered. (No need to twist yourself into an angst-y posture like Rodin's sculpture, "The Thinker." Take it easy.)

4. Sitting quietly with eyes closed, you will notice something, whether a thought, an idea, an image, an emotion, a physical sensation. Whatever this experience, put it into words and say them out loud.

5. Open your eyes. Research done.

Empath Quiz #2. ANSWERS

Please do not read the following until you have taken this quiz. Otherwise you will spoil its effectiveness when you actually *do* the quiz.

Okay, Brave Empath, think about what you said at Step 4. Which of the following categories comes closest to your experience? Choose from A, B, C, D, or E:

A. I noticed my body.

B. I noticed an emotion.

C. I noticed my thoughts.

D. I noticed other things around me, but nothing to do with myself at all.

E. I noticed a sense of myself, but not in the ways described previously.

Now move forward to that heading and keep reading for your answer to Empath Quiz #2.

A. *I noticed my body*

This sense of yourself could have involved feeling hungry or cold or handsome or fat or anything physical whatsoever, including pain.

Turn to our upcoming chapters that describe two different gifts for physical forms of empath talent, Physical Intuition (Chapter 11) and Physical Oneness (Chapter 12).

Can you relate to either or both? If so, you're an empath. If not, you're probably not. Regardless, you might want to read all of Chapters 11-25.

Exception: What if you are living with chronic or acute pain? That may dominate your attention. In which case, when you are feeling better physically, redo this quiz, and stay at Step 4 until you notice something other than physical pain. Then continue with the answers.

B. I noticed an emotion

This sense of yourself could have involved feeling one emotion or many. You may have registered a specific emotion like *happy* or *sad*. Or remembered an emotionally-tinged memory from your past. Or found yourself saying a wistful prayer. Or thinking about someone you either like or dislike. Or any other experience with a strong feeling attached to it.

Turn to our upcoming chapters that describe different gifts for emotional forms of empath talent, Emotional Intuition (Chapter 13) and Emotional Oneness (Chapter 14).

Can you relate to either or both? If so, you're an empath. If not, you're probably not. Regardless, you might want to read all of Chapters 11-25.

C. I noticed my thoughts

This sense of yourself could have involved insights about who you are. Or abstract beliefs about life. Or self-conscious thinking about who you are, in your opinion or the opinions of others. Or doubts about this author's sanity for asking you to do this quiz. Or doubts about your own sanity for taking this quiz at all.

You could have had thoughts about your work, or crossword puzzles, or what to have for lunch — whether one gigantic thought or a whole series of little thoughts one after another.

Bottom line: You were aware of thinking. Consider: Was the mental part stronger than either emotions or physical sensations associated with those thoughts?

> ~ If the *emotional* component to your thoughts was extra-strong, consider that you gave Answer B and go read the rest of that answer.

> ~ If the *physical* component to your thoughts was stronger, consider that you gave Answer A and go read the rest of that answer.

~∿ However, if that *mental* part was indeed stronger, turn to our upcoming chapters about Intellectual Empath Ability (Chapter 15), Spiritual Oneness (Chapter 25) or, actually, any of the empath abilities between Chapters 11 and 25. Yes, you might want to read them all and then evaluate.

D. I noticed other things around me, but nothing to do with myself at all

This sense of yourself could have involved wishing you were doing something other than this exercise. Or feeling distracted. Or fighting the desire to get up and check your electronic messages.

Or maybe you were thinking about other people, what they are doing now, or should be doing later; perhaps even remembering something rotten that people have done to you in the past.

What if none of your self-exploration in Empath Quiz #2 had much to do with yourself at all? There are three strong possibilities:

1. Someone is making you do this quiz, and you'd really rather not.

2. You have little or no prior experience with focused self-reflection set in present time, either psychologically or spiritually. In which case, feel free to attempt this quiz a few more times, just to get the hang of paying attention to your inner self. Eventually you will come up with an answer different from D.

3. You are not an empath.

E. I noticed a sense of myself, but not in the ways described previously

This sense of yourself could have involved noticing colors or some kind of inner light. Or hearing non-physical sounds or qualities of silence. Or being aware of your presence as not confined to your physical body. Even seeing yourself as a kind of cartoon. Or maybe you noticed an awareness of yourself as a pattern of energy, such as movement of scintillating little particles.

Turn to our upcoming chapters on Empath Talent with Astral Beings (Chapter 22), Spiritual Intuition (Chapter 23), Molecular Empath Ability (Chapter 24), and Spiritual Empath Ability (Chapter 25).

Can you relate to one of these? If so, you're an empath. If not, you're probably not. Regardless, you might want to read all of Chapters 11-25.

Empath Quiz #2. Q&A

Q. *You make it sound so simple, "You're probably not an empath." What if this upsets you?*

A. If the idea of not being an empath breaks a part of your heart, guess what? You probably are.

Because a non-empath will more likely say, "So I'm no empath? So what?"

Whether you are an empath or not involves your entire mind-body-spirit setup, which was created long before you picked up this book.

Not being an empath makes you no better or worse than people who are empaths, just different.

If you are not an empath you could still be a Highly Sensitive Person. (Those two categories are different, remember? Only 1 in 4 HSPs is an empath.)

If you're not an empath, and feel fine with that, you have no further need to read this book unless you are simply curious about empaths.

Of course, another resource for finding out whether or not you're an empath is Quiz #3 in our next chapter.

Q. *How did your Empath's Quiz #2 work, anyway?*

A. Each person has many layers, including some that correspond to layers of the human energy field or aura. This is different from your flesh-and-blood self.

Your AURA is a set of energy bodies surrounding your physical body, layers stacked one inside another like nesting dolls (sometimes called "Matroyshka dolls").

Different subtle bodies within your aura specialize in different things, e.g., Pure spiritual energy, intellectual learning, and emotions.

With your human consciousness being as flexible as it is, at any moment you can identify with any one of these bodies, having it feel like your personal sense of self.

By taking the "Who, Indeed?" Quiz, here is what happened with your consciousness. Automatically it shifted over to the energy body with which you currently identify most strongly. That's also the body you probably use most often for unskilled empath merge.

When we get to the "Coming Home" technique in a later chapter, you will learn more about the various layers of yourself and your aura.

Q. *Why did you ask if we can relate to descriptions of different types of empath talent?*

A. People are very good at recognizing their inner truth, at least when given the chance. If my descriptions make you go Aha!, you pass the test. You are what I call an empath. If my descriptions of being an empath leave you cold, forget it.

Q. *I don't mean to split hairs, but couldn't anyone do empathic travel, having those multi-layered subtle bodies and all? Doesn't that make all people empaths, regardless of whether we consciously believe in it?*

A. Definitely not. Consider the research Dr. Aron has done on HSPs. People are wired for life as Highly Sensitive Persons, regardless of whether they have prior knowledge of the term. In fact, when Aron began her pioneering work, nobody had heard of Highly Sensitive Persons.

What about clinical research studies about this Program for Empath Empowerment and all the other skill sets in Rosetree Energy Spirituality? They do not exist yet. I welcome collaboration with those who combine a scientific background with interest in conducting rigorous studies.

Meanwhile I invite you to trust what I have learned from case histories as an empath coach and healer. As a leader in this field, I have conducted many thousands of sessions that included doing Skilled Empath Merge, probably more such sessions than anyone else alive. You can be sure that I have read auras of empaths and non-empaths alike.

Incidentally, AURA READING means accessing information from the human energy field. I teach aura reading as a form of energetic literacy. (It is widely taught in very different ways, related to psychic development, clairvoyance, etc.)

Extensive research that I have done with energetic literacy includes researching what happens to people's auras during Skilled Empath Merge.

Non-empaths do not do Skilled Empath Merges, nor do they do unskilled empath merges.

For empaths, there are huge energetic differences between doing no empath merge, an unskilled empath merge, or a Skilled Empath Merge.

For all this, clear evidence is to be found by reading auras with fully developed, normal, human, energetic literacy.

As for evidence of whether or not you happen to be an empath, I have a third quiz for you. Curious?

CHAPTER 7

Empath Quiz #3. Simple But Poignant

Here's the simplest quiz of all. There is just one question, actually.

Empath Quiz #3. THE TV QUIZ

1. Imagine that a TV talk shows has flashed onto your screen. It's the kind with the highly dramatic emotional confrontations. Or imagine that you chance upon an ultra-violent reality show that humiliates the contestants really, really effectively.

Which of the following comes closest to your typical reaction:

> **A.** Thank goodness! Now I can watch something to spice up my day.
>
> **B.** Hmm, that might be fun, but what's on the other channels? Maybe I can find something even more intense.
>
> **C.** Help! Let me outta here.

Empath Quiz #3. ANSWERS

Depending on your choice, move forward to heading A, B, or C. Go, find your answer to Empath Quiz #3.

....

Answer A
....

One person's "Spice up my day" is someone else's emotional exhibitionism. With all respect, if you're among the millions of viewers who love confrontational talk shows or humiliating reality shows, you are probably *not* an empath.

Quite the opposite. You might be a highly *insensitive* person. Or simply not sensitive. Otherwise, you are carrying STUFF in your aura configured in such a way that you cannot feel much emotionally unless presented with something intensely dramatic.

Note: Even if you chose this answer you still may have an empath gift that doesn't involve experiencing human consciousness. Take a look at the chapters on Animal Empath Talent (Chapter 16), Plant Empath Talent (Chapter 17), Crystal Empath Talent (Chapter 18), Environmental Empath Talent (Chapter 19), Mechanical Empath Talent (Chapter 20), Medical Empath Talent (Chapter 21), and Empath Talent with Astral Beings (Chapter 22).

Answer B.

As a TV viewer who loves emotional drama — the more of it the better — you could belong to any of the following categories.

- You're young, and trying to learn what life is about.
- You're seeking CATHARSIS. (That's a term from classical Greek theater about emotional healing that can occur when entertainment frees up your tears or laughter).
- You have become disconnected from life, perhaps due to watching way too much TV.

Okay, there could be other causes, too. In any case, you watch TV as a form of entertainment unrelated to human reality.

Also possible: You could be volunteering to lift emotional burdens from the poor souls on the shows. In which case, you might be an empath... but way overworked and definitely not skilled yet.

Unless you belong to this volunteer category, you're probably *not* called to travel in spirit as an empath.

Except that you still might have an empath gift that doesn't involve experiencing human consciousness. So you might wish to take a look at the chapters on Animal Empath Talent (Chapter 16), Plant

Empath Talent (Chapter 17), Crystal Empath Talent (Chapter 18), Environmental Empath Talent (Chapter 19), Mechanical Empath Talent (Chapter 20), Medical Empath Talent (Chapter 21), and Empath Talent with Astral Beings (Chapter 22).

....

Answer C.

....

What, you feel revulsion towards TV programs with over-the-top sensationalism? Ta da! You're probably an empath.

For you, what is the relationship of these shows to your emotional life? It's like having a professional surgeon entertain herself by taking a romp to the butcher's shop. There's already drama enough in your life.

"Spill Your Guts TV" is a poor choice of entertainment for empaths.

Empath Quiz #3. Q&A

Q. *I'll tell you about one feeling that I have right now. I didn't like your test, okay? I'm not proud that I'm too unstable to be able to enjoy shows that normal people watch.*

A. Empaths often feel bad about not fitting in. We wish we could be like "Everyone else," i.e., not so super-sensitive. But if you have been born as an empath, it's high time you accepted it. Your peer group is other empaths, not the public at large.

Stop kidding yourself about this fitting-in business.

- Millions of people love confrontational talk shows so much, they find them addictive.
- Millions live for reality shows, the crueler the better.
- Other viewers find them mildly interesting. (Really, imagine that possibility!)
- Other TV viewers tolerate these popular shows, although all that conflict isn't quite to their taste. Much as you might discard a parsley garnish from an otherwise tasty dish of beans. (Again, can you even imagine such a possibility?)

None of these people are probably empaths. You are.

Q. *I always wondered why shows like this were on TV. Are you telling me that this is related to non-empaths being 19 out of 20 people? Is this quiz supposed to serve as a reminder that, even though I sorta expect that everyone is just like me, we empaths really are different?*

A. Bingo!

CHAPTER 8

Since You're In, Let's Get Technical

A PROGRAM FOR EMPATH EMPOWERMENT is built right into this book. In this self-paced manual, you will learn two of the three steps for becoming a skilled empath.

Strictly speaking, only the first two steps are required for becoming a skilled empath. They can change your quality of life more than any skill set you have ever learned, like finally learning how to turn that water faucet OFF, ending the drip-drip-drip.

The third step of Empath Empowerment is optional. Yet I doubt that you will choose to skip it. Because this is where you will learn to turn that water faucet ON, expertly saving that precious fluid. Like bottling your own gorgeous Bordeaux vintages, perhaps Chateau Lafite Rothschild or Eau de Brooklyn. For that systematic sequence of instruction, turn to the next book of this series, *The Master Empath*.

Survival skills first, entertainment later! Survival skills for an empath are exactly what you will get from this part of our Program for Empath Empowerment.

Now that you're quizzed and reasonably certain that you could be an empath, what's needed next? I'm going to start introducing you to a small number of technical terms needed to understand pretty abstract shifts of consciousness.

This won't be as hard as learning Chinese. More like working a new app. Let's take it one techie term at a time.

Techie Term 1. Empath

An EMPATH is someone with at least one significant gift for directly experiencing what it is like to be another person. Although you may have many different empath gifts, all of them switch ON or OFF the same way. So empath skill is developed the same way whether you have been born with one empath gift or many.

Altogether I have identified 15 different empath gifts. Whichever ones you happen to have, they were installed on the day you were born. Installed fully switched ON. What happens after that? Up to you.

Techie Term 2. Skilled Empath Merge

Before you gain control over this aspect of your life, unskilled empath merges happen many times every day, a kind of flying in spirit that may feel good sometimes.

Although Emily, John, and William didn't especially enjoy doing this, you might have. Even if later you had to pay a price.

Regardless, did you know this important technical point? Most unskilled empath merges happen without either conscious knowledge or good feelings. By far the majority of unskilled empath merges (yours included) happen super-fast, and at a subconscious level only.

What about the times that you do recognize consciously? Does it count as Skilled Empath Merge if you're purposely blending your awareness with somebody else? Maybe it's a glorious moment. You might find it delicious, exploring what someone else is like from the inside.

Uh-oh. Still not skilled. Which means that energetically you will pay a price. Every time.

And guess what else? Those conscious moments of flying in spirit as an empath are just the tip of the unskilled-empath-merge iceberg. Most empath merges are definitely not conscious.

I don't mention this to worry you, because you are going to learn how to stop this funny business. Still, it's time to know the truth and not sugarcoat it. Every single unskilled empath merge deposits STUFF in your energy field.

Techie Term 3. STUFF

STUFF is a practical term used in Rosetree Energy Spirituality (RES) for stored-up energetic garbage. These are blobs and globs of astral-level energy, deposited within your aura in a way that causes confusion for your subconscious mind.

All the healing skill sets I teach have this in common: They aim to remove STUFF permanently. In fact, my motto as an emotional and spiritual healer is this: "STUFF can always, always, always be healed."

To make that healing permanent, STUFF removal must be followed by energetic **PUT-IN**, adding subconscious energies and conscious knowledge that, together, awaken a stronger soul expression. Facilitating that kind of healing is my main area of professional expertise. Coaching empaths is one part of that, especially dear to my heart.

RES practitioners can discern many different varieties of STUFF. Within this profession, different skill sets are available to solve each type of problem.

Preventing and removing STUFF related to being an empath will not solve other STUFF-related problems. However, it is a big deal to rid yourself of the particular type of STUFF that clobbers unskilled empaths. Including...

Techie Term 4. Imported STUFF

This Program for Empath Empowerment addresses **Imported STUFF**. Which means STUFF belonging to *other people* that lands in *your* aura as a result of unskilled empath merge.

In *The Empowered Empath*, our emphasis will be on *preventing* Imported STUFF. Plus there will be some *permanent healing* of Imported STUFF. All this leads to a clearer energy field.

What can happen, just because you have vanquished Imported STUFF? For starters:

- Greater effectiveness at work or in school
- Establishing a stronger sense of identity
- Enjoying relationships more
- Greater personal power
- Spiritual awakening, living more in the present

You see, Brave Empath, Imported STUFF is really a bigger deal than some faucet that goes drip-drip-drip. This hidden energetic debris clutters up your subconscious mind and energy field in random ways, at random times, through problem energies belonging to random people.

No wonder being an unskilled empath is way confusing, both subconsciously and consciously.

No wonder, empath skills can transform your life for the better. And now that you know our basic techie terms, you're ready to learn something that may seem like a *really* technically-big-deal skill. (Although I'll help you to get comfortable with it right away.)

In our next chapter, you'll begin to learn an indispensable skill for empaths. You'll start to learn *how to position your consciousness.*

CHAPTER 9

Positioning Your What?

POSITION YOUR CONSCIOUSNESS. That's what.

Awareness, or consciousness, flows. You're so good at having awareness that it flows from the moment you first wake up until you drop off into Snoozeland. All your waking hours, consciousness is positioned in one direction or another.

No need to be self-conscious about this, particularly. Except sometimes a person can benefit from learning to direct, or position, consciousness just a bit differently. And I think you know the kind of person I mean.

Empath gifts direct the *subconscious* mind towards other people. Subconsciously positioning consciousness back at yourself — as the most important person in the room — now that's what will keep your empath gifts turned OFF.

Does this seem a bit technical? Are you clear about how your conscious mind is different from your subconscious mind? Let's explore this further. There will be a practical payoff for you, I promise.

When You Aim to Change SUBCONSCIOUS Positioning of Consciousness

Human consciousness flows automatically. Without your having to direct it. Yet sometimes it is helpful to change that direction of flow. In order to position consciousness differently, the first thing to understand is how surface-level conscious thinking differs from subconscious thinking.

You see, Brave Empath, your CONSCIOUS MIND amounts to just 2-3% of your mental potential. The remainder is subconscious.

Although some authorities today estimate the percentage for conscious thinking as high as 10%, I expect that greater refinement in scientific measurement will eventually make that 2-3% estimate quite standard.

Indisputably your conscious mind matters most for everyday life. Survival requires paying conscious attention to little details in the grand scheme of things, such as "Driving between the lines" while you go down the street.

As for your relationships with other people, they are largely defined by conscious, objective reality. Such as what people say and do; what can be measured or videoed or tattooed.

Conscious experience matters greatly, to empaths and non-empaths alike. By contrast, your subconscious mind is far more vast, amounting to the remaining 98% of your mental capacity. Within your subconscious mind are layers of functioning that are progressively more subtle, more abstract and delicate... and way more powerful.

A very small percentage of this subconscious functioning could be called your "Higher Self." For the practical ideas that follow, however, let's simply include "Higher Self" as part of the overall functioning of your subconscious mind. Keeping things simple whenever we can, yes!

Changing Your Mind. Which Mind?

To change the positioning of your *conscious* mind is relatively easy.

For instance, Brave Empath, what if I asked you to start noticing blue objects? You could easily train your conscious mind to do this. Scanning objects in a room, you might readily see many blue things. So your conscious attention could easily be positioned that way.

Not so easy and obvious? Changing *subconscious* habits for positioning consciousness.

This isn't like using physical vision. It's more like changing how you hold those little facial muscles underneath your eyes, part of your *obicularis oris*. Mostly this is an involuntary muscle, working all on its own. Automatically your eyes can round or narrow, due to those muscles.

However, you can learn to purposely move those muscles beneath your eyes. Just for fun, sometime, spend a few minutes in front of a mirror.

- Practice straightening out the shape to the lower eyelids of your eyes. Such a small scrunch...
- Then practice rounding that shape. Relaxing, ooching out, moving those funny-feeling, seldom-used muscles in a pretty subtle way...
- Afterwards, flop, let the shape of your lower eyelids return to normal, whether curvy or straight-ish or whatever. For this, no effort is needed. Having your eyelids relax in this manner doesn't only look normal. It feels normal.

Such tiny muscle movements! To move your obicularis oris on purpose takes practice. You could consider this experiment... an exercise in positioning your conscious awareness... on something that usually works subconsciously.

With training, an empath like you can learn to position subconscious awareness more appropriately. This new habit will not show physically. It's effortless, way easier than making faces in front of a mirror.

How to Position Consciousness
as a Skilled Empath

Brave Empath, you have begun Empath Empowerment Step ONE. Now comes the juicy part. It is important to learn specifically which empath gifts you have.

This will help your conscious mind to acknowledge what has been going on subconsciously all along. Well, hello. You deserve that much, don't you? I call that "Embracing your special empath gifts," officially Step ONE in this Program for Empath Empowerment.

After you accomplish this, Step TWO will bring a gentler sort of surprise. From inside, you will start to discover how a very gentle shift is all it takes to position consciousness in a way that improves your life. Just a tiny, delicate shift to your simple, naked, unadorned, very human consciousness.

This will be deeply personal, getting the knack for positioning your consciousness as a skilled empath. Whenever you make this gentle shift in consciousness, all your empath gifts will switch OFF automatically.

Does it sound mysterious? Maybe that's not bad. If positioning consciousness in this way were obvious, you wouldn't need to learn a thing.

Just because you haven't learned it yet, so what? That hardly means you can't. You are totally capable of learning, once you have a teacher who is capable of teaching. Of course, you can learn to manage your special empath gifts!

This Program for Empath Empowerment will systematically and gently educate you to position consciousness differently, preventing both unskilled empath merge and the Imported STUFF that inevitably follows.

- If you are new to studying consciousness, you can enter a new world of *self-discovery.*

- If you are *already fascinated by consciousness,* you will love the sophisticated information to come in this Program for Empath Empowerment.

- Developing powerful, flexible skills will allow you to make use of special characteristics of your consciousness *available exclusively to born empaths.*

~ You will learn *very specific, effective ways* to position your consciousness.

~ After you have become empowered in this way, you can easily learn Empath Empowerment Step THREE, how to do *Skilled Empath Merge*. Hint: This also requires positioning of consciousness, a version that builds upon the same positioning skills that keep your empath gifts turned OFF.

~ So even if your main goal is to become a Master Empath who learns loads and loads of techniques for Skilled Empath Merge — Oh yes, I can teach you, and that will be such huge fun — nevertheless, it must begin with Empath Empowerment Steps ONE and TWO.

Owning your empath gifts? You have accomplished that now. Brave Empath, you have begun to think like an empath, to assess problems you have had in a new light.

When you took our three versions of Empath Quiz, you began to appreciate that you have a lifelong degree of sensitivity. Not only are you a Highly Sensitive Person. You are a Highly, Highly Sensitive Person. And you have at least one gift for directly experiencing what it is like to be other people.

This is not a personal weakness but something absolutely magnificent. Own it!

Then you can really start to embrace it.

PART TWO

Embracing Your Empath Gifts

Brave Empath, it's so important to embrace your gifts. Not just to use their full potential. Also to avoid wasting time.

Many "guru-prescribed" activities are, in fact, unnecessary, don't work, and — if you understand what *really* makes an empath tick — *can't* work. These include such busywork as:

- Protecting yourself against "Psychic vampires"
- Using thoughts, feelings, or behaviors to manage your sensitivity
- Constantly trying to "Clean up your energy field"
- Doing grueling, ongoing work on your psychological boundaries

Besides all this, Brave Empath, you may have been doing many other things to compensate for problems caused by Imported STUFF. Only you didn't know that was happening. You just thought you were using a technique for personal development.

Very often this happens with energy healing. One example is how unskilled empaths can become dependent on using Emotional Freedom Technique, a.k.a. EFT or tapping.

What if you don't know which empath gifts you have? What if you don't yet have skills as an empath? Until you become skilled, any one of your empath gifts can make you feel bad, with totally unpredictable ups and downs all day long.

Many an unskilled empath has moved through this pattern with EFT: Initially, great results. Then tapping all day long, just for maintenance.

Sadly that isn't really maintaining results.

Initial results that lasted? Now they were true results. By contrast, habitual tapping could be a sign of diminishing returns.

And for an empath, it could also be a sign of trying to clean up Imported STUFF. Wouldn't it be better to prevent that icky in the first place?

Have you been tapping when you could be clapping? Let's go for clapping... because you feel great, and you feel like yourself.

CHAPTER 10

Your Pain Is Not Your Gift

Step ONE of Empath Empowerment began with core understandings about what it does, and doesn't, mean to be an empath. Now let's answer the juicy question: Which empath gifts do you have?

One chapter at a time, let's conduct a depth survey of 15 very different empath gifts. Get ready to write down your personal LIST OF MY EMPATH GIFTS, a list made with old-fashioned pen and paper. Alternatively, use a favorite electronic technology. However a list in your head will not work nearly so well.

Trust me here, Brave Empath. Make a physical list.

In the cause of embracing your special gifts, acknowledging them on a list is the least you can do. "Embracing" implies a certain physicality, or where is the fun? Embracing your gifts is not optional in this Program for Empath Empowerment.

Making a physical list will inform your subconscious mind, as well as your conscious mind, that you take your empathic nature seriously. You deserve to know about it in detail, for self-appreciation and also to reframe some painful parts of your past history.

Indirectly, making a list will help you subconsciously in one more way. Writing down the name of each gift will clarify what your empath talent is *not*. For example:

- ∿ There is no empath gift called "You have a disability."
- ∿ There is no empath gift called "Be ashamed."
- ∿ There is no empath gift called "You are weak."
- ∿ There is no empath gift called "You are fated to suffer."

Feelings like those are understandable. A constant drip-drip-drip could get anyone damp, discouraged, and discombobulated. Being an *unskilled* empath pretty much guarantees suffering... but only until you get yourself skills.

Let The Great Empath Gift Survey Begin

How many empath gifts might you have, out of the 15 I have identified in my role as Empath Coach?

Most empaths have more than one gift but not all 15.

Brave Empath, this survey can explain so much about your life so far.

With that goal, let The Great Empath Gift Survey begin! Read through a description of each gift. If you can relate at all, write that name on your List of My Empath Gifts.

Since each of these gifts involves consciousness, it is subtle. What, were you expecting something obvious like a tattoo or a neon sign? Fahgettaboudit.

Realistically what can you expect? An empath is someone with at least one significant gift for directly experiencing what it is like to be *another person*. I hope you have fun finding out which of those various gifts are yours.

In the following chapters, you will get to expand your definition of "Another person." Here's a hint: Not necessarily human.

CHAPTER 11

Physical Intuition

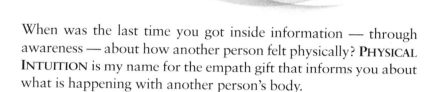

When was the last time you got inside information — through awareness — about how another person felt physically? PHYSICAL INTUITION is my name for the empath gift that informs you about what is happening with another person's body.

Brave Empath, I am going to do something brave, too. I am starting this catalogue of empath gifts with the one exception that proves a rule.

> ***All empath gifts are lifelong, for keeps.***
> ***(Except for Physical Intuition.)***

Physical Intuition is given temporarily to all human mothers, fathers, and other caregivers directly responsible for a baby. This temporary form of Physical Intuition lasts for just a few years, beginning when a new baby enters the caregiver's life, whether through physical birth, adoption, employment as a nanny, etc. Count this temporary gift as one of the spiritual rewards for committing to parenthood.

Of course, parents need this temporary dispensation for flying in spirit. How else can people care for babies without killing them?

Sleepy? "Waahhh!"

Wet? "Waahhh!"

Thirsty? "Waahhh!"

Learning the language of Cry is just the beginning.

> ~ Behold the *face* of the cutest little girl, adorable Baby
>   Boodles. Uncanny but true — when a father uses his

temporary gift for Physical Intuition, the father can tell that her *bottom* needs changing.

~ Courtesy of temporary Physical Intuition, Baby Boodles' father can see her *from the back* and tell that she needs a nap. (Looking from the front, most people can read body language. But pegging a kid's physical fatigue with one quick glance from behind? That goes beyond mere body language, doesn't it?)

~ Baby Boodles' mother, blessed with temporary Physical Intuition, can sniff her infant daughter's *feet* and know she is in for a rough day of teething.

Mysterious though such forms of knowing may seem, caring for babies is the most common example on earth of Physical Intuition. Or any empath gift.

Do parents maintain their temporary gift for Physical Intuition? No. Certainly by the time a kid is five, that temporary empath gift is gone. What can become a substitute? Guessing. And nagging.

Think back to when you were a teenager. Did Mom ever holler dressing instructions at you?

"Take your jacket. Listen to me. You are going to freeze without that jacket."

Rules about clothing, predictions, worrying — none of this bears the slightest resemblance to empath talent.

(Incidentally, healthy children actually stay warmer than most older people. As explained by Covert Bailey in *The New Fit or Fat*, scientists have discovered that, compared to adults, kids have far more efficient thermoregulatory functioning. So the jacket-less teenage Ms. Boodles may actually know what she's doing.)

When a mother, or anyone, incorrectly tells Boodles what she is (supposedly) feeling, it's enough to make you highly suspicious that anyone could possess such a gift as Physical Intuition. So let's be clear.

"I Know Just How You Feel"

Bossing other people around, based on claims of superior knowledge, has nothing to do with being an empath — neither Physical Intuition nor any other gift. In general, question anyone who tells you, "I know just how you feel."

Who knows for sure if that alleged "expert about you" is an empath?

- A real empath might know for sure... only after developing some pretty solid skills as an empath. Just what you are doing, Brave Empath!

- Who else can tell? Someone who has developed a different skill set, well-developed energetic literacy that can be used to research another person's aura-level gifts. Plus, this expert at reading auras must also clearly understand the full range of empath gifts. Today, most aura readers don't.

- Even that well trained kind of expert doesn't just "know" who's an empath by taking a casual look. Instead that aura reader will use a technique suitable for researching the presence or absence of empath gifts.

- Otherwise, what equips anyone to call somebody else an empath (or a non-empath)? Could be any random gossip or fuzzy thinking or perhaps a new kind of bragging because "empath" is starting to go mainstream as something desirable. Don't believe a word.

What's happening when Boodles' Mom claims to know how cold her daughter feels?

That is something else entirely. Maybe misdirected affection, psychological projection, a craving to control, or an overwhelming need to protect the family's status by having her child dress properly. None of which counts as Physical Intuition.

Physical Intuition, the Glory

What about empaths who *do* have the genuine gift — permanently, not just the temporary version? Using that gift on purpose, employing a technique for Skilled Empath Merge, an empath experiences directly what is happening with another person's physical body.

Here comes a useful technical term for us to start using for "The person at the receiving end of a Skilled Empath Merge." Brave Empath, let's start calling this a "DISCOVERY PERSON."

Which sorts of experience might you have while experiencing your Discovery Person, provided that you have Physical Intuition? Hint: This is not Medical Empath Talent, which will be discussed later.

Physical Intuition informs you about everyday human things, physical things like:

- Mia feels peppy, agreeably over-caffeinated.
- Alyssa has a different kind of vigor, more healthy and strong and in the prime of life.
- Julian looks to be about 60 years old. What a great example he is that "Sixty can be the new 40." Physically he feels in the prime of life, too.
- Alex feels way older than his physical age. Although his driver's license might document a chronological age of 25, there is a stiffness to his posture and movements. You can even feel there is stiffness in Alex's joints. Physically he feels more like a kid of 80.
- Susan's back hurts.
- Colin has a headache.
- Colton is one horny guy.

Sure, information like this can be very useful. You just know. Physical Intuition causes you to just know.

The skilled empath's advantage is using this knowledge to understand what makes a person tick. For business dealings, for friendship, for pacing your behavior with that Discovery Person... so very useful. For helping others, whatever your line of work in the world? Also potentially useful.

Incidentally, do you think that any of these folks might make a direct announcement to you about how they physically feel? Joke! They may not have even made that announcement to their own conscious minds.

Bottom line: Great advantages can result when a skilled empath has Physical Intuition.

Physical Intuition, The Most Common Pain

Every empath gift has a flip side, a kind of pain. With unskilled Physical Intuition, the problem is too much information (TMI).

Wouldn't it be nice to bump into your neighbor Sebastian without being reminded, yet again, how he's got a hangover? Definitely TMI!

And do you really benefit from riding on a train next to a seatmate who has a migraine?

My student Natalie used to dread riding the subways. She would sit next to Commuter A and experience certain kinds of discomfort until she could take it no longer.

It didn't seem to matter what Natalie did, either. She would try to read or listen to music. Unwelcome information kept coming non-stop. So Natalie would shift to a different seat. Until she couldn't stand that any longer, because Commuter B, next to her, would also have plenty of physical problems.

On to the next seat, adjacent to poor suffering Commuter C.

Natalie told me, "Sometimes I would use up every seat in one car. Then I would have to move to a completely different subway car and find a whole new bunch of places to sit. Commuting to work or back home, I was just exhausted."

Guess what else Natalie also told me, after she learned what you will be learning in this book? "Now I just ride the subway."

No more "TMI Musical Chairs" for her!

Plus A Different, Hidden Kind of Pain

Grace, a massage therapist, has told me that the best part of doing her work is "Taking a ride on the client's energy." Nothing she learned from her professional training compares with this intuitive learning about another person's body.

"It makes me so high," she told me, smiling.

I would encourage Grace to become a skilled empath, not merely a talented one. As such, she will stop all that joy riding... because there is a hidden price to pay. Remember that term "unskilled empath merge"? Later I will describe the specific forms of icky that result from unskilled empath merges.

Isn't that fair, if you want to fully understand what makes each empath gift distinctive? The good, the glorious... and the ugly. I don't want to pretty up what could have been happening to you, not if you have a gift like Grace's.

Just consider, how could Grace use her empath talent more appropriately? She can learn to keep her Physical Intuition turned OFF almost the whole time while she's at work. Mostly she could use her professional skills at massage, the skill set her client thought she was paying for.

To enhance that skill set, Grace might choose to use advanced empath skills to purposely do a one-minute Skilled Empath Merge on each client. Right at the start of a massage. Just one minute, not a full hour.

Gathering useful information. Not junking up her aura with Imported STUFF.

That sensible use of empath talent can really be fun. Using a dedicated technique to fly in spirit would protect Grace. Plus this quick and richly informative experience would provide her with much more precise information than her old habitual joy rides.

Frankly, smart and sparing use of Skilled Empath Merge would also be way better for Grace's mental health. After that initial exploration, no joy riding while she gives the rest of her massage. As a skilled empath Grace can use what she learned in her super-quick download to supplement the skill set she has been hired to use.

Actually the experience of one brief Skilled Empath Merge is way more *fulfilling* than taking a one-hour joy ride on another person's energy.

Besides, Grace is being paid to work as a massage professional, not a joy rider. To earn her credentials, she studied long and hard at massage school. Emphasizing that skill set, rather than random experiences of energy, can help Grace to progress professionally. Like becoming an expert driver of the car she owns, rather than cruising around in a borrowed automobile.

If you have Physical Intuition, consider it a highly valuable form of intelligence. Maybe you will only choose to use it personally; or maybe it can bolster your skill sets for work. As your training progresses in Empath Empowerment, you will learn to increase your insight... without paying a hidden price.

Already you're starting to get the picture, right? To protect yourself energetically, don't let your empath gifts make you a victim. If you possess even one empath gift, learn how to use it on purpose. You can do better than joy riding.

CHAPTER 12

Physical Oneness

Unlike Physical Intuition, which reveals your Discovery Person's physical life at a distance, PHYSICAL ONENESS brings a much more personal kind of learning. With this empath gift, sensations within your own body can change temporarily, a result of flying in spirit.

These sensations are information in physical disguise. Except what's with that, finding information about other people, displayed inside *your* body? Do you think that might complicate your life just a bit? And yet your potential for knowledge and service can be so glorious once you have mastered this gift.

Physical Oneness, the Glory

Brave Empath, when you have flown in spirit on purpose, having this particular empath gift is ultra-useful. Because you are purposely using a technique to learn about your official Discovery Person, no confusion arises. You can tell at once: Who owns that tickly feeling in your throat? Same deal for any other physical sensation that flickers by temporarily while you're in technique.

To experience the glory of Physical Oneness, your empath merge must be conscious. Then it becomes so easy to notice any interesting, temporary physical sensation.

Tickles or twinges or pain will then serve as information, like words in a newspaper. Clearly not about you, not your problem.

- ⌇ While in technique, you register the information.
- ⌇ After your technique ends, so do any physical sensations.
- ⌇ Neat and clean!

Meanwhile what have you gained, doing research as a skilled empath? Only the ultimate inside information. You know deeply because the experience was part of you; so many textures and meanings and feelings, a knowing delivered as close as your skin.

Physical Oneness, the Pain

For an unskilled empath, Physical Oneness can be physically inconvenient, to say the least.

Have you ever taken on aches and pains that belonged to somebody else? The most extreme examples I have heard yet came from one of my students, Mackenzie, a body worker.

For example, she did one of her regular sessions to help a client with asthma. That night, Mackenzie woke up in a panic, hardly able to breathe. She blamed her "bad" empath talent for the problem.

While I coached her, Mackenzie also told me this: "Breathing problems aren't all. What really gets to me are the stools. Some of the patients I work with are in chemotherapy, and they'll describe strange bowel movements. More often than not, they'll describe one and, I swear, very the next day I see the exact same kind of stool in the toilet. You know, coming out of my body."

Not that unskilled Physical Oneness is usually so extreme. Sometimes the experiences are so subtle that an unskilled empath won't even notice. For example, consider the plight of Blake, an empath with a gift for Physical Oneness. He has been invited to a very cool party.

A highly attractive specimen strolls by and engages him in some light banter. Blake's sexual signals go "Yes, yes, yes." By golly, Blake is starting to feel mighty attractive himself.

Except gradually Blake realizes that his lower back has been hurting like crazy. Which is something his particular back doesn't generally do. How to handle this?

Let's suppose that Blake is an unskilled empath. He never got the memo announcing his gift for Physical Oneness. No owl arrived from Hogwarts, either.

Of course, Blake isn't to blame for being unskilled, so far, as an empath. Folks don't become unskilled empaths because they take a class on empath skills only to flunk out. It's more like being illiterate or never learning how to drive a car. (In a parallel world where few people teach either reading or driving!)

Hold on. Actually, Brave Empath, you grew up in such a world! It was a world lacking Empath Skills 101. *The Times They Are a-Changin'*, so our empath children can have such an easier time than Blake.

Meanwhile, what can Blake do if his back is hurting in some weird, inexplicable way? If has not learned about Empath Empowerment, most likely he will improvise a way of coping. For instance, Blake might start to feel guilty for (supposedly) being a hypochondriac.

Really, what does it mean to be a HYPOCHONDRIAC? That's someone who fabricates an illness by blowing ordinary physical sensations out of proportion. By contrast, having Physical Oneness does *not* make anyone a hypochondriac. The symptoms are real. Although they seem to come out of nowhere, they do belong to someone. In this case, not to Blake but to that very hottie he is admiring (and all the Imported STUFF he picks up).

Even Worse Than Guilt Over Hypochondria?

Let's be thorough in describing the pain of unskilled Physical Oneness. So I'll take this example in a slightly different direction.

What if Blake knows something about being an empath, but the little he knows so far is inaccurate? A lot has changed since 2001, when the first edition of the first book for empaths was published. By now, millions of people are familiar with the term "Empath."

Conversations galore are happening all around the world. Just about everyone has heard the term "Empath," yet they don't necessarily understand what it is, nor have they developed skills that truly protect them.

Like many beginners, Blake might have heard, "An empath is someone who feels other people's feelings."

Brave Empath, haven't you heard definitions like that? By now you know better. For example, you're aware that Physical Oneness is not the only empath gift. You already know about Physical Intuition. Let's revisit our definition for this particular empath gift, so you can appreciate how very different it is from "Someone who feels other people's feelings."

Physical Intuition is the empath gift that informs you about what is happening with another person's body.

- ∿ "Informs you."
- ∿ "Another person's body."
- ∿ Important clues, right?

Physical Intuition does *not* involve personally downloading painful emotions into your personal experience. With this particular empath gift you do not necessarily feel any emotions.

Furthermore, every empath gift confers an ability, a potential, a something that the empath can eventually learn to use with skill. Each empath possesses at least one significant gift for *directly experiencing what it is like to be another person*. Period. You don't necessarily feel other people's feelings in any way.

This Program for Empath Empowerment could help Blake to develop skill that supports his gift. Then he can choose to experience another person or not. Equally important, by developing skill, Blake will not take on Imported STUFF.

Long before then, while Blake is unskilled as an empath, going to a simple party can become so complicated. Picture him there, crushing on a potential new date while his back registers a scary new kind of pain. Under those circumstances, what might he do?

- ∼ Blake might try asking himself, "Whose STUFF is this, anyway?" Which I would not call a skill at all, more like a consolation prize for lacking real skill as an empath.

- ∼ Or Blake might try psychological boundary work, as if social skills could prevent Imported STUFF. Hello! Blake's subconscious mind took on that STUFF long before his conscious mind got a clue.

Granted, it's interesting to probe for the source of Blake's STUFF. So what? Consciously playing with ideas about who caused his STUFF won't budge that astral-level debris.

- ∼ Another common strategy among today's unskilled empaths? Blake might feel sorry for himself or worry. Could he be a victim of psychic attack? Perhaps Blake will now worry that the back pain is a warning, and start fearing his crush at the party is secretly an energy vampire or toxic personality.

- ∼ Will self-pity or fear of psychic vampires prevent Imported STUFF? Not in the least.

Blake could do so much better for himself. He can avoid physical symptoms. No more drip-drip-drip.

Once skills are established, Blake's Physical Oneness will be routinely turned OFF, including at parties. His gift for Physical Oneness will bring information only when Blake purposely chooses to fly in spirit.

Being fully protected energetically, doing a dedicated technique for Skilled Empath Merge, phew! Blake will also spare himself the mess of having Imported STUFF land in his subconscious mind and aura.

Why overcomplicate life, using the conscious mind to try and fix subconscious energies? (An attempt that doesn't work, anyway.)

Blake's conscious mind — and yours — can accomplish many things. Not that one, though. Subconscious problems require skills that are effective subconsciously. In that context, conscious worrying cannot work.

While Developing Empath Empowerment

How about Blake's experiences while developing Empath Empowerment? Suppose that Blake is not fully skilled yet but learning. Perhaps he has been reading this very book.

Suppose that Blake has progressed beyond this chapter and learned the "Coming Home" technique. Before attending this particular party, he has been doing the "Coming Home" technique every day for a month.

Brave Empath, this skill (which you will learn in Part Four), automatically turns all your empath gifts OFF. "Coming Home" protects you from unskilled empath merge, with help that lasts for approximately 24 hours.

Learning this core technique could take you as long as washing your car or getting a mani-pedi. For the next couple of weeks, you might spend last 20 minutes daily. Continuing practice can reduce the time. Eventually you can receive the full benefit from just 1-2 minutes per day.

Becoming fully skilled as an empath is a matter of degree. Despite learning "Coming Home," which will provide your single best form of protection as an empath, you still might slip up from time to time, with empath gifts flipping ON. It takes a bit of time and practice for that OFF position to become established as a habit.

What if you slip up? Suppose that you are enjoying a fabulous party when suddenly you start to feel a strange new backache that seemingly comes out of nowhere?

As a semi-skilled empath, you would at least notice that something had happened. Then you could use the "Empath's First Aid" technique to get that STUFF out of your aura and physical system. (This technique is also coming up in Part Four.)

Brave Empath, you have already progressed at Empath Empowerment just by reading this chapter. "Empath's First Aid" and "Coming Home" will enhance your skill level.

First things first, though: Owning and embracing your gifts. Maybe reading this chapter has added a meaningful Aha! to your understanding. Have you learned that you have Physical Oneness rather than Physical Intuition? Or vice versa? Or perhaps you won't be putting either one of these gifts on your personal List of My Empath Gifts.

Either way, that clarity can help you to embrace whichever gifts you have, vital to this Program for Empath Empowerment.

Can you still be an empath without possessing either of these physically-oriented empath gifts? Sure. I ought to know. I don't have either one.

CHAPTER 13

Emotional Intuition

In life there is more than one way for a person to be outed. EMOTIONAL INTUITION outs other people. Emotionally. Constantly.

It's not as if the unskilled empath ever wanted to know. Inadvertently you learn so much. For instance, what is your friend Cameron really feeling?

Admittedly some non-empaths are great at *reading* emotions, especially Highly Sensitive Persons. Like them, empaths without Emotional Intuition can develop the skill of emotional intelligence. Because *all* people can develop a higher Emotional IQ (as discussed back in Chapter 2).

Emotional Intuition is different, though. If you can do it now, you have always done it. Far back as you can remember, uncanny insights have come to you about other people's feelings.

Regarding your friend Cameron, for instance, you are eligible for the glory version of knowing about his emotions. And what would that be?

Emotional Intuition, The Glory

Emotions are so tricky. Did you know that the English language has 3,000 words for different emotions? Yet we still don't have enough words for them all, a famous example being *Schadenfreude,* a German word for the sort of pleasure that comes from enjoying somebody else's suffering.

Knowing fancy words or not, when you have Emotional Intuition and you do an official technique for flying in spirit, wow, do you ever learn about the emotions of your Discovery Person!

But are you, personally, "Feeling what another person is feeling"? No, not with Emotional Intuition.

Instead, as yourself, you download information about another human heart. Maybe what your friend Cameron feels right now, with his many complex and even contradictory emotions, here and now.

For friendship, for business, for gaining wisdom, for service — oh, you can find so many ways to use the amazing privilege of access into Cameron's heart. If you were born with Emotional Intuition and then you complete this Program for Empath Empowerment, will you ever have an advantage in life!

Of course, no empath is born with skills. Lacking those skills, Emotional Intuition brings its own tricky, sticky, icky form of drip-drip-drip.

Emotional Intuition, The Pain

One sunny spring weekend you pull out your phone and call your mother. "Heeeeeeello," she groans.

Your next words? "Mom, what's wrong?"

Welcome to the world of *Unskilled Empath with Emotional Intuition.* Where you're privy to information you might strongly prefer not knowing. This version of TMI differs from the kind that arises through unskilled Physical Intuition.

Talking to your mother, it's like a weird kind of way-too-smart-phone. Imagine a new technology that teleports you directly into your mother's emotional distress. Does your mother feel sad right now? Hoo-boy, that's an understatement. Something about her voice has clued you into the entire emotional painting, vivid with shades of pathetic suffering. All you needed to hear was that one word. "Heeeeeeello."

At least, that's what can happen while you are unskilled with this gift. Emotional Intuition, unskilled, can switch on and off as if it has a will of its own. Without warning, you become the captive audience to somebody else's emotions.

In the case of your mother, the sound of her voice tells you the whole story. Is it anger? A guilt trip she is ready to lay on you? Fear? With Emotional Intuition, you could get hit with a dozen simultaneous variations on Mom Misery.

Maybe she wants to repeat a sad story that you have heard countless times before. She's hoping you will sympathize. Ha! That's like asking a graduate student in math to practice counting to 10.

What makes listening to your Mom's story so exquisitely painful (or exasperating) is the sheer redundancy. With this empath gift, you know what Mom is feeling full force... before she finishes her first sentence. When she recounts her sad tale, blow by blow, it's like hitting you with repeat blows from a sledgehammer.

"Then he said to me, 'You're wrong.' The nerve! Can you imagine how frustrated I felt?"

Imagine? Hardly.

Why would you have to imagine? You heard frustration loud and clear when she cleared her throat at the start of each paragraph. You heard frustration in every sentence, every period, every pause. Had Mom been describing Easter bunnies and perky little sunbonnets, you still would have heard the subtext of woe.

So Many Varieties of Misery, It's Almost Comical

Really, if it didn't promise such glorious potential, you might want to sob about this empath gift. Or else laugh like a loon.

Because Emotional Intuition doesn't stop with people you know as well as your mother. When you pay attention to *anyone*, you can learn what is going on with that person emotionally. Assuming that you have this gift, and don't yet have the habit of turning it off, anything can start you journeying:

- ❧ Tone of voice
- ❧ Speed of words
- ❧ Odors around the body
- ❧ Subtle variations in the person's facial skin tone
- ❧ The texture of her lips as Mom sits, sulkily quiet

Although facial expressions may be useful for emotional intelligence), how important are they if you have Emotional Intuition? Merely superfluous.

Emotional Intuition,
The Special Sneaky Kind of Pain

Actually facial expressions may be not just superfluous but confusing. Expressions can lie, like words that people use to describe their emotions. Sometimes lying purposely, usually not.

One way to tell if you have Emotional Intuition is when people tell you how they, or other folks, feel and you're quite sure it is *wrong*.

What, is it common for people to name one mood when, really, they feel something quite different? Do human hands have more than one finger?

"How are you doing?," you ask your co-worker Bruce.

"Just fine," he says, flashing a closed-mouth smile.

Silently you register, "Grumpy, long-term depressed, slightly bored, and temporarily flustered." What else? "Bruce isn't lying to you purposely. He habitually ignores and mislabels his true feelings."

Brave Empath, do you constantly notice communication gaps like this? Then unskilled Emotional Intuition might cause you to feel pretty depressed yourself. On a good day you might giggle inwardly from the perpetual TMI. Hey, Marcel Proust wrote novels.

Whatever your reaction, you're entitled. Only you're better off using skills to usually keep that potentially pesky gift turned OFF. You'll thrive when you can purposely use Emotional Intuition quickly and powerfully for a Skilled Empath Merge. One minute's worth, not all afternoon.

Sigmund Freud famously said, "Sometimes a cigar is just a cigar." Well, sometimes it sure would be nice to interact with other people and NOT know what they are going through emotionally. Empath skills make the difference.

Emotional Intuition
Versus Common Social Courtesies

What is the relationship of Emotional Intuition to other forms of emotional sensitivity? Embracing your empath gifts will be easier when you're not confusing them with these totally different experiences:

- COMPASSION means deep awareness of somebody's pain, combined with the desire to relieve it.

- SYMPATHY is a form of identification. Another person's mood triggers your own. You feel along with that person, which is what the word "sympathy" literally means. (Mirror neurons are involved.)

- APPEARING EMPATHIC? Here comes an especially important distinction, Brave Empaths. Appearing empathic is today's fancy term for "Being nice" or "Acting as though you care."

What do all three terms have in common? Absolutely nothing about being an empath. Behavior shows on the surface of life. Empath gifts show in a person's aura. Or not.

Compassion — like sympathy or appearing empathic — can be learned. These social skills draw on your past. By contrast, empath talent opens you up to your future.

In the emerging field of coaching empaths, some practitioners take an obviously empathetic approach. Empaths are sometimes treated as fragile and delicate, as if we empaths require sympathy. My approach is not to manage expectations about how an empath's life is, supposedly, going to be difficult.

Granted, that tender hand-holding can be very appealing. Well, Brave Empath, you will have to turn elsewhere for an Empath's Pity Party. I'd rather teach you effective skills to stop the subconscious drip-drip-drip.

Here's one final point of discernment about empath talent. None of it involves theorizing. Intellectually figuring out "What Bruce must be going through" can signal good intentions. It also can come across with all the grace of an early-model robot trying to waltz.

Emotional Intuition involves consciousness. All empath gifts do. For overwhelm related to any empath gift, your most productive approach is learning to turn that gift OFF, using techniques that involve consciousness.

Positioning an empath's awareness appropriately is what brings the greatest comfort. Avoid analyzing patterns of behavior... to manage distress... resulting from unskilled empath merges.

Knowing that help is on the way, you can relax and enjoy the rest of our tour of embraceable empath gifts.

CHAPTER 14

Emotional Oneness

EMOTIONAL ONENESS is an inside job. You take on other people's emotions as though they belonged to you.

Maybe you're often "malled" like Emily, who thought she just hated shopping. Perhaps you wonder if you have the wrong set of friends. Or you try avoiding negative people as if they were toxic. Well, thank goodness you found this Program for Empath Empowerment. You have something effective to look forward to. Even something glorious.

Emotional Oneness, The Glory

Did you ever wish you had an identical twin, a nice one? Imagine how well that twin could understand what you were feeling.

Some of us search for a soul mate, wishing that one special person could deliver a comparable kind of understanding.

Who hasn't longed to feel heard and seen and touched that deeply? Especially if you never had to say a word to be understood?

Well, a Skilled Empath with Emotional Oneness can be that sort of person to you. Alternatively, you can become that sort of person to others. What a privilege!

It feels so profoundly worthwhile when you can do this. Through this one empath gift alone, you can help others to fulfill one of the most universal human needs.

Every empath gifts matters. But this one can allow you to know the near-ineffable, regarding any person's emotions.

To clarify the distinction between Emotional Intuition and Emotional Oneness, let's suppose that your friend Allyson's feelings are like a juicy mango.

As a Skilled Empath with Emotional Intuition, you can give Allyson a superb, detailed description of all the flavors and textures, so much detail about the taste of that mango.

What's different for a Skilled Empath with Emotional Oneness? It's as though you eat an exact duplicate of Allyson's mango, tasting it directly. Then you have even more to describe and validate, more to use for helping her.

Emotional Oneness, The Pain

What's just as unique as your potential service to others with Emotional Oneness? All the kinds of emotional pain that flow from having this gift while you're still unskilled. It can feel like being a vacuum cleaner for other people's emotional suffering.

No matter how pleasant your friend's manners, how positive her conversation... when the two of you talk and she is suffering emotionally, what happens to you?

Ouch! Even a sweet, friendly conversation can leave you exhausted emotionally.

Before attaining skill, Emotional Oneness brings your subconscious mind cascading heaps of data, as if you start receiving unimaginable amounts of e-mail spam. Each random emotion feels as if it were generated by *you*, perhaps indicating something terribly defective about *you*.

Not true. Unfortunately it is normal for emotional life to be exhausting until you learn to turn this gift OFF. Another example:

You are riding a bus. Other passengers sit and gaze out the windows or play with their electronic toys. You, though? You don't have to look out any window to see "The sights."

On every side your bus-mates press upon you, their assorted moods dripping directly into your gut. One short ride may pull you into Emotional Oneness with:

- A deeply depressed mother, nearly asleep while clutching her toddler
- An angry divorcee who glares competitively at every woman in sight who might qualify as a trophy wife
- The weird and wacky playfulness of teenage boys after school
- Hidden giggles from a teenage girl who watches them
- Scariest of all, the numbed out, tranquilized emotions of a pleasant-faced businessman

Can experiences like this be nerve wracking? You bet. Sometimes you may wonder if, like that guy with the three-piece suit, you ought to tranquilize yourself into numbness. Please don't. Just keep on getting yourself skills.

The Very Weirdest Part

What's weirdest of all about unskilled Emotional Oneness?

Brave Empath, I have thought about this long and hard. I had to. Because Emotional Intuition and Emotional Oneness are both in my personal gift set, but Emotional Oneness caused me much more serious problems, back when I was unskilled.

When moods go up and down, for no apparent reason — that's awful. To some degree, *every* empath gift causes that. Which is why another term for "Unskilled empath" could be "Living in hell."

Note: Many an unskilled empath has worried, "Am I bipolar?" And sometimes such problems are diagnosed. If this has happened to you, keep taking your meds while developing empath skills on the side. Evaluate later with your doctor every few months. (Sometimes medication is discontinued after empath skills are established.)

Turns out, sometimes there is no medical cause for the manic feelings or the depression or the other versions of unpredictable mood swings. That especially holds true for empaths born with Emotional Oneness.

That said, mood swings aren't the worst thing about having Emotional Oneness without yet having solid empath skills. To me, what's the weirdest part? The *emotional confusion.*

Most folks, empaths or not, have intense feelings sometimes. Coping with them is hard enough when all of those emotions belong to you.

What happens when other people's feelings are constantly added to this mix? Added without warning or control, and often no conscious recognition of the process!

Torment is not too intense a word for it. With Emotional Oneness, every kind of emotional misery imaginable has been visited upon you, starting from the day you were born.

Meanwhile, it's quite typical to try and make emotional sense out of that emotional stew.

Good luck, figuring that out! Even if you do, any conscious figuring out is done after emotions (and Imported STUFF from others) have become your personal problem. Really, I don't think that *torment* is too strong a word for describing life this way.

Let's take the example of your friend Allyson, who might herself be an unskilled empath with Emotional Oneness.

Allyson has a secret. She considers herself a hopeless, neurotic mess. Emotionally she suffers intensely, and has since childhood. Sometimes Allyson asks herself, "Why do I feel so much pain? My life hasn't been that hard."

- ∿ Has Allyson grown up in the slums, in a crowded and filthy apartment, infested with rats? No.
- ∿ Were there gangs, gunfire and murder? No.

~ Was Allyson sexually molested? Raped? Pillaged?
No, no, no.

You get the idea, Brave Empath. In objective reality, Allyson's life hasn't been all that horrible. She can watch TV any day of the week and see loads of examples where other people go through (external) drama that's far worse than anything happening to her.

"I have no right to feel this bad," Allyson tells herself. "I must be crazy."

Well, she isn't. Neither was I, back in the day. How I wish that every confused, talented empath with Emotional Oneness would get the skills you are learning.

Embracing your empath gifts isn't easy if you have gone through this kind of confusion and suffering. Trust me here, Brave Empath, and don't blame your gift. All you need is skill. Then your life will change for the simpler.

The drained energies, intellectual confusion and self-doubt, an emotional stew that may have seemed inescapable — problems that have pained you all your life — all this is about to come under control.

Emotional Oneness *not* on purpose is misery. But life as a skilled empath is another matter entirely. If you were born with this gift, some day you will thank your lucky stars.

CHAPTER 15

Intellectual Empath Ability

INTELLECTUAL EMPATH ABILITY means a talent for energetically sharing another person's thought process. With unskilled empath merge, your usual way of thinking can change so drastically, it might temporarily seem as though another person's perspective is really your own.

Are you literally thinking that other person's thoughts, like mind reading? No, it's more that you experience the other person's thinking *process*.

Which is plenty. Can that ever be confusing, at least until you become a skilled empath!

Intellectual Empath Ability, The Glory

Because Intellectual Empath Ability is so abstract, maybe it's simplest to start describing this gift in terms of the nots.

- ∽ Intellectual Empath Ability is *not* the same as academic intelligence. Your IQ could be high or low. What matters is that your smarts wear traveling shoes.

- ∽ Teachers, salespeople, first-rate executives, technology wizards, and effective parents in large families... do *not* necessarily have Intellectual Empath Ability.

- ∽ But if they do have the gift, they can follow the maze of your thought process and guide you away from some dusty, lonely, intellectual corner.

With unskilled empath merge, Intellectual Empath Ability generally brings confusion. While Skilled Empath Merge can brilliantly expand your ability to communicate. Through consciousness you can learn how anyone's mind works.

Maybe you are wondering about effective communicators who are *not* Intellectual Empaths. Those super-effective teachers, sales-people, etc., how do they manage? Communication skills could keep them going, or maybe flexible thinking. Non-empaths may know their subjects so thoroughly, they can play bits of information on demand, moving into "Rewind" or "Fast Forward" as needed.

Perhaps one listener needs to hear the complete recitation over and over, while another prefers to hear one sentence and supply a personal paragraph that repeats the basic idea several times. Mental agility and good pacing, though commendable talents, are not the same as Intellectual Empath Ability.

What, when I make this distinction are you shocked, shocked? Very likely you really do have Intellectual Empath Ability. Based on personal experience, you expect that the only way to communicate is to do your habitual mind-meld.

Incidentally, this gift is *not* related to being a "Good conversationalist." Often intellectual empaths come across as indistinguishable from other people driven by intelligence: Nerdy, aloof, dry, or relentlessly precise. No glitter.

Answering even one of the following questions in the affirmative can indicate Intellectual Empath Ability:

- Are you interested in music, math, chess, and/or computers... especially because they highlight different ways to think?

- Do you intensely feel the challenge (or delight, or absence) of intellectual companionship?

- Do you have a knack for learning complex abstract ideas... from the *background* of conversations?

Concepts could be as contagious for you as having a yawn passed around the room. Jennifer, a computer consultant, told me, "Basically I'm not very good at computers, but I can travel to the consciousness of people who are... and move around where they do what they do."

Another aspect of Intellectual Empath Ability is the ability to see two or more sides to a story — then turn each one into a big, vivid, and complex story.

Intellectual Empath Ability, The Pain

Of course there's a downside to this form of giftedness, so long as you keep slipping into unskilled empath merge. Here's a hint: Does the word "indecisive" mean anything to you?

After slip-sliding into other ways of thinking, it can be hard to win an argument. Sometimes it can be hard to even remember what you thought when the argument began.

Why limit yourself to that point of view? Well, because it is yours. Everyone is entitled to a point of view, a perspective, a priority.

As an Intellectual Empath, it can be a short leap from "I don't know what I really think" to "I am nothing."

Other common consequences of too many unskilled empath merges?

- What I think isn't important.
- Other people don't respect my opinion.
- Other people don't notice me.
- Other people don't really care about me.

None of this is necessarily true. However it's hard to feel secure as a person until this wonderful gift is supported by skills. Before then your effectiveness at handling conflict can be compromised.

Sadly, Hamlet-like wavering does not inspire confidence in others.

The pain of Intellectual Empath Ability can also include a unique sad, lonely feeling. "If she really loved me, she would know how I think."

Actually not. Actually most people are not empaths. Even among empaths, most do not have this prize of yours, Intellectual Empath Ability.

Take comfort in that. Probably the people who love you most are not capable of reciprocating with your kind of insightful understanding.

It isn't about caring. Your gift comes easily to you. That doesn't mean other people are capable of the same empath gift. Lacking that, they cannot replicate perceptiveness like yours.

I have helped many an empath with this gift to rehab personal self-confidence. As empath skills grow, you may develop more respect for yourself, including that ingenious mind of yours. Results can help your career and social standing — not too shabby, considering the very abstract quality of this particular empath gift.

CHAPTER 16

Animal Empath Talent

ANIMAL EMPATH TALENT allows you to experience from the inside what it is like to be a member of the animal kingdom.

Without being taught how, you learn from your pet. You can learn different ways to be. That relationship with a dog or cat or turtle can become an inspiration, a love like no other.

One pet? You may wish to have many. You may secretly wish that life were like a lot of kid's books, where most of the characters are animals dressed up in human clothes.

Dealing with humans can be so messy. But animals? They're refreshingly direct, and so very much themselves.

How about meeting other people's pets, encountered by chance on the street? That can make your day.

Did you ever long for a radio station that just played love songs to animals?

Animal Empath Talent can be reason enough to get out of bed every morning.

Animal Empath Talent, The Glory

Each empath gift brings a unique capacity for profound learning and inspired service. For an Animal Empath, that service can be done directly with… animals.

One famous example is horse whisperer Monty Roberts, who has worked with more than 10,000 four-legged clients. Part of the inspiration for the novel *The Horse Whisperer* by Nicholas

Evans, Roberts has developed Join-Up, a nonviolent method of "starting" horses rather than "breaking" them. "Join-Up" could be considered a systematic use of Animal Empath talent.

If you're an Animal Empath, you may prefer whispering to pigs. Or ferrets. Whatever your creature of choice, you understand how it is to be that animal.

Perhaps you commune telepathically or stretch the limits of your human system to feel some of its perceptions. You can also appreciate what Animal Empath talent is *not*. It is *not* dressing your poodle, Queenie, in a white lace ensemble and feeding her sirloin on a silver platter. It is *not* imagining that your pet has feelings like your own.

Neither is Animal Empath Talent the same as being an animal communicator. One can learn animal communication as a form of psychic development. Studied that way, it's a skill.

By contrast, Animal Empath Talent is a wilder and freer kind of knowing. During a Skilled Empath Merge, you join with the animal's awareness. You may know his fears, his curiosities, or perhaps the sensations in his body.

That knowing can come as a oneness experience or an intuition experience, or both. In your habitual way, you explore a non-human form of consciousness. More power to you!

Power, incidentally, is where Roberts' aura shows its greatest distinctiveness. He succeeds at his work because he doesn't just communicate. He whispers. You see, he can whisper because he intimately knows the animal's deep experiences, quite an advantage for negotiation.

My aura reading research suggests that Roberts does his version of Skilled Empath Merge on whichever horse he is working with. Connected he remains, energetically, until he and the horse arrive at a friendly understanding about power.

Animal Empath Talent, The Pain

Power is one of those ways you are likely to suffer, Brave Empath, until you develop skill with Animal Empath Talent. Any of the following problems can happen.

Animal Empath Problem #1.
The pet's needs trump yours

Say that you are out walking your dog, Lassie. You need to walk slowly. Yesterday you strained your ankle. So today you really need to baby it.

Obediently Lassie sticks to your pace. Except your poor pooch feels so frustrated, it's upsetting. You force yourself to move faster.

After you make the sacrifice, maybe don't feel a thing until you get back home. Then awareness of your own pain sinks in.

And why didn't you feel a thing during the walk? Why didn't you take better care of yourself? What you noticed was Lassie's joy, romping and sniffing her way down the street. Definitely an unskilled empath-type problem — and I sure would love to help you get over that one.

Animal Empath Problem #2.
Upset by the strays

It is so common to encounter an animal that has been mistreated. Some might be vagrants in your neighborhood, like feral cats. With Animal Empath Talent you might feel guilt when you cannot take in any more pets. Guilt that keeps you from using you personal power to get more of what you need and want!

⁓ Sure, other animal lovers may speak of similar reactions. The difference is depth of experience. To non-empaths, observing a stray may be an upsetting sight, similar to seeing badly treated people on the nightly news. Being compassionate, a non-empath may wish to help.

〜 By contrast, with Animal Empath Talent, it's personal — like learning that a member of your family has gone homeless.

Animal Empath Problem #3.
Suffering along with neglected animals

Suppose that you're walking by a house when you hear a lonely dog bark, alone all day in the yard. Or you hear that dog, kept inside, barking valiantly to protect the property.

Yet being an Animal Empath, you hear more than the obvious. You hear the dog's loneliness, maybe even a sense of abandonment.

Many a loyal pooch is neglected. Not purposely. That dog's owner might keep that pet well fed and walked regularly, yet ignored. Some pets are bought for show, or provide a fun togetherness project for lovers who might just as well buy themselves a lawn statue. So many reasons cause people to inadvertently neglect their animals.

Now, you may not consider yourself a particularly emotional person. You might not care much for human adults who whine about their difficulties; human adults can do so much about their misery. By comparison, a pet seems like a helpless victim.

Yes, this vicarious suffering can be a very real problem for an unskilled empath. This personal suffering won't help any other creature one bit. And you might spin your wheels trying to help.

Animal Empath Problem #4.
Worried about the sick animals

Brave Empath, you have already read about gifts for Physical Oneness and Physical Intuition. You may have no such gift and thus be completely unable to relate to problems that are common for unskilled empaths who have those gifts. Yet with animals, energetic awareness of physical suffering could clobber you. Oops!

Whether you consciously know about an animal's problems or not, until you are skilled as an empath, you can suffer Imported STUFF from these animals.

Energetically their pain can become your pain. Physical pain could develop or you might start to worry, worry, worry about any random topic. (All this without once consciously knowing that animals were the source of your Imported STUFF.)

Animal Empath Problem #5.
Anger related to an animal's service

Ever notice how dogs often look like their humans? Of course they do. Every pet lives in service to the human "owner."

Dogs look like humans more than cats or goldfish because their bond is so strong, their energetic service so far-ranging.

Animal communicators and animal healers know a simple energetic fact of life. "Looking like the owner" is the ridiculously obvious part. Paying attention more deeply, it becomes clear how pets can take on physical illnesses and psychological problems... belonging to their humans.

With Animal Empath Talent, you don't need to be told about this kind of energetic connection. Although you never studied Healing Touch for Animals® or animal communication, deep within, you know.

You know because consciously you have sympathized with that pet's "obvious" suffering:

- Maybe you feel how a poodle is wearing his master's hatred almost like an overcoat, nobly trying to help that master calm down.

- Maybe you take one look at that cat. And immediately you know she is energetically overloaded. Why? Because her owner has a serious spiritual imbalance that grows worse by the day. Could be, this hard-working pet feels like a failure since her owner suffers so.

∼ Consciously you may have noticed such things and wished that, at a minimum, the owner had a clue about all that sacrifice.

Guess what? Subconsciously, by then, you have taken on Imported STUFF from that pet. And maybe the human as well.

Later, when we discuss unskilled empath merges, you will understand better why none of these energetic merges really helps anyone else, not long term. Would you prefer to do something helpful? Become a skilled empath, do Skilled Empath Merge, and then take action at a human level. You know, use your power!

While you're still doing involuntary, subconscious unskilled merges, Imported STUFF is messing up your life. Without helping anyone, human or animal.

Animal Empath Problem #6.
Anxiety that makes no earthly sense

Not to depress you, Brave Empath with Animal Empath Ability, but I have left the worst example for last.

When you have this gift, you can receive Imported STUFF from animals you never have noticed at all. Not noticed consciously, that is.

Lacking conscious knowledge about your gift and Imported STUFF? This has not protected you, not in the least. For example, suppose that a nearby property used to have lots of trees. Birds would fly there at nightfall.

Then a developer came, cut down all those trees, and built one more interchangeable chain store (like so many all over America). Where were all those the birds supposed to go?

Nobody thought about that.

Now, at dusk, those displaced animals fly around, circling wherever the trees used to be. You might not even notice them particularly.

In their bird-like way (not a human way) those birds are trying to figure out where to go for the night. And they live in terror.

When does that become your problem? While looking out the window to admire a sunset, you happen to see a few birds out the corner of your eye. Or maybe you hear some distant birdcalls.

Chance encounters like that can be enough to trigger a series of unskilled empath merges, straight into the aura of one bird, then another, then another. Imported STUFF finds a nesting place within you, causing chronic anxiety of a kind that has no appropriate human name.

Here's what matters most: This kind of anxiety will go away after you become a skilled empath.

Animal Empath Talent, The Worst of the Worst

No matter how much you love animals, being human, your conscious mind tends to focus on human frequencies of reality. Even with Animal Empath Talent, you still focus on human.

Consciously, then, you may underestimate the ongoing terror of animal life on earth. Despite your Animal Empath Talent, consciously you may underestimate the ongoing intensity of animal survival fears.

In English we have the saying, "It's a dog-eat-dog world." Certainly it is a "Fish-eat-fish world." For every form of animal life, there is plenty of terror to go around.

And here's one way that homo sapiens differ from other animals: Human fears are localized mostly in the individual. By contrast, animals participate strongly in collective consciousness for the species.

Maybe you have read in the Bible, "Not even a sparrow, worth only half a penny, can fall to the ground without your Father knowing it."

That's a Divine perspective, perhaps. What would be the bird perspective? When one sparrow falls, to some degree, every sparrow on earth registers a death.

Human empaths don't have either perspective, either a sparrow's or God's. However an unskilled Animal Empath will often merge in consciousness with the everyday tragedies of one favorite group of animals.

Brave Empath, this ongoing type of empath merge can become so intense that it causes you to neglect your own life, this incarnation's precious opportunity for personal development. Distracting you from life, liberty, the pursuit of happiness, and the use of your personal power to advocate for *yourself*.

Some Animal Empaths blow animal suffering way out of proportion. And they can't stop themselves — at least, until they become skilled empaths.

Can you relate to what I have described? On the bright side, you may wish to reread this chapter after you have become a Master Empath. Sometimes we can fully credit a familiar suffering... only after it has vanished.

CHAPTER 17

Plant Empath Talent

Some avid gardeners have it. And farmers. Sometimes it's great cooks. Also possible? You can barely make packaged ramen noodles, and right now you cultivate zero houseplants. Nonetheless you have PLANT EMPATH TALENT.

If you possess this magnificent empath gift, you can have it exclusively with one type of growing thing, like basil or roses. Or maybe you have it with every plant on this gorgeous green earth.

Either way, Plant Empath Talent allows you to join in consciousness with things that grow. Through consciousness, you enter into their slowly throbbing bodies and feel your human equivalent of what it is like to be them.

Or it might be more your style to receive information as your own person, knowledge clearly at a distance while still feeling like yourself (no confusion there). Except your personal energies still get scrambled due to Imported STUFF — a hidden sort of mess, not obvious experiences of being thrown off balance in everyday life. Nicer, sort of.

Hey, why leap ahead to the pain aspect, the STUFF, how life can turn unexpectedly weird until you become a skilled empath? Instead let's turn to...

Plant Empath Talent, The Glory

Doing Skilled Empath Merge with a plant can be such a treat, imparting useful information to supplement your existing skill sets at gardening or cooking or farming. Compared to your peers, you will understand more about your plant of choice, understand because of subconscious input from your empath merges.

A shining example of a skilled empath with Plant Empath talent was Luther Burbank, the horticultural genius who developed the Burbank potato, the Burbank tomato, and more. He also developed an edible form of cactus. As reported to Paramahansa Yogananda in *Autobiography of a Yogi*, plants listened when Burbank told them, "You don't need your defensive thorns. I will protect you."

Of course, you don't have to undertake such ambitious projects before you qualify as a Plant Empath. Also note: This gift is *not* the same as talking to your plants, commendable though that may be. Can you feel what it is like to *be* a particular plant? That's the requirement for being able to call yourself a Plant Empath.

And you don't need fancy skills at horticulture to benefit, either. Once I visited my friend Faith. On a tour around her apartment, she paused at a plant in her bedroom. Unlike other houseplants in her gorgeous apartment, this one was in trouble. Faith sighed. She told me, "I've tried everything to help this plant. I don't know what more I can do."

Faith knew a lot more about home gardening than me, but I figured it couldn't hurt to do a Skilled Empath Merge. Perhaps I might discover what Faith's plant needed by going directly to the source.

"I'm lonely," her plant told me. "I need to be with other plants, not all alone here in this room."

In our last chapter, you were introduced to the idea that house pets take on problems from their people. Well, house plants also serve their people. It so happened that Faith was single at this time, and going through a pretty lonely phase, socially.

In retrospect, I can appreciate the connection between the plant and her owner. At the time, I had no clue that Faith felt lonely. Incidentally, Brave Empath, that can be part of the joy of using any empath gift, once skilled. You learn things you never expected. And sometimes you get to help people you love.

Something else pretty fascinating? This plant's version of "I'm lonely" was not a human, emotional kind of lonely. It was plant loneliness, combining energetic, physical, and social components of being that plant.

Like every empath gift that is not about human consciousness, after you develop skills, hello! You can explore so many exotic versions of Otherness.

What happened to Faith and her plant? She took my advice and brought a couple more plants into her bedroom. As for that listless-looking, new friend of mine with the gorgeous green body? Faith reported, it perked right up.

Plant Empath Talent, The Pain

Friendship and love do not have to bring suffering. Similarly, empath gifts do not have to cause you pain. No empath gift necessarily dooms you to suffering.

Until you become skilled as a Plant Empath, however, conscious life is frequently soggy with pain, pain, pain and drip-drip-drip. How come?

Brave Empath, have you ever walked into somebody else's home and found a languishing houseplant? Have you ever walked by a vase of cut flowers, drooping in their vase, long past their prime?

Most people are NOT Plant Empaths. So it's understandable how they would allow such things in their homes. Or offices. Or gardens. Faith, for instance, is a Highly Sensitive Person with loads of great qualities. She has exceptional skills in different areas of life. Faith is, however, not an empath. Although very good to her plants, Faith has zero Plant Empath Talent.

So there's no reason to blame her for what she happened to point out during the tour that she gave me of her apartment:

The equivalent of a quadriplegic, sitting in a flowerpot, patiently waiting to die.

Folks who are otherwise very refined will keep around the equivalent of nearly dead people (or animals), proudly displayed in some very attractive vases.

Guess what? If you're a Plant Empath, that happens to bother you. Subconsciously, and maybe even consciously, you can hear the wails and screams... even shrieks... coming from a mostly hidden houseplant, stuck in some faraway corner, having a near-death experience... and not the nice kind, either.

No wonder, as an unskilled empath, you can visit someone like my lovely friend Faith, and later return home feeling as though you have been punched in the stomach.

No, that is not literally what happened to me while visiting Faith. Still, consider the implications. If you can relate to Plant Empath Talent, this alone could explain why — for years — and for no reason that crossed your mind —you have sometimes felt like a pathetic trampled patch of weeds.

Previously you never knew what would trigger these terrible feelings, the inexplicable stiffness in your legs, an inner numbness like feeling half-alive. Who would have known that, all along, the philodendron did it?

CHAPTER 18

Crystal Empath Talent

Moving on from animal and vegetable matters, yes, it is possible to be an empath with the mineral kingdom, too. CRYSTAL EMPATH TALENT allows you to experience directly what it is like to be an aquamarine or a diamond, a wise old rock by a river bed or, perhaps, a splendid pebble that empaths with different gifts might overlook in the woods.

Yet many a born empath with this wonderful gift might overlook the gift itself.

Personally, I had no clue until my friend James took me to a rock shop. I had never gone to that kind of store. Shelves displayed pointy quartz crystals. I thought, "Whatever." Then, like any casual shopper, I picked up a large piece of quartz and held it in my hand. Could have been a piece of plastic, for all I knew.

Suddenly that crystal took me on a journey in consciousness. Wow, and I thought I was just holding a rock! Only later did I learn that crystals are used for healing because of their lively vibrational qualities. Not every Crystal Empath has that dramatic sort of recognition. So let's go into more particulars.

Crystal Empath Talent, the Glory

Being a Crystal Empath could help you to design jewelry in an inspired manner. The gift is useful for mining or sculpting or working in the construction industry.

Or Crystal Empath Talent might make you the top salesperson for a jewelry store, with an uncanny knack for matching up customers with appropriate inventory.

Alternatively Crystal Empath Talent might help you to carve out a career as a sculptor. Perhaps fabulous work as a geologist. Maybe you might develop an uncanny knack for pouring concrete.

Really, Brave Empath, I could have named this gift "Mineral Empath Talent." But how inspiring is that? Such a name starts putting me to sleep, and I actually have the gift. Hence my choosing the slightly more glam appellation of "Crystal Empath Talent."

What can be absolutely glorious about this gift? Using it for healing, via Native American wisdom, shamanism, or other skill sets.

Admittedly this empath gift may not be the first one that you associate with wisdom traditions. Herbalists, with Plant Empath Talent, may be better known. Or you might think of Animal Empath Talent, so useful for native tribes and their leaders. However, Crystal Empath Talent has equally been a specialty of powerful holistic healers from time immemorial.

In ancient days, medicine men endowed with this gift, and armed with knowledge, would collaborate with samples of the mineral kingdom. A wise healer would hear the call of a seemingly insignificant pebble. He would pause, bend down, and welcome the stone to his personal collection of power tools. That simply, he would have acquired one more valuable resource for helping others.

Some holistic healers today do something similar, their technical skills for crystal healing amplified by the intimate knowledge available only to a Crystal Empath. Being a skilled empath exponentially enlivens any technical training you receive in a related field. That includes mining the mysteries of minerals.

Famed crystal healer Katrina Raphaell is a great example of someone whose Crystal Empath Talent supplements awesome technical skills. The crystal healers she trains are not necessarily empaths. Katrina can't teach that. She teaches how to facilitate energy healing by using the special properties of semi-precious and precious stones, polished gems, and crystals. Learning to do effective crystal layouts is both an art and a science.

Brave Empath, you might consider studying crystal healing a bit, just to find out if you also have Crystal Empath Talent. Otherwise you will have no sense of the amazing thrill it can bring. Regardless, if you do have this empath gift, you will have suffered your entire life from the impact of unskilled empath merges.

I will get to that, but first...

My Big Disclaimer about Crystal Empath Talent

Attuning to precious stones through empath talent is *not* the same as good taste in jewelry... nor the exuberant flair for self-decoration that demands wearing no fewer than 20 rings, earrings, necklaces, and bracelets — all meant to help you look good.

Sheer quantity of jewelry bears no relationship to being a Crystal Empath, nor does enthusiasm for body piercing. Crystal Empath talent involves a particular knack for travel into the consciousness of the mineral kingdom.

Consider the saying, "Diamonds are forever." To a jewelry collector, this may work on a sentimental level. By contrast, this Crystal Empath finds nothing about eternity in the experience of being a diamond. They have a very here-and-now, multi-level intelligence, alight with a transformative quickness. Beyond that, each individual diamond you meet will possess its own remarkable quirks.

Guess what else? Some fabulous fake diamonds are manufactured these days. Energetically they do more than just look good. New discoveries are marketed all the time. Don't discount them until you have picked up a sample and explored it. You may be in for a surprise. Then proceed to play with quartz crystals, calcites, pearls, amethysts.

If you do have Crystal Empath Talent, going to a big gem show or jewelry store can feel like taking a trip to Disneyland.

Crystal Empath Talent, the Pain

The problem is not personal hygiene. Not quite.

But by way of analogy, what if you had never learned to bathe? Your person would carry the familiar fragrance that human adults tend to have in their natural state.

Well, problems would follow, natural state or not.

Similarly, stones soak up energies. Crystals and gemstones, especially, soak up energies. They bring in gorgeous new energies, too, depending upon the properties of that particular bit of lapidary substance.

Brave Empath, you know about Imported STUFF. Guess what happens to your jewelry when you pick up some of that STUFF? Some of it goes directly into your diamond engagement ring or that lovely turquoise stone on the chain you are wearing around your neck.

Oops.

In Chapter 28, you will learn in detail what happens during an unskilled empath merge, how an empath imports STUFF without feeling a thing. (At least, without consciously feeling a thing at the time.)

Gemstones do something similar, whether precious or semi-precious or one of those manufactured marvels like cubic zirconia.

In short, you wind up wearing your pain. Some attractive decoration, such an auric adornment!

The day passes. You start your new day, oblivious to all the Imported STUFF still carried over from unskilled merges with the mineral kingdom. Bright and early, you take a shower (because, really, that previous idea about not washing was just an analogy).

Well, no such luck for your personal adornments. They are not energetically clean. Nor will they become clean until you learn how to cleanse them energetically.

How to Energetically Clean
Your Crystals

Jewelry cleaners will not suffice. Choose from the following three methods. If you have a fragile stone or delicate jewelry settings, avoid the third method. Besides, the first two are easier.

1.   My favorite approach is to use a specially designed purple plate. (To purchase one, go online for a reputable dealer of purple plates, as invented by Ralph Bergstresser.) Place your crystals on the purple plate and leave them for 15 minutes. Done!

2.   Or place your crystals on a crystal cluster. (Ask at a rock shop. Crystal clusters are gorgeous, and not necessarily costly.) Since they are self-cleaning, you won't have to clean that quartz healing appliance. Again, 15 minutes will suffice.

3.   Otherwise use a nonreactive container, such as a ceramic bowl, stainless steel saucepan, or glass container. Make sure this vessel is dry. Pour in several inches of sea salt or kosher salt. Bury your crystal in the salt. After 15 minutes or longer, take out your crystal and brush off any remaining salt.

     You may re-use this salt indefinitely, so long as you keep it dry. Cover your vessel between uses; this will keep the salt reasonably clean.

Although 15 minutes is enough to cleanse gemstones energetically, there's no harm in prolonging these energy baths. Here's what I do. After I take off any gemstone jewelry I have been wearing, or I finish using a crystal, automatically it goes right onto my large purple plate. Next day, I put away all my cleaned-up goodies. That simple.

Now there's a fine way to make that engagement ring come alive! (A clean diamond's song just might last forever.)

More Hidden Causes of Pain
for a Crystal Empath

Before you read the following, remember not to worry, Brave Empath. Old causes of pain are about to change, however hidden they used to be. My goal is to validate what you have been going through, if you were born as a Crystal Empath.

So far, you have been warned about hidden problems with your own cherished adornments and, maybe, healing tools in the form of crystals. Simple cleanup will take care of that.

But how about walking around as a not-yet-skilled empath, randomly doing unskilled empath merges? What might happen to you resulting from *other* people's jewelry?

What if you enjoy a posh night at the opera? Or maybe you simply ride a bus. Gee, Brave Empath, do you think some of those folks might be wearing diamond rings or other jewelry with gems or semi-precious stones?

You think? And do you think that all of these jewelry owners use one of our three cleansing methods?

Ironic, I know. Many jewelry lovers do a fine job of keeping their adornments physically clean. (Especially bank tellers, have you ever noticed? Well, those are people who value material life.)

Your typical jewelry lovers do the personal kind of washing just fine. They don't smell like cavemen. Yet their adornments are writhing in slow-motion agony.

Therefore, after your elegant night at the opera, you may well take home plenty of Imported STUFF.

Beyond that, consider other social situations and all the folks who are wearing exhausted, and potentially exhausting, jewelry. What about folks you know who get "malled" like Emily? These suffering specimens of humanity might have only this one empath gift.

Look, that's all it takes to feel really, really bad... at the mall and elsewhere.

No wonder you are wise to read every description of every single empath gift, not just the ones you have assumed might apply. Crystal Empath Talent. Who woulda thunk it?

Such a counter-culture idea, ahead of its time. Yes, for Crystal Empaths, the problem with getting "malled" isn't being hopelessly neurotic, nor are psychic vampires to blame.

The cause could have been imported pain from marital fights five years ago, twinkling out (still) from some very expensive diamond engagement rings. Rings that Emily walked right by... without once even noticing them. Afterwards Emily came home carrying *that*.

What if this sort of thing has happened to you? Don't blame the crystals. Don't blame yourself, either. Just keep on owning and embracing your empath gifts and, soon as possible, managing them.

This Program for Empath Empowerment definitely includes all the skills you need to manage energies from the mineral kingdom. When you stop the drip-drip-drip, you're protected whichever glorious gifts you possess, and no matter whatever anyone else has purchased from life's Jewelry Department.

Crystal Empaths, save your depth experience of gem-consciousness for times when you do Skilled Empath Merge.

A Special Treat, Juicy as an Emerald

In preparation for when you become a Master Empath, you can start now to save photos from the Oscars and similar gatherings, where much-photographed stars are wearing priceless gems.

Or start taking your own photos at museums that display legendary gems, such as The Hope Diamond, on display for free at the Smithsonian Institution in Washington, D.C.

Of course, you don't require famous crystals to be inspired by Skilled Empath Merge. Once you learn how, you can research any person, any gemstone.

However, famous celebrities may gradually seem less important, and not just their gems.

Why? Because you can receive inspiration from so-called "ordinary" people in your life right now.

You can become like a young child who enjoys a simple pebble just as much as some big, fancy toy. Empath skills can awaken your heart of delight, even as you keep all your hard-won knowledge as an adult.

Certainly, with empath skills, you'll be protected from sorrowful diamonds. While the wisdom that beams from an inexpensive quartz crystal can transport you.

CHAPTER 19

Environmental Empath Talent

What if you were born with ENVIRONMENTAL EMPATH TALENT?

Then you have a gift for linking your consciousness with the body of Mother Earth. One way to tell if you have this gift is to recall what happens while you take a walk someplace beautiful.

Exploring nature, most people see or smell or touch or taste... while their consciousness stays right on the surface of physical reality. Travel provides us with plenty to enjoy. But let's be clear. Swapping around your environment does not necessarily mean the same thing as making a shift to your consciousness.

A selfie taken at home could be Photoshopped to make it seem you traveled just about anywhere. For instance, Lily is a Photoshop wizard. She takes a picture of herself and her partner Liam. Then she adds fresh backgrounds to create a slideshow, their virtual world tour:

- Lily and Liam stand, beaming, at a beach at a Caribbean resort.
- Next it's off to the Sonoran Desert, with Lily and Liam pose in an identical manner, only now they are standing next to a huge saguaro. Such a great picture — after all, the saguaro is the largest cactus in the United States.
- Ooh la la! Now Lily and Liam are standing (amazingly, still in that very same pose) very close to the base of the Eiffel Tower.

Perhaps the electronic tinkering is done so well, each pseudo-travel image looks believable. Neither Lily nor Liam changes a bit in their consciousness, though. Lily and Liam at home they remain, looking good in their pictures.

Fair enough. However, as real-life travelers, Lily and Liam may not change in consciousness, either. They may fly with the rest of their tour group. They may speak exactly like tourists. Read their guidebooks like tourists. Shop like crazy. Adore the food. Acting like real tourists because they *are* tourists.

Yet they do not fly in consciousness.

Indisputably they hear Caribbean surf; they sweat from lush tropical heat. Are they experiencing in their consciousness how it is, the special excellence of being in that particular part of the world? Nope.

For that, a person needs Environmental Empath Talent.

Environmental Empath Talent, the Glory

In more ways than one it's a trip, having Environmental Empath Talent. Do you find that you feel differently when located at a forest, ocean, mountain, or desert? As you hike, does it thrill you to move from one ecological system to another?

Do the smells, the plants, the animals stop you in your tracks? Do you become a captive to wonder?

That's the upside and the inside. There's also a downside. For an unskilled empath with Environmental Empath Talent, you may have suffered for years without knowing the real cause.

Environmental Empath Talent, the Pain

When a glade of trees near you is cut down to make way for yet another shopping center, it can hurt. Likewise, you may suffer due to destruction of rainforests on another continent entirely. Far-fetched? Not really.

All on earth are connected in consciousness. Until you get yourself skills, you will suffer needlessly, depending on how much talent you have as an Environmental Empath.

Aware of the cause. Or not.

Consciously aware of your subconscious suffering. Or not.

What is the worst part of all? None of your Imported STUFF as an empath will create meaningful, permanent healing for anyone else, whether animal, vegetable, mineral, or environmental.

Granted, voluntary suffering on behalf of the environment can be beautiful. It can have great meaning, depending on a person's religious path. Joanna Macy, for instance, encourages the practice of "Despair Work" in her deeply devotional book, *World As Lover, World As Self*.

"To experience anguish and anxiety in the face of the perils that threaten us is a healthy reaction." she writes. "Far from being crazy, this pain is a testimony to the unity of life, the deep interconnections that relate us to all beings."

Learning to become a skilled empath is religion-neutral. With skills, you can practice your religion, giving and getting at least as much as before.

If you believe in Despair Work, you will do it at least as well after you have become a skilled empath. Also you will do it more effectively than all the non-empaths who also (unwittingly) practice Despair Work.

By all means, contemplate the misery of a particular ecosystem. Send prayers or do whatever else pleases you. Just don't walk around living with drip-drip-drip.

Brave Empath, regardless of your religious affiliation, know that Environmental Empath Talent without skill can cause immense personal suffering, psychologically, even physically, and at totally random times.

Unfortunately this particular kind of suffering, related to Imported STUFF, doesn't significantly help anyone or anything. (With all respect, I don't think Despair Work helps either, although it could be tremendously meaningful to the practitioners.)

By contrast, turning this empath gift OFF most of the time, and then turning it ON — only in a protected manner, with skill — this can help you to be of service. Effectively.

As a skilled empath, you might take up environmental activism with an insider's knowledge of priorities. For you, that could be best part of this training to own, embrace, and manage your special gifts as an empath.

Every Environmental Empath deserves to taste nature's flavors of joy. To do this with clarity and energetic protection, just keep moving forward in this Program for Empath Empowerment.

CHAPTER 20

Mechanical Empath Talent

With **MECHANICAL EMPATH TALENT**, you can join in consciousness with machines. You're a natural at making them work. Perhaps your gift will work better with one type of machine than another. So what?

Even if you only relate to one type of machine, this can be a fabulously useful talent to possess. And potentially lucrative, too.

As with other empath gifts, a Mechanical Empath isn't necessarily talented at experiencing how *all* machines operate. You might be just work well with computers or sewing machines. The point is that you do.

Mechanical Empath Talent, the Glory

In olden days, Brave Empath, you might have traveled everywhere by horse. You might have owned a few horses. Today you are far more likely to own a car.

Many mechanical helpers are owned by you, actually. Not necessarily chickens, goats, or horses but a mobile phone, a computer and TV, a refrigerator.

Probably there has never been a better time on earth for living with Mechanical Empath Talent. So many machines assist us, while technology continues to advance so very fast.

From a spiritual perspective, every complex machine has its own consciousness, much like a farm animal. Its mechanical body works a certain way. Each machine has its equivalent of normal health versus illness.

With Mechanical Empath Talent, you can learn to do Skilled Empath Merge with the machine of your choice: Learn how it is doing, operate it brilliantly, maybe assist with repair.

Ever dream of designing computer hardware or software? Lucky you! A skilled Mechanical Empath can research and solve problems as nobody else can.

Teaming up with your favorite type of machine, you may become extra-creative and resourceful. Spontaneously you may develop a knack for making that machine work. You can learn about it in abstract ways, more like a feeling than conscious analysis. Resulting insights will relate to the special quirks of that particular sort of machine.

In addition, Mechanical Empath Talent can combine with other empath gifts, like the one in our next chapter.

Mechanical *Intelligence*? Having that type of intelligence can be a great career asset. But also having Mechanical Empath Talent? Now that's really something!

Mechanical Empath Talent, the Pain

Despite all the glory, despite your potential to make loads of money in today's technological marketplace, let's talk drip-drip-drip. For an unskilled empath, Mechanical Empath Talent brings a very distinctive problem.

Machines often have glitches, ouches, pain. Not necessarily fun at all. You may know from experience how hidden problems in machines can become Imported STUFF in you... bringing you suffering without your necessarily fixing anything in objective reality.

What do I mean, pain from a computer or car? Does it seem weird to you, thinking that a machine can suffer? I'm about to give you an answer that makes sense to me. First, here's fair warning. The following ideas are is far-out, compared to the rest of this Program for Empath Empowerment.

If the following explanation makes you uncomfortable, skip forward to the next chapter.

Otherwise, here's what I have come to believe about machines from an energetic perspective. Each small or large appliance you own has a **DEVA** (pronounced DEHY-vah). This is an astral-level being, less well known than flower fairies or some other elementals, but just as real.

While a flower or horse has an auric field, machines do not. However, it needs an energetic component to be able to operate strongly on earth, and so elementals help. Thus your car, Black Beauty, has a deva. I'll call that deva (and also the car itself) "Beauty" for short.

Let's say that Beauty is a very nice, second-hand luxury car. When strangers see it on the road, or when parked, they react to it as a luxury car. Unfortunately many passersby hate the idea of all that luxury belonging to you, not to them. So many a stranger has grumbled audibly about your "horrible" car.

Plus your best friend, Riley, is a real car snob. Whenever you give her a ride in Beauty, she starts complaining loudly about your horrible, undependable car.

Given these kinds of criticism, after a while, it's only human for Beauty to underperform. Okay, this deva isn't human, exactly. However, a deva is a deva. And, in this regard, a deva responds much as a human would.

Haven't you ever worked in an office where everybody picked on one particular machine and it kept breaking down?

Or maybe your high school had a vending machine that was constantly the butt of insults, kicked around both figuratively and literally. What a surprise! "That worthless piece of junk" kept breaking down.

Machines may not have feelings but their devas sure do.

Brave Explorer, do you see where I'm going with this?

Supposing that you have Mechanical Empath Ability, what happens when you take a ride in Black Beauty, and it is feeling really sorry for itself? What happens when you pass by that much-kicked vending machine?

Imported STUFF. That's what. Imported STUFF can come to you from an astral-level being, the deva of any machine. (The very same deva that telepathically helps you to understand how its machine operates.)

But no repining! When you have skill as an empath, this particular talent becomes so worthwhile. As an Empowered Empath you reclaim your life energetically as being about you:

Loving your life. Learning every day. Growing as a person. No longer distracted by chronic drip-drip-drip.

What if you progress all the way through our next book in this Program for Empath Empowerment and become not only skilled but a true Master Empath? Such extra fun can you have then! Whenever you wish to experience more with your consciousness, just do a very brief, circumscribed Skilled Empath Merge on the machine of your choice.

If you had a deva it would applaud at such times. Actually, you don't.

But you do have a soul; plus you have a personal team of Divine and celestial beings. And they can get pretty thrilled about all your empathic research — just like you, the human.

CHAPTER 21

Medical Empath Talent

MEDICAL EMPATH TALENT brings an ability to notice minute details of the physical body... and without trying to show off.

With this gift, you have always been physically aware. Even before you learned anatomical names for body parts, you sensed them. By now, you probably know many of those anatomical names, just as Artist Molly would make it her business to learn color names like "Cerulean Blue."

During sessions of aura healing, I will often ask my client to choose any random body part and describe the physical sensation. That's when I hear chiropractor Anthony tell me, "Two inches beneath my zyphoid process: It feels tight." Or elementary schoolteacher Kayla says, "The underside of my diaphragm is a bit achy."

Huh? Where the heck is that? That's my response, along with admiring that kind of effortless awareness.

Of course, many people are more physically aware than Rose Rosetree, and some non-empaths are physically aware enough to feel an ache in the diaphragm, just like Kayla.

Being a Medical Empath is more than that, though. With this gift you experience directly what happens with other people physically, minutely noticing their aches and pains and tingles. Aware of the progress of an illness. Perhaps allowing the body to speak to you and tell you what it requires to feel better.

Maybe it's a oneness experience, maybe an intuition experience. Either way, this becomes your direct experience.

Far more famous today than Medical Empath Ability is being a medical intuitive, which is altogether different. So let's clarify that distinction next.

Being a Medical Empath Versus a Medical Intuitive

What is the difference between that psychic specialty compared to being a Medical Empath? MEDICAL INTUITIVES are psychics who specialize in receiving health-related information. In this type of psychic reading, they investigate a client's problems, energetically staying within their own personal boundaries. Famous medical intuitives include Caroline Myss and Dr. Mona Lisa Schultz.

Both are psychics, not empaths. Take Myss as an example. I have read her aura from photos and videotape; her hard-edge aura is crisply delineated.

Delightful as this is, can you appreciate how this differs from what an empath does? Medical Empaths, skilled or unskilled, can energetically merge with their clients.

When a skilled Medical Empath imparts diagnostic information, the content might seem identical to advice from a medical intuitive. However, the process of gaining knowledge is way more personal.

It's more likely you have heard of Myss or Schultz than Dr. Brihaspati Dev Triguna… unless you're involved in Ayurvedic medicine, in which case you might consider him a major celebrity.

Triguna been trained to do *nadivigyan*, the ancient science of pulse diagnosis. During this procedure, the Ayurvedic physician's consciousness walks around in the patient's body.

Talk about inside information! Of course, learning the skill set of pulse diagnosis doesn't make Triguna — or anyone — a Medical Empath. You must be born with it. Doing Skilled Empath Merge on Triguna, I am awed by the devotional quality of his energy field. Aurically his Medical Empath Talent is a really big deal.

Medical Empath, The Glory

Be they trained as pulse readers, doctors, nurses, computer programmers, whatever, Medical Empaths show certain distinctive abilities in their auras:

- The specific empath gift for being a Medical Empath
- Plus Physical Intuition and/or Physical Oneness
- Plus mechanical ability
- Plus the kind of intelligence that can soak up information about how the physical body works.

Sound great? Don't envy this too much. Medical Empath Talent isn't necessarily convenient.

Medical Empath Talent, The Pain

Doctors today don't generally make house calls. Except you might feel like that kind of doctor if you have been blessed with Medical Empath Talent. At least so long as you are unskilled.

Medical Empath Talent can make you feel as though you're continually making house calls. Or, depending on the people you encounter, you might feel like a walking emergency room.

Olivia, one of my students, told me about her checkered path as an unskilled Medical Empath. "By training, I'm a nurse. Soon after my training I discovered something they never covered in nursing school. I could tell when people were ill. It was as if I could feel what was going on in their bodies. This took no effort at all. It kind of hit me over the head.

"I would walk by a patient and smell something at the throat or belly or feet. This would tell me which part of the patient was sick. Immediately I would know who was getting better and who wasn't. It was uncanny, how I was right every time. Lab tests would prove it.

"Eventually I started to tell other nurses and doctors about what I knew. Big mistake! They weren't prepared to receive my help. In fact, they convinced me I was crazy. I even spent time in a mental hospital. Afterwards I got out of nursing. For so many years, I have struggled to seem normal."

For Olivia, becoming a skilled empath made it safe for her to use her talent on purpose, then to trust it.

Brave Empath, for you, skill may simply mean that, whatever your empath gifts may be, you are not on call 24/7 to provide free services. Your gifts are turned ON only when you choose, using a technique that you choose, for just a minute or two at a time. Then you're done.

Another one of my students, Jake, is an oncologist. Knowledge about Medical Empath Talent wasn't included in his medical training any more than Olivia's. Yet Jake has become a skilled empath. So being a Medical Empath no longer torments him.

Altogether Jake's life is much better now. He researches at will in order to learn which patients have cancer, where it is, when it has gone, and if it returns. The only downside?

"I had to stop telling my colleagues what I know," Jake confided in me. "Other oncologists think it's weird. That's a shame. Knowing what I know... really makes me a better doctor."

It's very flashy to be able to join your consciousness with someone in order to come up with a medical diagnosis. And Jake's right, the opportunities for service are great. However, Brave Empath, I hope you understand by now that Medical Empath Talent is just one empath gift. It is *not* required that you must have it in order to qualify as an empath.

What if the sight of blood makes you hurl? What if you lack enough mechanical ability to put together a broken clothespin?

Not to worry. This Program for Empath Empowerment can help you to use the brilliant empath gifts you do have. Those other gifts are just as valuable (although not as flashy) as being a Medical Empath.

Medical Empath Talent isn't even required for you to have two other kinds of empath talent related to physical knowing, Physical Intuition or Physical Oneness. And, of course, empaths do *not* have to become medical healers.

Moreover, having any empath gift does not equate to a meant-to-be, as in, "Because I can experience these things, God has decreed that this must be my grand purpose in life."

Or "Being a Medical Empath means that I am spiritually called to define myself in terms of my gift."

Or "I must earn a living this way."

Or "Because this is a spiritual gift, I am supposed to use it whenever I encounter someone in need."

No, no, no, no! God has given you many gifts. Who gets to decide which you will focus on now? You alone.

For instance, you might want a day job that pays the rent well, involves little drama, and is the opposite of working in an emergency room. You might choose to use your Medical Empath Talent no more often than once a year. Altogether a fine use of free will! Actually you might evolve fastest, spiritually, in just that way.

Brave Empath, you came into this lifetime with more gifts of consciousness (and other kinds of talent) than you can possibly use. When it comes to setting priorities for your lifestyle, please, allow yourself to decide. Nobody else but you.

As you develop empath skills, real friends will support your chosen lifestyle. Neither shape your life, nor ruin your life, but support your life. Brave Empath, that's what real friends do.

CHAPTER 22

Empath Talent with Astral Beings

I'm curious, Brave Empath. Have you ever felt overwhelmed while standing in a crowded room? Probably you haven't seen the half of it, not consciously. Subconsciously, though, you always registered the complete crowd. Angels, ghosts, and other kinds of astral beings live among us. They are especially prevalent in places like hospitals, churches, gambling casinos, and bars.

Will all that astral traffic matter to you consciously? Your answer to that second question depends on talent as well as training. For context, let's start with "VIBRATIONALLY NORMAL HUMANS." These folks live on earth as though no astral beings share the planet. Maybe, for entertainment purposes, a ghost story is told while sitting around the campfire. That's about it.

For vibrationally normal humans, conscious perception falls comfortably within the range of human-level frequencies of energy. Which is why most folks have little to do with astral experiences, except for what occurs naturally during sleep and dreaming, generally forgotten on waking.

Vibrationally normal humans don't consciously suffer from problems related to astral beings, so there is no burning need to develop any skills for relating to astral-level beings, not unless that person develops a metaphysical hobby.

However, some folks are wired differently from birth.

- Born psychics may easily slip into experiences of clairvoyance, or information about the future, from spirit guides.

~ Mediums and channelers serve as mouthpieces for astral entities, serving clients in ways that depend on whichever skills have been developed.

~ Alternatively, some of us are not psychics. We just are born with Empath Talent with Astral Beings.

What does it mean to have EMPATH TALENT WITH ASTRAL BEINGS? You can directly experience what it is like to be an astral being, or you can experience information from astral frequencies in a very personal way.

Having this gift, you don't necessarily seek out skills as a channeler, medium, or psychic. In fact, you may have zero desire to pursue any form of psychic development. Yet you don't live in quite the same way as vibrationally normal humans. (Brave Empath, you're already familiar with the concept that empaths can have just one gift, not necessarily all of them. Plenty of empaths are vibrationally normal humans, while others have Empath Talent with Astral Beings.)

Empath Talent with Astral Beings, The Glory

Human life includes so many astral-level experiences. What happens if you're an empath with a lifelong talent for direct experience of what it is like to be another person who lives at the astral level?

Your version of Empath Talent with Astral Beings might emphasize a oneness-type experience or an intuition-type experience or both. (Just like Physical Oneness in contrast to Physical Intuition.)

Okay, you may be wondering. *This gift allows for direct experience of astral beings, but which kind of beings?*

If you're a student of the paranormal, you know there is great diversity among astral beings. Here's a short list.

Ghosts

Those are former humans, now physically deceased, and still residing on earth. Another term for GHOSTS is "Stuck Spirits."

Empath Talent with Astral Beings can open up direct experience of ghosts. When you combine empath skills with separate skill sets to work with ghosts, you could do magnificent shamanic healing, lead rituals involving help from ancestors, do paranormal work, even give ghost tours.

By contrast, consider Robert Monroe, Founder of The Monroe Institute. He was not an empath but worked brilliantly to develop psychic-level skills and Hemi-Synch® technology for exploring astral experiences. Interest in astral beings does not necessarily mean that a person has any talent as an empath.

Temporary astral visitors

EXTRA-TERRESTRIAL ASTRAL ENTITIES sometimes visit earth, off and on, for any purpose that suits them. Some of these beings prefer to actively collaborate with humans in order to reach an audience.

Empath Talent with Astral Beings can open up direct experience of these E.T. entities, helpful if you are interested in pursuing mediumship or channeling or other psychic work. Empath skills make an enormous difference if you wish to pursue any of these skill sets. My advice? Learn empath skills first. (Or if it's too late for that, become a skilled empath as soon as possible.)

Well, hello! Of course you are doing just that.

What else matters, if you're interested in collaborating with E.T. entities? Definitely protect yourself further by developing skills in the related psychic field. Don't expect your spiritualist teacher to have any empath skills whatsoever — or to necessarily be an empath. Nor is it wise to assume that, as a skilled empath, you can safely make up your own rules about dealing with entities.

Elementals

The nature spirits called ELEMENTALS could be either elves, devas, fairies, or angels who specialize in protecting Mother Earth. With this version of Empath Talent with Astral Beings, empath skills plus related human skills can help you to collaborate with them to heal the earth.

One outstanding example of Empath Talent with Astral Beings is the late Eileen Caddy, Founder of Findhorn in Scotland. This empath was especially sensitive to the devas who help to grow plants. Caddy collaborated with these elementals to grow world-famous gardens in the sandy Scottish soil, famously producing 40-pound cabbages.

A contrasting example is a non-empath who works brilliantly with what she calls "nature intelligences." Machaelle Small Wright is a prolific writer and the Founder of Perelandra in Virginia. Although careful to speak non-metaphysical language, Small Wright is a psychic who specializes in working with elementals.

So what if her work hasn't been complicated by dealing with empath gifts like Empath Talent with Astral Beings? That hasn't stopped Small Wright from developing flower essences by receiving messages from elementals, then following their instructions. Work like this does not require experiencing what it is like to *be* the deva of a garden.

I have met each of these talented women. Both Eileen and Machaelle have developed communities that inspire many spiritual seekers who are NOT VIBRATIONALLY NORMAL HUMANS.

When it comes to empath talent, these New Age leaders could not be more different from each other. Machaelle is brainy, tough, and strongly individualistic. To my perception, she is not even a Highly Sensitive Person, let alone an empath.

By contrast, the late Eileen Caddy had such sensitivity; when I sat in the room with her, she reminded me of a melting soft-serve ice cream cone. In my opinion, Eileen was a mega-talented empath, with strong self-taught skills for using Empath Talent with Astral Beings, plus skills that she developed for working with devas.

At the Scottish community she co-founded, chatting up devas is part of the culture. You want the ancient washing machine to work? Go chat up the deva of that appliance. Only then will it help you clean your clothes.

Findhorn is primarily a spiritually-oriented community, not aiming to foster psychic development. The comparison between Eileen and Machaelle exemplifies why it would be confusing to equate psychic skills with being an empath.

Here's one way to think about it: Although someone with red hair might love to study mediumship, plenty of red-haired folks have no desire whatsoever to do that.

This Empath Talent + Other Empath Gifts

Empath Talent with Astral Beings can be useful in combination with certain other empath gifts, once empath skills are developed.

For example, how might appreciating the deva of a washing machine combine with being a Mechanical Empath?

If you're a *Mechanical Empath only,* your experience of that deva is focused on using the washing machine. Doing a Skilled Empath Merge could help you to repair that appliance (provided that you also have the particular skill set for repairing washing machines).

Alternatively *Empath Talent with Astral Beings only* would be useful for insights when you were doing a Skilled Empath Merge with the washing machine. No income for you, doing mechanical repair work. (You might not even be able to make the spin cycle operate.)

With *both* empath gifts, you could learn personally from devas in addition to being able to fix their associated machines. Sweet!

Other great combos are Empath Talent with Astral Beings plus being either an Animal Empath, a Plant Empath, or a Crystal Empath. Extra-big fun, potentially!

Empath Talent with Astral Beings is also useful in combination with skills for *healing astral-level STUFF*, such as using an effective skill set to cut cords of attachment.

Again, I think it is important to distinguish... when an empath has the consciousness gift for experiencing what it is like to be somebody else (in this case, somebody astral) versus... what happens when somebody uses either a psychic talent or practical skill set with no empath circuits involved.

The latter would be useful for researching information coming from astral frequencies. Psychic work is often accomplished by a Not Vibrationally Normal Human who is not an empath.

One famous example of a psychic — and non-empath — is Barbara Brennan. She has developed a skill set within energy medicine to clean and replace cords of attachment.

By contrast, I am an example of someone with Empath Talent with Astral Beings who is not a psychic. This empath gift helped me to develop skill sets like 12 Steps to Cut Cords of Attachment® and Vibrational Re-Positioning®.

When I facilitate cutting cords, Empath Talent with Astral Beings provides a depth experience of cord dialogue. This enhances the cord-cutting skills and enriches my client's experiences.

One of the defining characteristics of Rosetree Energy Spirituality is that it does not involve psychic work. In RES we facilitate healing at the astral level by collaborating with Divine-level beings.

Although the skill sets in RES were developed by a skilled empath whose gifts include Empath Talent with Astral Beings, all these skills for aura healing can be learned fine by non-empaths, or by empaths who don't have this particular gift for experiencing the astral so directly.

Brave Empath, these are examples from the professional field I know best. No doubt if you work in a related field, you can describe something similar. Empath Talent with Astral Beings can bring a special juiciness to your knowledge and experience. It combines beautifully with other empath gifts.

Empath Talent with Astral Beings, The Pain

The more involved you are in experiencing astral beings, the more likely you are to pick up STUFF from them through unskilled empath merges.

This STUFF can result in your becoming distracted or confused. Consequently, Empath Talent with Astral Beings — more than any other talent that you might have as an empath— can weaken your energetic commitment to being human.

Altogether, Brave Empath, it's complicated having Empath Talent with Astral Beings. Don't let that discourage you. Every technique coming up to prevent or remove Imported STUFF will work for every single empath gift you've got.

Some day you can look back on the messier aspects as "*Just a little drip-drip-drip. I'm so done with all that now.*"

CHAPTER 23

Spiritual Intuition

SPIRITUAL INTUITION allows you to explore spiritual experience as it really is, no illusions — especially how other people seek contact with a Higher Power.

Your friend Harper, for instance. What is the texture of her silence? How does beauty impress her? Spiritual Oneness allows you to feel how differently someone else stands in the presence of God while wrapped in one particular individuality. This Otherness is not necessarily like your own way of reaching out to the Divine.

Brave Empath, note that this empath gift provides an intuition-style experience, like Emotional Intuition or Physical Intuition. In a later chapter we will consider a related gift, Spiritual Oneness. As an empath you may have either of these spiritually-oriented empath gifts, or both, or neither.

So let's explore more fully what is involved in Spiritual Intuition. How can it ennoble all your other empath gifts?

Spiritual Intuition, The Glory

Spiritual Intuition is so much more interesting than COMPARATIVE RELIGION, the study of different spiritual paths.

Customs of a religion have little to do with its spiritual excellence. *Experience* is the key with Spiritual Intuition, as with all forms of empath talent. Without this particular gift, comparing different theologies might be the best a curious spiritual seeker could do. By contrast, Spiritual Intuition brings direct experience.

Long before knowing you were an empath, you may have enjoyed attending services at different houses of worship or singing hymns from different religions, buzzing like a honeybee to reach the sweetness of that particular path.

This isn't just beginner's luck. And, no, everybody doesn't do it. Spiritual Intuition provides direct experience of someone's distinctive way of connecting to the Divine. Everybody hugs differently. Likewise we connect in a unique manner to Spiritual Source.

Witnessing this sacred love is seldom obvious, like news crawl at the bottom of a TV screen. The knowledge dawns. You feel or see or otherwise know. As skill sweetens this gift, you may become very grateful for what you are privileged to experience.

Of course, Spiritual Intuition isn't limited to experiences at a house of worship. With a dedicated technique for Skilled Empath Merge, you can research — whomever, wherever, whenever — and do this safely. Effortlessly, you'll distinguish the dutiful rule-follower from the frightened fanatic or the true mystic. Direct experience also makes it easier to discern social add-ons to religion:

- Skilled Empath Merge reveals how some people experience nothing at all spiritually. Yet they are leaders in a particular congregation. How can that be?

- Some quiet people in your faith community may have the most exquisite connections to the Divine. While other members of the congregation don't seem to value them. Why, why, why? The short answer: Folks act from their level of consciousness, that's why.

Spiritual Intuition helps you to accept reality here at Earth School. Yes, EARTH SCHOOL is one of my names for this big one-room schoolhouse where each human lives. At this challenging academy for spiritual evolution, the grades are not labeled accurately. Illusions are rife. Actually, these confusions contribute to the spiritual learning. Each of us gets to decide what is true.

Here's a hypothetical. It isn't likely to happen here at Earth School but, just for fun, imagine: 100% of the members of a particular religious congregation are empaths, and every one of them is a skilled empath with Spiritual Intuition. Golly, do you think the pecking order for that group might honor those with clearest experience of the Divine?

Spiritual Intuition, The Pain

Just because a gift is spiritual doesn't make it comfortable for you, not until you get skills. Spiritual Intuition is no different from other empath gifts in these two respects:

- Before you get skills, "Big Insight" is not mainly gained by your conscious mind. Mostly unskilled empath merges happen subconsciously.

- Every unskilled empath merge deposits STUFF in your aura. STUFF is imported rapidly and, again, mostly subconsciously.

Then come quirky factors related to Spiritual Intuition that can make the drip-drip-drip particularly awful:

- Fear of going to hell could be shared by so many believers at your mosque or church, despite seldom being discussed out loud.

- Social competitiveness within your religious congregation could be crazy-making. At any religious gathering you attend, high status of certain members may not match up with your sense of spiritual anything.

- Perhaps you start worrying that Minister Mateo isn't all he is cracked up to be.

- And the biggest leaders in your faith community might (rightly) strike you as phony.

- Also, upsetting though this might be to admit to yourself consciously, some of the missionary-like folks you know from this group... give you the creeps.

Subconscious whispers like these tend to be true. Such whispers come courtesy of Spiritual Intuition. These whispers would have begun long before you found this Program for Empath Empowerment. Could be, for years you have been taking on wildly confusing Imported STUFF courtesy of other people's religious insecurities. Every time you attended a service or Bible Study, the inner mess got worse! How ironic is that?

Is it possible that some fine, upstanding members of your group might have worried subconsciously that they're not worthy? Or they have even feared being tricked by Satan? Can guilty secrets like these come to *you* along with their Imported STUFF?

Heck, yes! This aura healer has helped many clients of different faiths who told me, in so many words, "I am going to Hell for sure." Talk about irony! These clients are doing relatively well, taking initiative to clean up their STUFF. Whereas their religious "betters," whose faith seems exemplary, can have some really, really messed up auras.

Going to a church supported by such pillars? Energetically that provides far less inspiration than expected, and way more Imported STUFF.

Spiritual Intuition, the Really Sneaky Pain

As if it weren't enough to suffer from all the aforementioned grief, here comes another tricky dynamic for all unskilled empaths. Imported STUFF from others is always translated into *your* vocabulary and values.

Perhaps you don't worry about hell. Think that will protect you from related Imported STUFF?

Think again. Every human personality has distinctive vulnerabilities regarding chosen lifestyle, cherished goals, and long-term belief system. Maybe your ultimate fears right now involve sex, money, sanity, or losing favor with the folks you admire most.

∼ How about not being pure enough to get results from Law of Attraction?

∼ Or good enough to attract the right spouse?

∼ What if your weight has become the single biggest topic for personal torment?

Then *that* is the sort of worry you'll have, due to Imported STUFF. Random unskilled empath merges propelled by Spiritual Intuition... will import energies related to other people's spiritual insecurities... and then be translated into your own personal topics of torment.

Shall we celebrate how tricky this is? Open up your hymnal and turn to Empath's Hymn #10,008: "From All Those Confusing Labels at Earth School, Deliver Me, Oh Lord."

STUFF in your aura due to imported religious insecurities may be overflowing more than a megachurch collection basket on Christmas. That dynamic will continue for as long as you *do* have the gift of Spiritual Intuition and *don't* yet have empath skills. Dare to own that fact of spiritual life, Brave Empath. Then embrace the glorious possibilities, because they are just as true.

Of course you are getting skills. So far, you are at the necessary owning and embracing stage of Empath Empowerment. You might want to pause and compassionately acknowledge how much you have suffered so far.

If you have the gift of Spiritual Intuition, there is no question whether you have been suffering all along — and probably fearing some terrible weakness within yourself. Although you probably had no clue that empath anything was involved.

Lack of skill is not who you are. All that suffering is not "A part of you" or "A character flaw" or even "A deep-seated neurosis." Soon you can afford to laugh and call that old distress by its rightful name: *Just some of the silly old drip-drip-drip.*

Empath gifts demand skills to work properly, that's all.

CHAPTER 24

Molecular Empath Ability

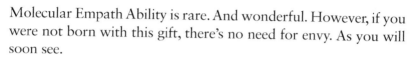

Molecular Empath Ability is rare. And wonderful. However, if you were not born with this gift, there's no need for envy. As you will soon see.

MOLECULAR EMPATH ABILITY means that the very substance of your aura consists of superfine energies which easily blend into the auras of others at an equally superfine level.

Therefore, any time you do an empath merge, skilled or not, you will experience your Discovery Person at a deeper level than happens with any other empath gifts.

What do you win?

Exceptional ability to validate the experiences of others. A Molecular Empath will often describe profound things to friends, articulating truth at a level that they cannot consciously access or express. What a great opportunity for service to others!

Molecular Empath Ability, The Glory

Uniquely a factor with this empath gift: Whenever you do an empath merge you will effortlessly move others forward in their spiritual evolution. This happens whether you are skilled yet or not. It's a kind of energetic entrainment.

Molecular Empath Ability, The Pain

Of course, results of jump-starting evolution for others may not be quite so beneficial for the Molecular Empath. While unskilled, this gift can cause you to suffer some of the deepest human pain and insecurity imaginable.

As an unskilled empath, you subconsciously experience this pain directly, one empath merge at a time. Of course, the resulting Imported STUFF is extra intense. Beyond that, what else?

Other people may *subconsciously* notice what is happening. While they are on the receiving end of a Molecular Empath's unskilled merge, *consciously*, those folks may feel that they don't like you.

- Not like being known so deeply
- Not like being invited energetically to evolve faster
- Not like you for doing those deep unskilled empath merges (inwardly sensed although not consciously noticed)

Feeling uncomfortable, people can lash out... even when the Molecular Empath hasn't said a word. Has this happened to you, as a Molecular Empath?

Then it's high time you understood. Solve that lifelong mystery, as well as preparing yourself for the future. It helps nobody to blame yourself for this kind of reflexive subconscious negativity from others.

Of course, all defensive reactions to your being a Molecular Empath will cease when you stop doing unskilled empath merges like a steady drip-drip-drip.

Brave Empath, are you finding it difficult to relate to this description of empath talent? Most likely you do not have this particular empath gift. Thus far, I have encountered fewer than 100 Molecular Empaths, either folks whose auras I have researched in person or others I researched with remote techniques like those you will learn in *The Master Empath*.

Here is a typical pain story. It concerns a sweet, unskilled Molecular Empath who knew nothing whatsoever about her gift. When I was hired to give readings at an upscale Christmas party, Leslie was the last to approach my table. Startled to encounter her Molecular Empath Ability, I described it, both the glory and the possible pain. Leslie's aura lit up with a gigantic Eureka! Then she told me this:

"I work on Capitol Hill. Learning about Molecular Empath Ability explains something about my relationship with Newt Gingrich."

(Historical Note: When Leslie told me this story, Gingrich was at the height of his political power, serving as the Speaker of the House of Representatives.)

"Newt has told me that I'm the only person he's ever met who frightens him."

Watch out, politicians, wherever you are! Actually, here's a warning to anyone hanging out with a Molecular Empath. That person may subtly jump-start your spiritual growth. (Whoever is on the receiving end can, of course, resist.)

Back at you, Brave Empath, what if you suspect Molecular Empath Ability? The process of becoming skilled is the same for you as for any other empath. You simply need those skills more.

Backlash from people who resist or resent or otherwise react negatively to your unskilled empath merges? Ouch, can that ever sting!

CHAPTER 25

Spiritual Oneness

Already, our final empath gift on this list of 15! I have listed them in no particular order of importance, since each one is magnificent.

Spiritual Intuition was considered a couple of chapters ago. Maybe you can guess what is different with SPIRITUAL ONENESS.

Both empath gifts bring direct experience of how another person connects to the Divine. With Spiritual Intuition, this knowledge comes at a distance. However, a funny little disguise occurs with Spiritual Oneness. That other person's spiritual experience seems to belong to you.

Oops, no prior announcement! *Gotta love Earth School!* (Personally dealing with Spiritual Oneness, this empath finds consolation with this wacky motto. You're welcome to use it, too.)

Spiritual Oneness, The Glory

This empath gift helps you to serve as a spiritual teacher, even if you have never attended an accredited "Divinity School." Spiritual Oneness brings an intimate knowledge of anyone's personal development, especially helpful once your native gift is enhanced by skills.

Who in your life will benefit when you're fully skilled? Only every one of your friends and lovers, parents and children, business relationships, even random acquaintances — that's all.

Automatically an empath with Spiritual Oneness connects to that other person at his or her level of consciousness. A high degree of perceptiveness about that person's spiritual life comes automatically, even without your doing an empath merge. And when you *officially* do a technique for Skilled Empath Merge, you will gain even greater conscious clarity about that person's spiritual experience.

Spiritual Oneness is especially powerful when supplemented by other empath gifts. For example, suppose that you are at work and talking to your boss Katherine:

- ~ Spiritual Oneness + Intellectual Empath Ability helps you to spontaneously speak Katherine's inner language, including spiritual nuances or overtones that can uplift her.
- ~ Spiritual Oneness + Emotional Intuition helps you to display sensitivity to Katherine's inner feelings, including spiritual nuances or overtones that can uplift her.
- ~ Spiritual Oneness + Physical Oneness helps you to spontaneously pace your communication. Your words can be extra compatible with how Katherine feels physically at the time, whether great or not-so-great.
- ~ Meanwhile the spiritual nuances or overtones in your voice and body language can uplift her.

Maybe you're wondering, what does any empath with Spiritual Oneness receive in return for being of service to others?

Even a chance encounter can become a magnificent source of learning about the innumerable faces of God... expressed in human form.

Spiritual Oneness, The Pain

What's not so great? Before skills, innumerable unskilled empath merges include the special qualities of Spiritual Oneness. Some of the resulting Imported STUFF will come from other people's religious fears. Fears then translated into your own inner language!

Remember our earlier description of how Spiritual Intuition can cause an empath to internalize religious or spiritual fears, then label them in terms that seem completely unrelated, like worrying about weight?

Exactly the same dynamic occurs with this empath gift. Only, of course, the fears can turn extra sneaky with Spiritual Oneness. Because you experience the exact quality of that particular fear and, weirdly, feel like it's coming from you.

For example, meet three popular flavors of spiritual anxiety:

- ～ Mason tries valiantly to seek wisdom from angels.
- ～ Kaylee pauses countless times every day to ask, "What would Jesus do?"
- ～ Samuel is downright desperate for guidance. Desperate, get it?

You do get it, if you're not skilled yet with Spiritual Oneness. Whatever your favorite way of seeking spiritual reassurance, you will be driven to overuse it. Feeling lonely, unaccountably isolated from others — you name it. And, oh yes, you have plenty of personal names for that.

Reacting to Imported STUFF from Spiritual Oneness creates deep kinds of misery.

In my experience helping clients, I have observed that "I must find my purpose" usually indicates a form of spiritual anxiety. After the client stops carrying so much subconscious STUFF, that fear abates. Meanwhile, that client's spiritual fears keep broadcasting like a powerful radio signal.

With unskilled empath merges, you keep listening to other folks' subconscious radio shows like, "So Scared I Am Wasting My Life and Disappointing God." Developing skill with Spiritual Oneness, you may lose a great deal of anxiety.

In the past, you may never have considered that so many worries of yours really belonged to other people.

Connecting with Divine Beings

By now, Brave Empath, you have been formally introduced to a dazzling array of empath gifts related to spiritual and psychic aspects of life. Concluding our survey of empath gifts, let's clarify something important.

- ∿ Spiritual Intuition allows a skilled empath to savor different ways that other people connect to the Divine.
- ∿ Spiritual Oneness brings an even more direct, personal experience of how people connect to the Divine.
- ∿ In addition, some empaths possess Empath Talent with Astral Beings, traveling in consciousness to experience directly what it is like to be an angel, a ghost, the deva of the cabbages in your garden, and so forth.

All these gifts have their beauty, yet many of you may be wondering, what about connecting directly with a Divine Being, like Jesus or Buddha or Athena, Allah or Almighty God?

What about being able to connect *not* as an empath but simply on your own?

Of course you can. And whichever empath gifts you do or don't have. And regardless of whether you are an empath or not. Every human being is capable of consciously making a Divine connection.

Perhaps you have already found a way to do this on your own. Otherwise you can learn.

One resource is going to be taught to you later as part of this Program for Empath Empowerment, the technique called "Get Big" in Chapter 40.

Meanwhile, Brave Empath, it's important to understand this:

Of course, you can consciously connect with Divine Beings — whether skilled or unskilled as an empath, whether in great shape psychologically or while not doing so well.

What's the catch? We connect at our current level of consciousness.

∿ A miserable drunk who has just hit bottom? Sure, he can connect to God.

∿ A loving father, sleep-deprived from taking care of his infant? Sure, he can connect to God.

Connections like these may not be terribly intense, dramatic, or clear. Yet they count as authentic connections. Regarding that lack of clarity, it's not fair to blame either God or the seeker of God.

Which degree of clarity will you have while attempting to pray or worship or read scripture or otherwise connect to your Highest Ideal? That will depend upon many complex factors, including your level of spiritual awareness; how much STUFF is stuck in your subconscious mind; whether or not you are using self-authority to value your authentic experiences.

SELF-AUTHORITY means acknowledging what is true for you, here and now. Self-authority flows from many sources: How you feel emotionally, responses of your physical body, worldly wisdom, common sense, intuitive hunches, and paying attention to what people literally say and do. Ultimately all self-authority is a kind of self-acceptance.

What else will help you to honestly explore spiritual connection with your Highest Power? Learning skills, like "Get Big," will help.

And what detracts most from connecting to the Divine while you are still unskilled as an empath? Your subconscious mind will be riddled with Imported STUFF, on top of all the other kinds of astral STUFF that you have accumulated. What an awful volunteer job, taking on pain from random people whenever you go to your church or synagogue or mosque.

As a skilled empath, you can anticipate way more spiritual clarity. Plus the process of learning to do Skilled Empath Merge will improve your ability to do techniques designed specifically to experience or co-create with God.

Just thought you might want to know.

CHAPTER 26

How Sure Must You Be About Your Gifts?

Brave Empath, take out that List of My Empath Gifts you have been making. Whatever you wrote during our survey, trust it.

Maybe you listed just two or more gifts. Maybe you wrote down many. Possibly you wrote down only one empath gift.

Regardless, you're an empath.

Did you ever write down a question mark along with the name of an empath gift? What if you are not sure that you really, truly have even one of the empath gifts on your List of My Empath Gifts?

Please don't worry. You're not on the witness stand in front of Judge Judy.

Besides, all empath gifts are subtle. They involve consciousness. Dead certainty is for identifying corpses, not subtle shifts of consciousness.

One way to appreciate Step ONE in this Program for Empath Empowerment is embracing, right? Allow yourself to cozy up to your gifts and start liking them, trusting them, loving them.

Have you ever heard from me that certainty is required? Or that an empath gift must seem as obvious to you as a jumbo tattoo? Maybe looking at your right arm and seeing a huge submarine labeled with the names of all your empath gifts?

Nope, that's not happening. I call you a "Brave Empath" because courage is required for developing empath skills. Probably you have not felt rock solid confident.

Fair warning: That may continue along with your progress, during Empath Empowerment Parts TWO and THREE. Your training, your growth, will involve the subtle domain of consciousness. Unless you already have background in meditation, aura reading, or other subtle reality skills, even Step ONE of this training might feel foreign to you.

Look, when developing awareness of awareness, everybody must begin somewhere. You have entered this Program for Empath Empowerment from wherever you are in your personal develop-ment. If you are rereading this book, once again, you'll participate based on your current level of personal development.

Therefore, I congratulate you... whether your response to our 15-gift survey was clear or hazy, comfortable or not quite.

Know that you are growing in your discernment of important aspects of consciousness. How much owning and embracing have you done so far? This much is your triumph, and the basis for *managing* your empath skills.

Definitely expect the results of this Program for Empath Empow-erment to be real and human, not nearly as abstract as our Empath Empowerment Step ONE. Continue and you will gain those very human results.

One of My Secrets as a Teacher

Why don't I end all suspense? Why don't I offer a service where I tell clients and readers which empath gifts they have?

It would be easy for me to do that. Client Cliff sends me a photo. I read his aura, then reply with an email listing his empath gifts. Or I could validate over the phone, researching with energetic literacy and listing his every empath gift.

Oh, how some of you readers might like that!

Such relief, when the fancy authority figure has removed all self-doubt. I'm reasonably sure that a service like this would be accurate for my customer, plus totally easy for me. Maybe a fine income stream!

What is my response to such a business proposition?

NEVER.

Here's why, Brave Empath. That very same self-authority which you have used thus far will be required for Empath Empowerment Parts TWO and THREE. Only you will need to trust it even more.

My advice? Trust your self-authority now. Get used to it.

When the first edition of this book was published, there were no other empath coaches. At least nobody else who wrote books about empaths, other than science fiction writers.

By now, plenty of empath coaches have stepped up to meet demand. As you know, 1 in 20 people on earth has been born as an empath. That's a big market, with plenty of room for empath authority figures.

To date, though, I have not identified other empath coaches who use skills based in consciousness. You will, however, find plenty of experts who will tell you to work on your boundaries, analyze your problems psychologically, or perhaps invite you to worry about the energies of (alleged) psychic vampires. Maybe you will be told to cleanse your aura repeatedly or wear a special crystal.

To this empath coach, only subtle shifts in consciousness will really turn your empath gift(s) OFF. Or prepare you to have the experience of Skilled Empath Merge — safe and subtle and utterly amazing.

Are you willing to dare, to explore? To learn something really *new*? I am rooting for you, Brave Empath.

Whatever your empath gifts, they deserve recognition. Every bit of empath talent comes with a drive to use it, a sense of calling that will not quit.

Yet many of the empaths I've helped up to this stage didn't necessarily feel great about their gifts. Many tried to shut down their
sensitivity, improvising techniques that torqued other aspects of
life away from normal functioning.

Sensitivity is not your enemy. Ever.

Sensitivity just needs to be supported by strength and skills. This
matters for any Highly Sensitive Person and is especially relevant
to every empath on earth. Because all of us are not just Highly
Sensitive Persons. We are Highly, Highly Sensitive Persons.

CHAPTER 27

Do You Spot the Pattern?

Ultimately every empath gift is good for something.

Something superb. Purposely flying in spirit is bliss. Before then? It's a very personal story, way more complicated than a simple drip-drip-drip from a faucet. You have begun to understand what has been happening due to natural gifts run amok. Now let's summarize some of the implications, perhaps bringing even more compassion for yourself and your history.

Brave Empath, what have you put on your List of My Empath Gifts, drawn from our survey of 15 different possibilities? Maybe you have begun to spot some patterns to your history, patterns that used to involve considerable pain.

Another kind of pattern applies to every empath. It concerns the very nature of empath gifts, how they work. In general, empath gifts can bring information in three distinctive ways.

- A *oneness* gift as an empath
- An *intuition* gift as an empath
- An *informational* gift as an empath

With a ONENESS GIFT AS AN EMPATH, information that you subconsciously download seems to be personally about you. Despite really being about whoever is at the opposite end of your empath merge. Yowza!

No knowledge on earth is more powerful than the direct kind. At Earth School we learn most intensely through direct experience. Hence the popularity of support groups, wisdom from those who have been there — whichever "there" is the specialty of that particular support group.

Being a skilled empath with a oneness gift brings an intense education. However, being *unskilled* with a oneness gift? Energetically you get clobbered even more intensely than happens with the two other types of empath gifts.

Let's use the example of Physical Oneness versus Physical Intuition. Not yet skilled, you are doing an unskilled empath merge with your friend Wilbur. With the former, your experience might be, "I have a headache." Not "Wilbur has a headache." Which is not just inconvenient but potentially scary.

With an INTUITION GIFT AS AN EMPATH, the information you download is clearly about the other person, not yourself. For example, with Physical Intuition, "Hmmm, isn't that interesting about Wilbur? He has a headache."

Most empath gifts are neither an intuition gift nor a oneness gift. They are INFORMATIONAL GIFTS AS AN EMPATH. Your informational download comes as a random mixture of oneness and intuition.

Let's use the example of Intellectual Empath Talent. As in, "Wilbur is thinking sluggishly." Or, sometimes, "What's wrong with me? My thinking feels off. Better not play Lumosity right now!"

While still an unskilled empath, you might toggle back and forth in a really confusing manner, like "Wilbur and I are so mentally dull right now. What a coincidence!"

Most empath gifts are those ultra-confusing informational gifts. Which is why the name for them didn't include either "Intuition" or "Oneness."

Calling your gifts by their rightful names cuts down on confusion and makes it easier to embrace them.

Also, Brave Empath, maybe you can appreciate more than ever how unhelpful it can be to refer to empath talent as being an "Intuitive Empath" or using similar terms. Confused descriptions will not help you to master your special empath gifts.

Why Not Call Yourself a Psychic Empath?

Talk about confusion, what does being an empath have to do with *psychic ability*? Exactly nothing.

Information from the psychic level is what people call a sixth sense. It involves specifics, like flashing on the location of your lost suitcase or predicting that tomorrow it will rain.

By contrast, empath talent could be considered an opportunity for accelerated spiritual evolution. Whenever you work or play as an empath, your consciousness shifts. Consequently your way of experiencing life is forever altered (even if the changes are so subtle that your conscious mind registers nothing).

From what I have observed, developing skill as an empath can greatly hasten spiritual awakening.

Apart from this metaphysical distinction, there is a practical difference involving *personal identity*. Psychic experience adds to your collection of information, while Skilled Empath Merge changes the knower.

A third difference concerns *timing*. Psychic insights pop like a photo flash. By contrast, Skilled Empath Merge allows insight to dawn. Gradually.

Before becoming skilled as an empath, sometimes you may have felt a kind of slowly dawning insight. Gradually you start to notice a feeling like "There it goes again."

In that moment you consciously recognize that you have been traveling. Either you wake up to someone else's experience in terms of *your* body-mind-spirit package or else you awaken inside *another person's package* entirely. Well, that's interesting....

This relatively slow-motion timing comes with one delightful advantage over a quick psychic flash. Skilled empaths have the choice to linger, especially if using a safe technique designed for Skilled Empath Merge.

A fourth difference between psychic abilities versus empath gifts? *Practical benefits.* I may as well break it to you now. If consciousness gifts were just a competition for practical usefulness, psychics would win hands down.

For example, in her fabulous books, Laura Day emphasizes how valuable psychic information can be for making business decisions. Well, don't expect empath talent to help you to pick winning stocks.

Accuracy (truth that you can test) is a non-issue. Genuineness (truth that resonates within you) matters far more. Empath talent reveals the deepest truth you can hold. Like virtue, this had better be its own reward.

Service is a fifth point of difference. For a psychic, service is optional — desirable, prudent, definitely wise, yet optional. I think of Betty, a friend who used her considerable psychic gifts in a way that may surprise you.

Betty was a madam. She employed psychic abilities to tell which phone calls for services came from detectives. For years Betty's accuracy prevailed, helping to avoid confrontations with the law. Eventually she sold her business to a non-psychic. Within two weeks, police raided the joint.

Ethically mixed situations like these are perfectly compatible with psychic development, even if not ideal. Empath talent, however, will gently nudge you to live within the law. This style of knowing is more personal. Questionable choices will produce consequences that come back to you fast and hard.

Perhaps the most fascinating difference between psychics and empaths is *detachment*. When it comes to giving service, psychics help others best by staying neutral. The gold standard for information is crystal clarity.

In *Anatomy of the Spirit*, Caroline Myss explains, "For me, a clear impression has *no* emotional energy connected to it whatsoever. If I feel an emotional connection to an impression, then I consider that impression to be contaminated." Her record as a medical intuitive and teacher demonstrates how a psychic can work without descending into the deeply personal experiences of an empath.

For some of us, however, a more personal form of service is inescapable. Even preferable.

Fortunately there's enough work for us both, those who work as psychics and those who use empath skills. Were you to train yourself to fit Myss's mold, after great struggle, you could probably rid yourself of the "contaminated" perception that comes from sharing direct experience with the people you help.

In doing so, unfortunately, you'd lose about 80% of your effectiveness as an empath... and even more of your joy.

Such a prediction isn't merely theoretical. This kind of numbing has happened to several empaths who eventually wound up as my students.

Before finding this Program for Empath Empowerment they made heroic efforts to force their soul-level gifts to match up with requirements of their famous psychic teachers. Those well-meaning empaths were trying to turn apples into oranges.

Surely the orchard of God's helpers has room for us all. Some of us do psychic work, others serve as empaths, and still others do psychic work sometimes and, other times, use a completely different skill set in order to do Skilled Empath Merge.

Avoiding Confusion as a "Psychic Empath"

If psychic experience differs so greatly from being an empath, why does anyone use the term *psychic empath*? In my opinion, the origin is talent without skill.

A psychic will start playing around with the interesting concept of *being an empath*, then appropriate the term as one more selling point in the crowded paranormal marketplace.

Of course any psychic could be among the 1 in 20 human beings born as an empath. My client base for empath coaching has certainly included many a psychic.

So let's consider the example of Braden, a professional psychic who has respected his psychic gift enough to back it up with serious study. Because he also has several gifts as an empath, certain experiences flow from using his training as a psychic, while other experiences result from his being an unskilled empath.

Braden might interpret this mess as meaning that he is a "Psychic empath." Will that really bring him a competitive advantage, selling his services?

This sure won't be a selling point to anyone who knows about empath skills. Calling himself a "psychic empath" reveals a problem. Unintentionally Braden reveals that that, although talented, he doesn't know enough yet to make the most basic distinction between two entirely different skill sets.

What do I recommend if you are an empath who also loves psychic-style exploration? Go deeply into this Program for Empath Empowerment. Gain this separate skill set. Empath skills can supplement all your good training as a psychic. Just beware the "Psychic empath" type of mix-up.

Here's a real-life example. Psychotherapist Belleruth Naparstek has written a brilliant how-to about psychic work, *Your Sixth Sense*. Unfortunately she implies that those who call themselves "Empaths" are using a euphemism for the (supposedly) more controversial term, "Psychic."

I think it's more likely that training for this talented woman has not included empath skills. In one anecdote, for instance, Naparstek described how, while talking with a patient, she began to feel a lump in her throat

"How did *her* lump get into *my* throat?" she wondered.

How, indeed! To this empath coach, what happened to the therapist was a typical example of unskilled empath merge. It brought temporary relief to her patient. Afterwards, unfortunately, Naparstek would have to handle the Imported STUFF. She noticed when it entered her energy field. Later, perhaps, she stopped noticing it — which doesn't mean the STUFF was gone. Far from it.

Most likely too, within a few hours, that original lump in the throat came right back to Naparstek's patient.

Even when an improvised method for empath merge is done purposely, and with the sweetest intentions, that won't protect an empath from Imported STUFF.

- ∾ When a well-trained psychic helps others, the model for giving service is quite clear: Clean, accurate, information transfer.
- ∾ What kind of service can a skilled empath bring? What can we do safely? How much can we contribute, helping others? Maybe these answers are more complex.

Certainly, Brave Empath, you are one step closer to finding out. Embracing your gifts in Part Two of this Program for Empath Empowerment, you have readied yourself to learn one of life's spiritual mysteries.

Which hidden dynamics used to happen whenever you used to slip into unskilled empath merge? Let's explore that next.

PART THREE

Understanding Your Empath Gifts Even Better

Brave Empath, eventually you will be so grateful for every one of your God-given gifts as an empath. Although each gift is unique, each one of them works in the same manner. Here are the basic facts of life for an empath.

1. Each empath gift is given to you for life.

2. It comes to you switched ON.

3. Until you get skills, automatically, you will do countless unskilled empath merges every day. Drip-drip-drip!

4. Sometimes this flying in spirit is semi-conscious and feels good. Still it's an unskilled empath merge.

5. Most of your unskilled empath merges happen subconsciously only. Your conscious mind doesn't feel or learn a thing.

6. Regardless, every unskilled empath merge deposits Imported STUFF in your aura.

7. Unskilled empath merges are a habit for all born empaths. With skills, you can change that. Automatically you keep your empath gifts turned OFF. No more drips, just a wonderful faucet that you can control.

8. Whenever you choose, you can purposely turn your empath gifts ON. Do this safely by using a technique for Skilled Empath Merge.

Now that you have begun to embrace all your empath gifts, you're ready to understand more about how they work. Here is what you will learn in Part Three:

- ∼ Which energy dynamics, exactly, occur during unskilled empath merge?
- ∼ How can you prevent this from happening?
- ∼ Why will it be *effortless* for you to manage all of your empath gifts?

How Empath Merges Work

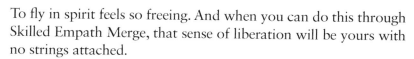

To fly in spirit feels so freeing. And when you can do this through Skilled Empath Merge, that sense of liberation will be yours with no strings attached.

Before then, unfortunately, you may do plenty of unskilled empath merges. Even if you have no clue they are happening. Even if they do not feel as if you are doing something wonderful, with a lovely name like "Flying in spirit."

How much do you know about unskilled empath merge? In order for me to learn the secrets I'm about to share with you, I spent more than a decade, coaching clients worldwide.

Your version of learning will be so much easier, Brave Empath. For your next step, just take this quiz.

EMPATH MERGE QUIZ. Test Your Knowledge

Answer TRUE or FALSE to the questions below. Then keep reading.

1.	Even if you haven't developed skills yet, instinctively an empath knows how to stay safe while flying in spirit.	T	F
2.	You can always choose whether or not to do an empath merge.	T	F
3.	Probably you don't do many empath merges while with other people.	T	F
4.	You would never do an empath merge with a stranger unless that person were really inspiring.	T	F

5.	On occasion you might do an empath merge just to lift someone's pain, help somebody out.	T	F
6.	It is Christian (or otherwise spiritually virtuous) to give someone the gift of an empath merge.	T	F
7.	If God gave you talent as an empath, you are obliged to use it for flying in spirit.	T	F
8.	If you feel bad after doing an empath merge, it's because you healed that person.	T	F
9.	Could be, one major reason friends love you is how you give to them as an empath.	T	F
10.	Unless you feel it happening, you are not doing an empath merge.	T	F

Expand Your Knowledge

Sure, we'll get to the answers to this "Test Your Knowledge" Quiz. In Chapter 31.

Unconventional as a way to proceed? Sure. But I'm teaching you something unconventional, and you're embracing something unconventional as well.

Just the process of answering these quiz questions could have stirred up some erroneous assumptions within you, Brave Empath — conscious ideas, and also maybe some subconscious expectations, that are totally understandable.

Understandable but, also, flat-out wrong.

Let's clear the way for an understanding that helps you better.

And let's introduce conscious words for subconscious experiences that you may never have thought about previously. Aligning with the truth about empath merge will prepare you to manage your empath gifts as nothing else can.

Your Next Informational Download

Every empath is born with talent. Until that empath also develops skill, an unsuspecting empath will do hundreds of unskilled merges each day.

What, exactly, happens to a empath's consciousness during one of these empath merges? To find out, investigate at the level of the human energy field. That's what I did.

Descriptions that follow are based on research using the system of Aura Reading Through All Your Senses® plus adding a somewhat advanced technique for capturing *what happens within a split second*. (If you're interested in learning more about this, you might want to google the aura healing technique of Vibrational Re-Positioning®.)

Gee, use aura reading? To learn about what happens to an empath's consciousness? Might seem pretty abstract. Because it is. To bring life to this description, I will describe what happens when unskilled empath Isabella hangs out with her boyfriend Sigmund.

Both these good people have soul-level gifts galore. Isabella's gift set includes three empath gifts, while Sigmund is no empath.

At the astral level of their auras, corresponding to the subconscious mind, both Isabella and Sigmund are evolving beautifully in their human lives. However, both have accumulated quite a bit of STUFF.

As you may remember, STUFF means stored-up fear, pain, anger, etc. It is both energetic and emotional. Subconscious STUFF can always, always, always be healed with effective techniques.

What Is Required to Heal STUFF Permanently?

Brave Empath, permanent healing of STUFF is definitely possible. Energy spirituality, energy medicine, and energy psychology all contain techniques to permanently remove this astral-level debris.

In this energy healer's opinion, human consciousness has evolved a great deal in our lifetimes. For healing to succeed now, in this Age of Energy, it isn't enough to do ENERGY CLEARING, which moves out STUFF from a client's aura. Energy clearing brings immediate relief, not permanent healing.

For permanent results, STUFF *removal must be followed by* PUT-IN. This means adding something energetically beneficial at the astral level, plus aiding the client to consciously learn something relevant and meaningful. It's powerful when conscious Aha!s support energetic replenishment at a subconscious level.

An aura reading is not a healing. Why not? A reading provides information. This does not budge STUFF. Nor does reading a client's energies insert anything at the level of the subconscious mind.

Sure, any aura *reading* — including one done by means of Skilled Empath Merge — can be perceptive, fascinating, illuminating, absolutely delightful. It just does not provide aura *healing*.

Energetically, this is a clear difference. A reading is not a healing because readings impact a client's conscious mind only. Whereas aura healing happens subconsciously.

And when you have skills for researching those astral-level, subconscious frequencies, it becomes quite easy to tell the difference. STUFF is either healed or not.

Intelligent people can flatter themselves that their conscious insights are so brilliant, that must heal subconscious problems.

Sorry. Not true. Not unless that intelligent person has also learned a skill set that produces actual healing.

So no empath merge provides *permanent* energy healing. However, here's the really tricky part. Immediately after an unskilled empath merge, there can be a *temporary* energy shift for the person at the other end of the empath merge. More accurately, this could be called *temporary relief* rather than "healing."

Gee, think this energetic fact of life might add to an unskilled empath's confusion? Let's make this distinction even clearer.

Unfortunate Energetic Quickies

Technically what distinguishes an unskilled empath merge from a Skilled Empath Merge?

Both require empath talent. Both can happen when an empath like Isabella sits in a room with another person. Both can happen whether that other person, like Sigmund, is an empath or not. Person means person, that simple.

During an UNSKILLED EMPATH MERGE, Isabella's aura expands to encompass Sigmund's aura. Almost like giving him a hug with her energy field!

This energy hug is random and entirely subconscious. More like a reflex than a volitional hug.

Hugging on purpose is done physically, and with active participation by the conscious mind. Unskilled empath merge happens without conscious intent, like when a doctor smacks beneath your knee to check a physical reflex, causing your leg to jerk.

Back at our example of Isabella's reflexive unskilled empath merge, what happens next, after her zippy moment of flying in spirit to hug Sigmund aurically?

Isabella's energy field returns to normal size around her physical body. Usually Isabella is totally unaware that she has done this. The aura-level hug happens subconsciously. Moreover, unskilled empath merges typically take way less than one second.

Nevertheless, an unskilled empath merge can sometimes take longer. In that case empath Isabella might consciously notice what is happening, however vaguely. She might have a familiar warm-fuzzy feeling or sense a pleasant kind of upliftment.

This would be a PROLONGED UNSKILLED EMPATH MERGE, lasting for several seconds or, even, minutes. Some unskilled empaths develop the habit of doing them routinely.

In duration, this is the opposite of most unskilled empath merges. I like to call them SPLIT-SPLIT-SECOND EMPATH MERGES for short. (The longer name would be "Split-split-split-split-split-split-split-split-split-split-split-split-split-split-split-split-split-split-split-split -split-split-split-split-second empath merges.") (Approximately.)

SPLIT-SPLIT-SECOND EMPATH MERGES happen way too fast for conscious detection.

Will this brevity somehow protect an empath from suffering the consequences? Nope.

Regardless of duration, each unskilled empath merge results in Imported STUFF for the empath. Does Prolonged Unskilled Empath Merge deposit more than the super-quick varieties? Probably.

All the more reason to detect it, stop it and, over time, prevent it completely.

CHAPTER 29

Prolonged Unskilled Empath Merges

Split-Split-Second Empath Merges don't show to a casual observer. But Prolonged Unskilled Empath Merges do, at least to a trained observer.

Vision patterns can provide a clue. For instance, what if you see Isabella staring for a long period of time at Sigmund? What if she is staring almost like a baby, with rapt attention? This might be a Prolonged Unskilled Empath Merge.

More complication, though! Isabella might just like Sigmund's tie. Or Isabella might be stoned on weed. Only aura reading would definitively reveal what is happening with Isabella's consciousness.

When an unskilled empath merge is prolonged, would Isabella necessarily know what she's doing? Does she sense how her auric field expands into hug position, akin to blowing up a large balloon that surrounds another balloon? Probably not.

If Isabella verbalized her mostly subconscious, warm fuzzy feeling, more likely she would call it, "I really love him." Or "Losing myself in Sigmund is what it means to be a really good friend."

Unless Isabella has studied with Obi Wan Kenobi (or the equivalent), she will not consciously notice random fluctuations in energy fields, a.k.a., "The Force." That would be a good thing, actually.

Outside a "Star Wars" movie, it isn't particularly healthy to dwell on auras all day long. Even the spiritually Enlightened do not do this. Reading auras all day long leads to spiritual addiction, which you can learn more about at my blog.

What Changes After Unskilled Empath Merge?

Once Isabella's aura reverts to its usual dimensions, she returns to her normal sense of self — for the moment. Until her next unskilled empath merge, which could happen any second.

Even then, there's a tricky after-effect. It follows every single unskilled empath merge. "Returning to normal" means returning to a slightly different form of normal. Because some of the Imported STUFF in Sigmund's aura has transferred to Isabella's own energy field. Where that STUFF becomes her personal problem, long term.

Temporarily, Sigmund feels better subconsciously. He might even feel better consciously. Why wouldn't he?

Here is what happens in one hypothetical example of Split-Split-Second Empath Merge. When some of his psychic-level STUFF has just been transferred to Isabella, that includes:

- 25 blobs of psychic coercion, each one related to feeling sexually inadequate
- 15 small frozen blocks fraught with anxiety
- 12 negative thought forms contributing to low self-esteem

All of these globs and blobs and blocks of stuck, negative energy are now Isabella's problem. Remain in her aura they will... until she receives depth energy healing.

Sadly, Sigmund's relief is temporary. He has received an energy clearing, not a true healing. There has been no PUT-IN, neither energetically nor in terms of a meaningful conscious Aha!

So Isabella has paid a pretty steep price for brief glimpses of Otherness, hasn't she?

Although this example is hypothetical, I have helped real-life clients to remove exactly the sorts of STUFF described here.

For years, the presence of all this STUFF perplexed me. How could certain clients carry so much random astral debris? Then I figured out the common denominator. All those clients were unskilled empaths.

If this hidden side of being an empath disturbs you, good. Now you know why I urge all my clients and students to make empath skills a priority in their personal development (assuming that they are empaths in the first place).

As a teacher, I offer instruction in many practical skill sets for aura healing and deeper perception. Yet whenever an empath asks me, "Where do you recommend that I start?" my answer is the same. I urge my student to gain Empath Empowerment.

Many an empath is bent way out of shape energetically, due to volunteer work like Isabella's unskilled merge with Sigmund, leaving her aura stuck with all those dismal energy souvenirs.

Randomly picking up Imported STUFF is unavoidable... until an empath learns how to support inborn talent with skill, and routinely keep empath gifts OFF.

Incidentally, you may be wondering about those empath gifs *not* related to human beings, like Animal Empath Ability or Crystal Empath Ability.

By now you appreciate that unskilled empath merges occur when an empath like Isabella is in the room with another person. What happens if you have one of those empath gifts not-about-humans?

Then you busily do volunteer work with the "person" who is an animal or crystal, etc. These are human-frequency objects, having a form in objective reality, and with energy fields as well. Sure, they can contain energetic STUFF.

Hello! That STUFF can (and will) move directly into your aura.

With skill, Brave Empath, you will simply enjoy your consensual wisdom downloads. Managing your special gifts as an empath? Definitely that means taking on wisdom, not Imported STUFF.

CHAPTER 30

What Happens During a Skilled Empath Merge

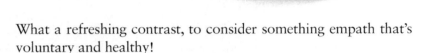

What a refreshing contrast, to consider something empath that's voluntary and healthy!

Nobody slip-slides into Skilled Empath Merge. This requires choice. You select one technique that you have learned. Then you do it purposely. Afterwards the technique is over. (You consciously stop doing it.)

Thus, each short-term voyage in consciousness is structured to have a distinct beginning, middle, and end.

Imagine that, as a skilled empath, Isabella wishes to probe the consciousness of her friend Sigmund. She chooses the "Deep Listening" technique (which you can learn from the follow-up book in this series, *The Master Empath).* She asks Sigmund for permission to learn about him from the inside, using her consciousness. After doing the technique, she will report back to him.

Let's suppose further that Sigmund agrees. Then Isabella does what she has said she would do. So inspiring, and insightful for them both! In some ways, this consensual empath merge could be better than sex: Pure consciousness pleasure, with no complicated feelings afterwards.

(In case you're wondering, Brave Empath, does one need to ask permission to do Skilled Empath Merge? Only if that particular technique requires an obvious physical position, like putting your ear to the other person's chest or hand, as happens with the "Deep Listening" technique. Otherwise you can employ a remote technique, using a photograph. *The Master Empath* can teach you more than a dozen techniques for Skilled Empath Merge, most of which are totally incognito, done with a photo or electronic image.)

Whichever technique you select to use on any particular occasion, what will happen in general when you do a Skilled Empath Merge?

A Divine blessing will protect you. Yes, every technique for Skilled Empath Merge will allow you to co-create with your favorite form of Highest Power. That protection is layered in many different ways. And it works.

Behold that Skilled Empath Glow

Continuing with the example of Isabella, what happens aurically during her Skilled Empath Merge? During the first few steps of "Deep Listening," her aura takes on an extra glow of Divine protection.

Once prepared, her aura encircles Sigmund's. How long does this sort of auric hug last? Isabella consciously chooses, based on what feels comfortable to her at the time. Usually the duration ranges from 10 seconds to a minute.

Not long, you'll notice, Brave Empath. Yet even the shortest Skilled Empath Merge will last significantly longer than a Split-Split-Second Unskilled Empath Merge.

Afterwards Isabella's aura returns to normal dimensions, completely separate from Sigmund's. And what changes within her energetically as a result of doing this Skilled Empath Merge?

Nothing. Sigmund's STUFF remains in Sigmund. Isabella's aura remains normal, too.

Even the Divine glow gradually subsides. However, Isabella does learn something consciously.

~ In terms of *content,* she learns about what it is like, right now, being Sigmund.

~ In terms of *process,* she exercises her ability to consciously fly in spirit.

~ *Mastery of her empath gifts* progresses as well. Mastery develops every time that Isabella uses her talent as it was meant to be used. This skill becomes cumulative.

~ If Isabella has additional skills for helping Sigmund, her personal *efficacy* can also grow considerably.

That efficacy is a really important advantage, not just for self-esteem but for accomplishing great things in life.

Supplementing her Skilled Empath Merge, Isabella may well use her friendship skills. Definitely, that counts as EFFICACY, a way to be effective in life.

Effectiveness must be earned. Efficacy does not happen as the result of some lucky accident. It happens because a person has developed a valuable skill set, then uses it purposely to produce a desired result.

So, after ending a Skilled Empath Merge, Isabella might apply any other helpful skill set that she has learned, like massage therapy or giving Sigmund a fabulous haircut or effectively cutting a cord of attachment.

All her efficacy will be enhanced, thanks to first having done that Skilled Empath Merge. Isabella's skills will adapt in *subtle* ways, since she has just experienced from the inside what it is like to be this completely different person.

Automatically she will apply her skills based on Sigmund's unique "Who-you-be," rather than expecting Sigmund to be "Just like me."

This will help to make Isabella's actions way more effective than otherwise. More efficacy, informed by deep knowing — that can be your destiny too, Brave Empath.

Let's note further, deep knowing like this is not a psychic experience, astrally based. Rather, Isabella has made a brief journey in consciousness to explore both Divine and astral frequencies of Sigmund's aura. Flying in spirit in this way supports her human life; this doesn't make her seem floaty or odd.

A skilled empath's kind of knowing is simple, direct, energy intensive, yet structured in a way that supports the humanity of the knower.

No wonder the results help Isabella to get her life together; just the opposite of the spaced-out, energy-entangled lifestyle of an unskilled empath.

Brave Empath, Skilled Empath Merge can be combined with all your life skills to help you become extra-successful, period. This is what I mean by BECOMING A MASTER EMPATH.

Applications abound for love, business, and friendship — bringing you a real competitive advantage. (For specifics, see *The Master Empath*. But, please, only make use of that workshop-in-a-book after you have learned more about how to turn your empath gifts OFF.)

Right now, at this stage of progress in this Program for Empath Empowerment, I have a challenge for you. Brave Empath. Let's return to our learning-in-progress, that Empath Merge Quiz.

Do you wish to change any of your answers before moving forward to answers supplied by Rose, your friendly empath expert?

If so, do that right now. Because some very blunt, detailed answers are coming next.

CHAPTER 31

Empath Merge Quiz.
ANSWERS

Brave Empath, you deserve to know the energetic truth. Your whole life, you've been doing unskilled empath merge. Yet how much have you really known about it?

....

1. Even if you haven't developed skills yet, instinctively an empath knows how to stay safe while flying in spirit.

....

FALSE

By definition, no unskilled empath merge is safe. Sorry.

While unskilled, some empaths will suffer more than others. The *number of empath gifts* is a factor. The more gifts you have as an empath, the more you will suffer.

An additional factor is your degree of empath talent. Independent of the number of gifts, each empath's talent could be gauged overall on an **EMPATH TALENT SCALE** that ranges from 1-100. I have coached empaths Andy, Ben, and Charles. They are at 4, 40, and 99, respectively.

The stronger your empath talent, and the larger your number of gifts, the more Imported STUFF you will pick up from an unskilled empath merge.

Hey, I don't make the rules. I help empaths to triumph within those rules, a.k.a. "Teaching empaths skills that work."

2. You can always choose whether or not to do an empath merge.

FALSE, MOSTLY

Usually an empath has no choice whatsoever. So many unskilled empath merges happen in random fashion, done with strangers, lasting a millisecond.

Hardly what I would call "Always choosing"! Sometimes, though, even an unskilled empath has some degree of choice.

This choice concerns whether the empath is going to stay in the merge for an extra-long period of time, longer than a split-split second. Remember our discussion of Prolonged Unskilled Empath Merge? That brings a sweet sense of connection, a pleasurable and familiar conscious experience related to empath merge.

Provided that you do notice this — and granted, most empaths do not — the state of connection can be prolonged intentionally. Which could become a habit, a bad habit.

Personal Teaching Tale: Back in the day, I sure did this. A lot.

For instance, I remember being introduced to Barbara. She was clearly uncomfortable with my body language. (As for my weird aura at the time, dripping with STUFF — this would also have been noted subconsciously by Barbara. Hardly alluring either.)

Obviously trying hard to be polite, Barbara told me, "You have such an interesting way of staring at everyone. I have never seen a person go so long without blinking. How do you manage to do that?"

Maybe it seemed as if I was on drugs. Nope. I just had that difficult combo of zero empath skills, a lot of empath gifts, and a high degree of talent on that 1-100 Empath Talent Scale.

Can you relate, personally, to the idea of Isabella (or me, back in the day) staring almost like a baby, with rapt and unblinking attention?

Brave Empath, that would be surprising.

It's unusual to catch yourself doing this, even if the habit has become pretty extreme. More likely, from now on you will notice *other* people doing this. You will see your buddy Jayden do it, or some random stranger at a Starbucks.

What will you observe then, with this Prolonged Empath Merge? Jayden stares, not blinking much, appearing deeply involved in the conversation, maybe seeming as if stoned on pot.

Only an aura reader knows for sure, but Jayden might well be an empath, prolonging his unskilled empath merge.

Why unskilled? No Skilled Empath Merge needs to take more than a smallish number of seconds, maybe one minute at most. Eyes will be closed while starting and ending the technique. Afterwards eyes open. The empath returns to normal. Yes, normal. Not spacey.

Although Skilled Empath Merge takes so little time, it is plenty powerful. Once complete, the educational interlude accomplishes far more than any unskilled empath merge, however lengthy.

3. Probably you don't do many empath merges while with other people.

FALSE

Not do many of those merges? Says who, your conscious mind?

Remember, Brave Empath, unskilled empath merges are not performed by your conscious mind.

It's more like a reflex for your aura, comparable to muscles that work involuntarily. (Muscles that could be trained to work voluntarily, like your *obicularis oris.*)

What, you assumed that empath merges either were rare or never happened at all? Not surprising. Look, once upon a time you didn't even know the word "Empath," let alone "Empath merge."

The very idea that "Probably you don't do many empath merges"? Are you laughing yet? By now I hope you can appreciate what a huge problem these are for every single unskilled empath.

You can afford to laugh, Brave Empath. Soon you will learn how to manage your talent. With skill, it can become so effortless — and routine — to keep all your empath gifts turned OFF as a matter of habit.

4. You would never do an empath merge with a stranger unless that person were really inspiring.

FALSE

Brave Empath, I am still gathering information about unskilled empath merges. I dream of formal, funded, well-designed research studies. Meanwhile, case studies will have to do. And so far thousands of sessions with clients have revealed surprising dynamics involving unskilled empath merge.

Just one example is a type of problem with subtle energy, very healable, a problem that I have often helped clients to solve. It happens in certain cases when aura healing sessions require that I analyze the contents of a cord of attachment. This analysis is required as part of the 12 Steps to Cut Cords of Attachment®. Step 9 of 12 requires that you research whichever bits of stuck energy were in the freshly-cut cord. These are called CORD ITEMS.

Well, here's a common problem with Cord Items, a dynamic that only affects empaths: Sometimes a cord of attachment contains a Process-Oriented Cord Item that switches empath gifts ON. Until that cord of attachment is removed permanently, every time it cycles through my client's subconscious mind, it will initiate having all empath gifts switch ON.

Now, a skilled empath will automatically compensate for this because the habit has become so strong, flipping that inner switch back to OFF.

Otherwise, what happens to an unskilled empath when a cord of attachment contains this particular kind of Process-Oriented Cord Item? You guessed it. Every time.

You see, an unskilled empath merge occurs every time the contents of that particular cord cycles through the empath's subconscious mind, which could be 50 times in one day. And that's just one cord of attachment.

Overall what have I learned from researching with the full range of skill sets in RES (not just cord-cutting)? "I do empath merges with strangers only when they are really inspiring" is an appealing illusion constructed by the conscious mind.

In reality? Such fastidiousness is highly improbable.

An unskilled empath like Isabella will slide into empath merges with random strangers due to physical appearance or behavior that captures attention. Not necessarily because of inspiration at all.

Really, that's just the beginning. Most empath merges are initiated by complex astral-level dynamics, driven by the subconscious mind, with no conscious component whatsoever.

Let's use the example of Isabella seeing Luke, a handsome stranger rollerblading down the street.

Subconsciously Isabella can tell if Luke might be dangerous, violent, or strongly unstable emotionally.

How? Subconsciously every human alive reads everyone else's aura. As if each of us were a runway model in the fashion show of life, constantly displaying our every energetic characteristic. My term for that is AURIC MODELING.

Of course, information from auric modeling remains subconscious only. At least, the info is hidden from conscious awareness until a person develops the skills to access this info consciously — by developing energetic literacy. (Fluent, effort-less, accurate aura reading is your birthright, Brave Empath.)

Auric modeling is just one of many potential triggers for sending an empath like you into an unconscious, unskilled empath merge.

What Else Triggers an Unskilled Empath Merge?

Yowza, those pesky, random unskilled empath merges! I'm still exploring what causes them. I'll freely admit that this has not been the major focus of my research into everything empath — since I would much rather help empaths like you than spend time investigating all possible causes of suffering.

For what it's worth, here is my latest thinking in the summer of 2014. Triggers for an unskilled empath merge can include any of the following:

- The empath's conscious mind becomes interested in another person, becoming curious for any human-interest-type reason.

- More likely there is a subconscious reason — at the level of auric modeling. Perhaps Luke's aura includes certain kinds of suffering that are familiar to Isabella, based on her past experience. Subconsciously she could be drawn to this.

- Or subconsciously Luke's aura might remind Isabella of difficult people from her past.

- Or Luke's auric modeling is unusual... and in a way that relates to Isabella's personal set of gifts as an empath. "Look, he's got Intellectual Empath Ability. Just like me!"

- The higher an empath's giftedness on the Empath Talent Scale, the more likely she will be drawn to empathic exploration of someone with unusual or extreme problems.

So Isabella's empath merge with Luke might simply be triggered by the rollerblading or his handsomeness.

Alternatively she could be fascinated by what a mess Luke's aura is, displaying kinds of trouble that are noticeable due to her gift for Intellectual Empath Ability; kinds of trouble that are particularly fascinating since Isabella is so talented empathically, a 99 on the Empath Talent Scale.

Let's suppose that Luke's thinking process is jumpy and disorganized, rife with complex patterns of STUFF. Encountering this unusual set of aura characteristics, Isabella's unskilled empath merge is triggered. A subconscious split-split-second thought might go, *I wonder what it is like to be confused in that way?* Or *He's suffering so much in his thought process. I sure wish I could help him.*

Whatever sets that empath merge in motion (and, remember, I'm still learning about this), those unintended, unskilled empath merges sure do happen. And definitely not caused just by inspiration.

Also not related to inspiration? How Imported STUFF is picked up after every single unskilled empath merge.

One More Contributor to Confusion (And Definitely Not Inspiring)

Brave Empath, we're still pausing mid-Quiz Answers, adding just a bit more practical understanding. What follows is quite technical, but bear with me if you are interested in understanding just how messy unskilled empath merges have been for you.

When Isabella sees Luke rollerblading down the street, suppose that he happens to have the same age and build as Isabella's last boyfriend, Eric. Suppose further that Isabella still has her cord of attachment to Eric.

No stretch of imagination needed there. A cord of attachment connects you to every romantic interest you have ever had. That cord persists, aura-level, unless you have used an effective technique to permanently remove that cord of attachment. Otherwise, it's significant, whatever happens to be in your cord of attachment to someone like Eric. This specific set of cord items cycles through your subconscious mind whenever you encounter somebody who reminds you of him. Energetically that's a fact of life.

Guess what happens, related to STUFF, when rollerblading Eric prods Isabella's subconscious mind? The complete sequence of cord dialogue from Isabella's cord to Eric will cycle through Isabella's subconscious mind, as cords of attachment are wont to do.

And further, just because this sort of thing really does happen quite often, let's suppose that this particular cord of attachment includes the process-oriented cord item, "Empath gifts turn ON."

Hey, that's all it takes. You know about that light switch factor. Any empath's gifts are either OFF or ON. Well, wham! Isabella's go ON.

Brave Empath, you can appreciate what a lot of complicated factors could set up *your* next unskilled empath merge with a stranger.

Whatever has happened with your personal situation in the past, you can be sure of these three things:

1. Your habits have been subconscious, involuntary.
2. Conscious inspiration had little, or nothing, to do with it.
3. Long-term energetic habits have caused you to do innumerable subconscious empath merges with strangers.

Okay, back to more Quiz Answers.

....

5. *On occasion you might do an empath merge just to lift someone's pain, help somebody out.*

....

TRUE, also FALSE

First, the TRUE part. Sure, feeling sorry for someone might trigger a Split-Split-Second Empath Merge or even a Prolonged Empath Merge.

Mostly, though, the answer to Quiz Question 5 is FALSE. Let's be clear. Does an unskilled empath ever help anyone energetically?

Not long term. Not significantly. Sorry.

It's one thing to bring a bit of temporary relief. Altogether different is facilitating the permanent removal of STUFF, complete with adding appropriate PUT-IN.

To illustrate, here is a story from one of my workshop students in Japan. Maxi-san worked as an acupuncturist. She told this story.

"I am a very, very talented empath. When an acupuncture patient comes to me, as I put in the needles, I learn about all her pain. I feel this in my body.

"Immediately my patient feels so much better. Unfortunately I am overwhelmed. I must go to another room and lie down for 20 minutes. Yes, this is something I have learned to do while my patient receives the healing treatment.

"Lying down helps. My pain subsides. Here is my problem, though.

"When I go back and remove the needles from my patient, what happens? The empath healing has worn off. My patient doesn't feel better any more.

"So I have come to this workshop to learn a way to take away my pain that does not put it all back in my patient. I want to keep helping my patients as an empath."

Empath talent? Clearly, Maxi had that. Yet she didn't understand what you are learning now. What really happens subconsciously and energetically with empath merge?

Maxi-san didn't make the distinction, yet, between doing a Skilled Empath Merge versus the unskilled variety. Consequently she thought that an energy reading was an energy healing. Sensing information about a patient's pain — however accurately — may bring emotional validation. However there will not be any significant or permanent energetic relief.

Moreover, Maxi-san had no clue that she was doing a Prolonged Unskilled Empath Merge. Or that coping by means of a nap might have brought her conscious relief but wouldn't budge the new STUFF that she had just imported from her patient.

It's easy to confuse feeling relief after a nap with removing the cause of feeling bad. Sleep does help with many kinds of healing. However, no amount of napping will remove significant aura-level STUFF.

One more sad fact, if we're going to look at Maxi-san's tale with an eye for potential improvement: Like many a talented empath, Maxi-san was improvising a way to combine unskilled empath talent with her valid skill set as an acupuncturist.

That improvised method didn't work as intended. Actually, being so involved in her experiment may have been distracted Maxi-san from growing professionally as an acupuncturist.

If her patients didn't notice results by the end of a session, that wasn't merely a problem related to the healer's lack of empath skills. Evidently Maxi-san wasn't doing that good a job as an acupuncturist. Because acupuncture — all by itself, with no extra techniques mixed in experimentally — happens to be a powerful skill set. At least, this holds true if the healer is focusing on her job.

With more skill, Maxi could take a minute or two for a Skilled Empath Merge near the start of her session. This could inform her work as an acupuncturist. Then she might then do a better job than otherwise, using her expertise at acupuncture.

After removing the needles and taking her client's pulses, Maxi-san might undertake a second Skilled Empath Merge to assess what changed, and maybe she might tell her client about the difference. (Brave Empath, are you curious about other ways to effectively combine empath merges with professional work? That's called "Sequencing" and is explored later, in my training for Master Empaths.

What's useful to know for this part of the Program for Empath Empowerment? It is very common for unskilled empaths — whether acupuncturists or not — to create theories where empath merges supposedly bring magical healing. Interesting theories, sure.

True? Probably not.

Beware sprinkling bits of empath merge into your life. Even if it feels good.

Self-authority is not a substitute for skill. Ideally the two support each other.

When you have skill *as an aura reader*, you can accurately assess the dynamics of any healing session; moreover you have a valid framework to gauge results for your client. When you are skilled *as an empath*, you will not be tempted to misinterpret or glorify the consequences of unskilled empath merge.

Well done, Maxi-san, taking that workshop so that she could start developing empath skills! I hope she has improved her efficacy with patients.

....

**6. It is Christian (or otherwise spiritually virtuous) to give
     someone the gift of an empath merge.**

....

TRUE, also FALSE

What could be more personal than deciding what you believe is virtuous?

One example: Does your belief system exalt sacrifice? If so, this Quiz Question 6 would count as true.

Suppose that empath Ben sees that his friend Gloria is suffering. Even if he doesn't have empath skills yet, he might sense how to do a Prolonged Unskilled Empath Merge. Further, he might consciously have figured out that he will pay a personal price, and feel terrible afterwards. Yet, out of duty — or his love of God — Ben might do plenty of Prolonged Unskilled Empath Merges, simply in order to be a good friend.

As a conscious rationale, Ben's choice might go, "If I can make Gloria feel better, even for a few moments, what does it matter if I must pay for it afterwards?"

Of course, a rationale like that could also be called "Co-dependency." A lovely religious faith can be mixed in with co-dependency, like pearls in the mud.

Brave Empath, after you have become a fully skilled empath, you can help a friend like Gloria without suffering as a result. You can help her better. Which is why, personally, my answer to Quiz Question 7 is FALSE.

Back in the Renaissance, singers of sacred music sometimes chose to become castrati, all the better to praise God through their voices. Yet they also could have grown up to sing like glorious tenors or basses or baritones.

When we revisit personal history, many of us can find similarly bad choices that we did for love, mostly because at the time we didn't know better.

Regarding your religious and ethical values, Brave Empath, here's a suggestion. After you have lived for several months as a skilled empath, sit for an hour and write a list of your current beliefs.

With a freshly cleaned-up aura, not perpetually picking up STUFF from others, some of your values might change. You may choose less human sacrifice, more joy for yourself, and far more effectiveness as a helper.

....

7. If God gave you talent as an empath, you are obliged to use it for flying in spirit.

....

FALSE

You might not agree with me about this Quiz Answer, Brave Empath. And that's fine. Because your self-authority rules, right? Besides, you are going to learn how to fly in spirit with Skilled Empath Merge, which will be a safe way to use that lifelong empath talent.

However, here is what I think about Quiz Question 7... and I have thought about it a lot.

Seems to me, the only way God can give anyone talent as an empath is to have it installed from Day One. (Some human gifts are just like that, although most are not.)

Learning how to develop skill to support empath talent? That part is up to us. If you do believe strongly in God, maybe you agree with one of my favorite sayings, "Heaven helps those who help themselves."

God made you an empath, but only you can make yourself a skilled empath. That's just how it is.

What else would be an example of a gift that works on its own, where you might or might not believe that you have a right to take control? Fertility.

The Catholic Church does not favor contraception. Supposedly if a sexually active married couple can possibly produce babies, neither partner has the right to limit the resulting family responsibilities. Yet that hasn't stopped the majority of the world's Catholics from using effective methods of birth control.

Fertility is a sacred gift, few would argue. Yet I don't see too many families today with 14 children or more. Do you?

Many a good Catholic would say, *I believe in right to life — my life. As a parent, I have chosen to have just two kids so that I could do a better job by each child. I'm a better parent because I am not exhausted, cranky and, quite possibly, insane.*

To such a parent, that is a sacred way to address fertility.

This new Age of Energy isn't the Middle Ages. Adults living today can develop situational ethics, choosing the lifestyle of a skilled empath as part of our adult thinking. This Program for Empath Empowerment encourages you to use self-authority to uphold your values, deciding for yourself what is truly virtuous.

8. If you feel bad after doing an empath merge, it's because you healed that person.

FALSE

Temporarily that other person might feel better. So you might have answered, TRUE, Brave Empath.

But does a brief feel-good experience really count as a healing? Fact is, neither unskilled empaths nor skilled empaths really heal people. Energy healing requires a dedicated skill set.

Seems to me, the skill set of Empath Empowerment comes as close to *self-healing* as you can get, but really that's prevention.

Learning to habitually turn your empath gifts OFF will prevent your taking on STUFF from others. This could be considered a way to prevent Imported STUFF, greatly decreasing your need to receive healing.

However, FALSE is the better answer to Quiz Question 8. Because temporary healing is not real healing.

Has this distinction been confusing for you, Brave Empath? At this stage in Empath Empowerment, it's often wickedly confusing. To help you better understand the potential confusion, let's use the example of Unskilled Empath Harry and his good friend Sally.

Visit 1, when Harry meets Sally

What happens during Visit 1, right after Harry has done a Split-Split-Second Unskilled Empath Merge with his friend Sally?

　　　⌐ At the conscious, observable level of human reality

They are having dinner at a restaurant, chatting away like the good friends they are.

Harry and Sally have been enjoying a great conversation, as usual. Sally has been emotionally wired, physically jittery, sweet as she could be — although not comfortable in her own skin.

〜 Sally's aura, right after the unskilled empath merge

Five pounds of STUFF, at the psychic level, leaves Sally's aura.

Subconsciously she has received a welcome temporary healing. She feels much better. Consciously she figures that is just the effect of being with her good friend Harry.

Not possessing knowledge of what will happen within the next half hour, Sally has no clue that equivalent STUFF will soon return.

〜 Harry's aura, right after the unskilled empath merge

Five pounds of STUFF have just been added to his aura, at the psychic level. Subconsciously, Harry has begun to pay the price for his reflexive volunteer work.

Not possessing knowledge of what just happened to his aura, and consciously having a great time due to being with his good friend Sally, here is what Harry thinks:

Gee, my stomach is all tied up in knots, and I'm feeling so jittery. So annoyed at myself for being weak! A real man wouldn't feel like this. I have analyzed my issues and know that I get anxious from being in public places, like this restaurant. Well, I'll have to keep working on that. At least visiting with Sally can distract me from being such a mess.

Visit 2, when Harry meets Sally

This time, Harry and Sally are taking a walk, chatting away. Oops, he does a Split-Split-Second Unskilled Empath Merge.

What happens next, energetically?

〜 At the conscious, observable level of human reality

As usual, they are having a great conversation, personal and lively and honest. Both friends feel energized by their relationship.

〜 Sally's aura, right after the unskilled empath merge

Five pounds of STUFF, at the psychic level, leave Sally's aura. This could, actually, be the very same five pounds of STUFF she temporarily lost during their previous visit, given how it reconstituted soon afterwards.

Let's say that these five pounds of STUFF happen to relate to issues that Sally worries about a lot. Here's a summary:

Go on a diet. Eat less today. You really must lose weight.

You spend too much money, Sally. You have to stop wasting your money. It's shameful.

Mom is right. You aren't getting any younger, and that biological clock is ticking away. When are you going to give her grandchildren? Plenty of your other friends have children by now. What is taking you so long?

Sadly, Sally has the habit of pressuring herself all day long with subconscious grumbling like this. When Harry did the unskilled empath merge, five pounds of this STUFF did leave her auric field. But consciously she learned nothing, changed nothing. No skill set was used by Harry to facilitate permanent healing. So all she receives now is a temporary respite.

Bottom line for Sally: She feels great. Being with Harry always makes her day. Partly, this is due to the friendship, which she notices consciously. Subconsciously, Sally is getting the usual lift from a temporary healing.

〜 Harry's aura, right after the unskilled empath merge

An additional five pounds of STUFF further complicates Harry's aura and subconscious mind.

Now he begins to fuss inwardly, translating the worry and self-criticism into his own subconscious vocabulary. Perhaps that Imported STUFF will create worries like these:

Am I ever going to get ahead at work? Why can't I act more aggressive?

When, if ever, will I be able to commit to a relationship? My girl-friend says that's my problem. What if she's right, and this is a permanent flaw in my character?

As usual, Dad is on my case about saving for retirement. Could I be making a big mistake? But I don't want to be cheap. My friends go out just as much as I do; I'm no more wasteful than they are. Are all of us headed for trouble?

Subconsciously, Harry worries, and maybe consciously too. None of this has Sally's name attached. Why would he consciously connect any of this with his wonderful visits with his buddy Sally? (Or with his doing unskilled empath volunteer work?)

Energetic Homeostasis, Like It or Not

HOMEOSTASIS is a term you may remember from biology class back in school. It means that a living system tends to return to its usual state. Energetically and psychologically, people can have a version of homeostasis, too.

So the previous examples of Visits 1 and 2 are typical examples of ENERGETIC HOMEOSTASIS. Soon after Sally receives her temporary respite, that five pounds of STUFF returns.

Does Sally notice the impact of Energetic Homeostasis? Probably not. Consciously she's too busy enjoying the visit. Subconsciously the replaced STUFF doesn't feel weird or new to her. It feels normal. Because, at this time in her life, it *is* normal.

Energetic Homeostasis is a common factor in the energy flows between people. To facilitate permanent healing requires skill, not just friendship or caring.

After the visit, sure, Harry feels bad. Sadly, that's not because he used skill to change Energetic Homeostasis for Sally.

Brave Empath, this hypothetical example can help you to understand why FALSE is the more accurate answer to tricky Quiz Question 8.

9. Could be, one major reason friends love you is how you give to them as an empath.

TRUE, also FALSE

Sure. Who doesn't like to get something for nothing? It's human nature.

Totally TRUE, then. Your volunteer work as an unskilled empath could be a major factor in some of your friendships right now.

FALSE is a better answer, however. By the time you move into the lifestyle of a skilled empath, some so-called "Friends" may abandon you. They will gravitate towards new "Friends" who are unskilled empaths and, therefore, provide exactly the same sort of subconscious freebie.

How about the friends who remain? Count them as real friends, the ones worth keeping.

10. Unless you feel it happening, you are not doing an empath merge.

FALSE

Brave Empath, did you laugh while answering?

By now, you know a great deal about the hidden, subconscious mechanics — the incessant volunteer work — affecting every unskilled empath.

You can afford to laugh, especially if you have started to recognize the full extent of this problem.

It is very personal, the chronic suffering of an unskilled empath.

Psychotherapists even have a term that fits: BLAMING THE VICTIM.

Okay, psychotherapists sort-of have a term for this. Blaming the victim is commonly used in therapy. Only it isn't necessarily used to describe empath anything.

Blaming the victim applies to any situation where a suffering person wrongly attributes blame.

For example, Oscar receives verbal abuse from his wife, then worries that he deserves it. Or Violet is raped, then agonizes.

Was the rape really her fault?

Could she have asked for it?

Was it really a rape?

Whatever the circumstances might be, blaming the victim is wrong. Often unskilled empaths will blame the victim regarding Imported STUFF. This results automatically from every random unskilled empath merge, whether it be super-quick or prolonged.

Sure, empaths will suffer from all that STUFF. Typically, though, we blame ourselves. Even if we have never heard the word "Empath."

Feeling bad, due to all that astral-level STUFF, we can call ourselves plenty of names, worrying that we are oh-so-delicate, even dysfunctional.

Really, you are not to blame for those unskilled empath merges. Other people are not to blame, either. Blame the process itself, Brave Empath. Then learn how to stop it.

Sure you can. You are in a Program for Empath Empowerment. Where you happen to be doing just fine.

CHAPTER 32

Ten Reasons Why Something So Bad Feels So Good

After flying in spirit into the mess of someone else's aura, you might feel inspired *anyway*. Imported STUFF or not.

That's because the very process of flying in spirit usually causes an empath to feel liberated. During the process, at least. Here are 10 reasons why:

1. You have moved out of the box of your consciousness into the box of Joe's consciousness. Such variety! It adds spice to life.

2. If your experience was *unpleasant*, at least it was temporary. Back at your own experience, you can feel better by comparison. Returning to your everyday sense of self, your consciousness positioned comfortably back at your usual subjective reality, it's as though you just took an exotic vacation.

3. If the experience happened to be *pleasant*, you gained inspiration. Like viewing a lovely painting at the art museum. While flying in spirit, you might feel caring.

4. As an unskilled empath, you might even define your passing mood as "My friend Joe really needs me." Or some other pleasant thought flickers across your conscious mind. Really, who doesn't feel good at the thought of helping somebody? (Even if your good deed is more a wish than a reality.)

5. After the empath merge, you may sense that you have helped that person. In a temporary way that is true; otherwise it is sooooo not true. (Brave Empath, you understand that part better than most folks today, having read those practical details in our Empath Merge Quiz Answers.)

6. Flying in spirit feels natural to you, having been done so easily. By comparison, so much else about life is hard. Even counting from 1-10 takes more effort.

Now, Brave Empath, please don't be offended at the remaining four reasons on this list. Keep in mind, flying in spirit is very different for an unskilled empath compared to how it will be after you have learned to keep your gifts OFF.

7. Flying in spirit may *feel* spiritual, as if you are doing something that brings you closer to the Divine. In a way that is true, but in a way that is not true at all. (Until you have lived for a while as a very skilled empath, this may be hard to believe. For now, just keep your mind open to the possibility. Also, you will understand the Divine component best after reading *The Master Empath*.)

8. Sense of identity for an unskilled empath might be a bit distorted. That personal sense of self could be vague or confused. Borrowing Joe's sense of identity, even for that split second, could make you feel more whole as a person.

9. Before you become a skilled empath, you might also identify more with the *process* of flying in spirit than with simply being yourself. The latter can feel very limiting to an unskilled empath, since we are capable of readily sampling such different human experiences.

10. It's fun. Variety keeps away the dreaded, common experience of same old, same old.

Other things being equal wouldn't you rather have 20 meals a day, 20 "Favorite" foods, maybe even 20 faithful lovers, at least 20 cats?

Seriously, Brave Empath, all of us want to be more, to have more. That's not greed necessarily, just human nature. Well, flying in spirit allows you to sample consciousness.

Safe sampling will become way more fun later, when you do only Skilled Empath Merge. Actually, regular everyday life for a skilled empath can also become huge fun... long before you start doing Skilled Empath Merge.

The techniques you're about to learn in Part Four will start you *managing* your special empath gifts. Managing means ending the drip-drip-drip. Can you begin to imagine what it will like to spend your waking hours without the confusions of subconscious Imported STUFF?

Once you start turning your empath gifts OFF, that will automatically turn ON something else — something distinctive, fresh and fascinating, even sacred — your sense of self.

PART FOUR

Manage Your Magnificent Empath Gifts

If you need to blame someone, blame God.

Even almighty God might have some limitations. Because it appears that the only way God can bestow any empath gifts is for every one of them to be installed in the turned-ON position.

Actually, I don't blame God. I love God. And it really doesn't need to be anyone's fault why, on this Learning Planet, certain things work as they do. The sky will always point upwards, for instance. Why fight the system when that same energy could be applied to working the system, even triumphing?

Empath gifts are installed in the turned-ON position. No lamentations, then. Right now, Brave Empath, you can learn skills to purposely turn those gifts OFF. This will protect you from picking up STUFF from random, unskilled empath merges.

Have you ever met someone totally burned out from business travel? At first, Zachary adores the prestige, the variety, his chance to see the world and get paid for it. A decade later, Zachary feels differently. Money can't buy him a sense of home. He realizes how much he has missed.

Unskilled empaths can have a similar experience. Subconsciously we are enriched by variety from sampling consciousness belonging to others. Consciously we may be vaguely aware of the pleasures from Prolonged Unskilled Empath Merge. We might even suppose that we have healed others, unaware that the relief we have brought is so very temporary.

Now is the time to find your way home. To learn one technique after another that anchors awareness in a present sense of identity. To learn how to position awareness habitually at your own human life.

Imagine a life where your empath gifts don't run you. Just the opposite.

Or don't imagine, Brave Empath. Now let's start exploring how to turn your empath gifts OFF.

That begins with an unexpected upgrade, improving something you might not have thought needed improvement at all.

CHAPTER 33

You Can Manage Consciousness Gently

What follows is a simple technique to help you manage your flow of consciousness. After you try it, keep reading and then (as you will be doing with every technique that follows in this book) join my virtual classroom for a session of Questions & Answers.

Make your choice about doing a technique, then commit.

Brave Empath, keep reading about this technique only when prepared to take 5-10 minutes to actually do it. Otherwise skip ahead to the next post-Q&A heading in the chapter. (In this case, it would be "The Consciousness Theater for Any Human Adult.")

Notice, Brave Empath, this is your recommended strategy for every technique presented henceforth in our Program for Empath Empowerment. Either commit to actually doing the technique or else skip it for now.

Preparing to do this or any technique in our Program for Empath Empowerment:

- Make reasonably sure that you will not be interrupted. Turn off electronic gizmos. Alert your roommates. Fling pets from the room. (Okay, Gentle Empath, you might prefer gently carrying Fido out of the room. Definitely close the door afterwards.)

- Sit comfortably, feet on the ground or supported by a good, firm pillow.

~ Avoid chewing gum. Or tobacco. Or cookies. Or other food, drink, cigarettes, etc.

~ Read through all the steps of the technique in advance. While techniquing, open your eyes to peek at those steps again, as needed. Close your eyes quickly after each peek and you will be doing just fine.

~ What about fretting over "Supposed to"? As in, "How am I supposed to feel while doing this?"

Fugeddaboutit. Just do the steps, Brave Empath. Afterwards we will have our Q&A.

Technique: HEY, YOU

Who are you, really? What does it mean to become conscious of your consciousness?

Brave Empath, do the following steps nice and sloppy and easy: All steps, the complete technique, once. Then proceed immediately to the Q&A section that follows.

1. Beginning this effortless technique, sit comfortably and close your eyes. This will automatically *direct your attention within.*

2. To bring a bit more clarity to your experience, *take a few deep breaths.*

3. Sit there for a while. Then ask yourself this question once, *"What do I notice?"* It could be thoughts, emotions, physical sensations, energy, images, whatever — in any combo. Continue gently noticing whatever you spontaneously notice, not trying to make anything happen.

4. After about one minute, put names to the *type* of experience you were just having. Was it thoughts, emotions, physical sensations, energy, images, what?

5. Say out loud whichever type(s) of thing you just noticed.

6.   Think, "Technique officially over" *Open your eyes.* Automatically this will direct your awareness outward, toward objective reality.

Q&A. Hey, You

Q.   *Trying to put this consciousness thing into words makes me feel stupid. Why can't I just call whatever happened "Whatever"?*

A.   Languaging your experience will enhance it in the long run. Stretch yourself.

Q.   *But what if all I have to say is "Boring"? Nothing amazing happened. All I got was a quiet kind of state. For all I know, I was asleep.*

A.   Were you drooling on your shirt? If not, don't call it sleep. "A quiet kind of state" sounds more accurate. The point is, you just described finding your screen of consciousness. You experienced underlying consciousness.

Usually your screen of consciousness is kept busy running a "movie." All those attention-grabbing interactions with other people and situations are noticed with eyes open, not while doing "Hey, You."

Discovering how the experience of your inner screen of consciousness could be quiet — that's important.

Don't let that quietness fool you into belittling a major spiritual discovery.

Deep down, you are consciousness. Maybe some others in our virtual classroom could have flashier ways of describing it. So what? You just made conscious contact with your consciousness. Excellent!

Q.   *Can you give examples of the kind of things people notice when you teach them the "Hey, You" Technique?*

A.   Sure. Just don't compare yourself to anyone else. Each of these is a fine answer, and there are innumerable others.

- ∾ Silence.
- ∾ A new sound of silence within ordinary silence.
- ∾ Darkness.
- ∾ Light.
- ∾ A discovery that you, the real you deep inside, are a kind of dancing light.
- ∾ Random thoughts.
- ∾ Random emotions.
- ∾ Worrying about my thoughts or emotions.
- ∾ Noticing flows of energy inside my body.
- ∾ Seeing cartoons.

Q. *So which of these experiences of consciousness is the best kind to have?*

A. Every one of them. Any one of them. Or something else entirely. What happened to you while in technique, whatever you noticed effortlessly with your consciousness: That is the best.

You realize, this very human kind of experience can happen effortlessly. Doing this technique, you did not have to work in any way to make it happen.

Q. *But what if I did work hard?*

A. That was a misunderstanding. Please go back and do the technique again.

I think you'll discover that your consciousness is plenty lively all on its own, with no effort needed.

Q. *What do we actually DO with this consciousness? Like, what happens to my consciousness when I'm not paying close attention to it like just now?*

A. Now that deserves a good answer. :-)

The Consciousness Theater for Any Human Adult

Just because you are human, your consciousness travels to classrooms and offices and bedrooms, breakfast and dinner, play and work.

Everything you do while awake could be considered a movie shown on the screen of your consciousness, as if you were a portable movie theater, as if the film actually transported your movie theater on location.

One thing that does *not* occur spontaneously? Clear, crisp labeling.

What *does* happen usually, when you are not doing a technique to purposely shift consciousness, like Skilled Empath Merge? For a well-balanced human being, consciousness is mostly about Me-Me-Me: My thoughts, my feelings, my ideas, my beliefs and values, my physical sensations, noticing my energies, etc.

Being human, often you will notice the physical environment (e.g., pets, plants, machines) and other people.

While your consciousness is positioned on the surface level of human reality, you might also notice another person's words, actions, expression, body language.

For instance, suppose that your friend Joe is telling a long joke. You might notice Joe's cute gestures, his smiling expression.

Following this kind of experience, any human adult can generate interpretations about what is noticed about other people. Your personal interpretations about Joe might include:

- ◦ Thinking that Joe's jokes are way corny.
- ◦ Feeling loyalty to him, including affection for his pathetically bad joke telling.
- ◦ Having an idea about a joke that you might tell Joe about sending him to "Remedial Clown School."

All this happens within your personal movie theater. Without a word of warning, the direction of your consciousness can shift from your "Me-Me-Me" movie to the "What Is Happening to Somebody Else," movie, then back again to lively entertainment with the "Me-Me-Me" show.

This is a typical human flow of consciousness, when being with somebody like your friend Joe.

This kind of flow, so easily taken for granted, is supported by your consciousness. Consciousness flows automatically for every human with at least average intelligence and relatively normal mental health.

So naturally, this happens flow of consciousness happens to empaths.

Only something else happens to the consciousness of an empath, and I mean *every* empath, from birth. This is something that does not happen to non-empaths.

It does not happen to most Highly Sensitive Persons. It happens only to the HSPs who are also born as empaths.

We Highly, Highly Sensitive Persons have incarnated with a different sort of consciousness theater.

Besides the regular experiences of consciousness for a regular person, we start life as unskilled empaths. Usually we continue until death as unskilled empaths. Unless — like you, Brave Empath — that individual decides to use those special consciousness capabilities *with skill*.

What is an important thing, usually taken for granted, that you were born knowing how to do with your consciousness? Hint: Using this wisely is vital for becoming a skilled empath.

CHAPTER 34

Like Yourself Better

Being human, you were born knowing how to attach all experiences to yourself. Not necessarily like married couples who are "Joined at the hip." More like the process known as "Identification."

This spiritual term, IDENTIFICATION, concerns something that happens automatically because you are human. Identification works like tagging a photo on Facebook with your name.

It's as though the words "Me-Me-Me" are attached to every perception, every experience, through every sense, at every waking moment. And also while replaying incidents from your past.

- You might feel like Joe's joke telling "rubs off on you."
- With psychological projection, you feel about Joe now might be blamed on something that came up like a hiccup from your subconscious mind.
- And with unskilled empath merge, whomever you wind up hugging astrally causes you to feel as though you just explored something else about Me-Me-Me.
- Incidentally, that sense of identification goes double for Oneness-type empath gifts.

To some degree, identification happens to all human beings. However, identification mixed with unskilled empath merge causes empaths to get really confused by all the travel into other people.

Ironically — or not — until you gain skills as an empath, you may not know much about your personal identity, your true version of Me-Me-Me. How come? You are so used to identification with other people's ways of being.

You may not even *like* who you are. Due to religious or spiritual training, you may have come to dislike yourself or feel unworthy. Admittedly, that could have happened for plenty of other reasons as well.

The point is, a pesky version of identification is a specialty of us unskilled empath, which makes it hard to know yourself or like yourself.

Now is the time to start liking yourself a lot. Finding yourself interesting, loveable, worth knowing, adorably human, even fascinating. Healthy human identification... with yourself... as somebody you actually like.

Liking Yourself, Loving Yourself

Who is this person, you? How well do you like yourself?

Speaking English, we're fortunate to have two very separate words, love and like.

Do you LOVE yourself?

Probably. That would be the unconditional kind of love, a recognition that deep down you are such a good person: Funny, fun, sweet, and all your other adorable qualities.

Soul-level qualities, they could be considered. The familiar deep-down love for your essential goodness could also be called UNCONDITIONAL LOVE. As the unique soul you are, Brave Empath, you may find it easy to love yourself.

Now for a very different question: Do you LIKE yourself?

Depends, doesn't it?

- Getting out of bed on a Sunday morning, hung over from your festivities the night before? Maybe not liking yourself totally.

- A friend says, "You're great." You think, "Hey, I really am special."

∼ Another friend says, "It isn't you. It's me. We must break up." You think, "Oh, it's me alright. How can I live with myself? Do I even like this person?"

Could liking yourself seem harder than loving yourself? Definitely, and for good reason. You are a spiritual being having a human experience.

Unconditional love for that spiritual being is simple. Wrapping your mind and heart around your ever-changing, way-complicated, human existence? That's CONDITIONAL LIKING. Which can be so very much harder.

Even for non-empaths, conditional self-liking is pretty difficult. Think of non-empaths you know who have managed to live with a sturdy sense of self. How do they pull it together?

∼ Consider your buddy Natalie. Her sense of comes from *things* that she owns: Familiar things, pretty things; jewelry with sentimental value; a gorgeous painting in her living room. When Natalie wants to feel better about herself, she goes shopping and buys something new to like. Maintaining this form of conditional liking could be hard, especially paying for all that shopping! Hard, but manageable.

∼ Or think of Charlie, your employee at work. His sense of self is power-related, based on *comparing his status to that of others.* When Charlie is one-up, he likes himself. When one-down? He doesn't like himself nearly so much. Even so, Charlie can plot and plan to win the next competition. The very fact that Charlie constantly struggles to win — that could be reason enough to conditionally like himself. Competing like this would be hard, but sometimes fun, and altogether quite manageable.

∼ How about you? Is your sense of self really so simple? Does it depend entirely on *one or two outer aspects of life,* like your appearance or financial status or relationships or the thrill of your sex life? Your personal sense of identity could be way more nuanced. Which would be typical for an empath.

Conditional liking for yourself while you are an unskilled empath? To the degree that can start developing now?

Do you ever have a treat to look forward to, Brave Empath!

Goodbye, Earthquakes

Have you ever lived through an earthquake? Even a tiny one on the Richter scale can deliver quite a shakeup.

We humans expect the earth to be stable beneath our feet. Most of the time it is, so we take that for granted.

After an earthquake, even a brief one, what automatically happens to your easy certainty? A certain kind of trust has been shaken along with the ground.

What if you were to live through an earthquake without paying much attention?

Subconsciously you would still notice, correct? Subconsciously, a certain kind of trust would be shaken along with the ground.

Well, moving in consciousness into another person's energy field produces a comparable consequence.

When this happens without your control, the subconscious shift in identity cam destabilize your sense of self.

No, the physical ground beneath your feet does not give way. However, your everyday sense of being "Me-Me-Me" shifts over to "What Is Happening to Somebody Else." Temporarily, the standard human experience of "Me-Me-Me" is disrupted.

Conditional liking for yourself is shaken.

Well, this is about to change for good, Brave Empath. Let's start to build up a stronger sense of yourself in very appropriate human ways.

A Funny Thing about "Who am I?"

Do you remember Empath Quiz #2, about "Who am I?" That was an exercise in consciousness. Assuming that you have had prior experience with meditation or other spiritual exercises, you probably found that technique pretty easy to do. Even for a beginner, it might have been fairly easy. Why?

For us empaths, one appeal of spiritual exercises is that we tend to do them very well. Once we learn the basic skills, we can usually out-perform the non-empaths.

The reason is simple. Every human of average intelligence can learn to do spiritual exercises. Every human is designed with amazing — even genius-level — consciousness. However, we empaths are wired from birth to fly in spirit with that consciousness. This is why we excel at spiritual exercises that *move* our consciousness.

Especially we can excel when we get out of our own way, when we don't work hard or try to produce particular outcomes.

Whenever you develop skill at a *spiritual exercise*, you awaken self-awareness as a soul. This deepens unconditional love for yourself as an eternal, distinctive soul.

By contrast, the technique you're about to learn goes in the opposite direction, exploring your quirky *human individuality*, which is evolving through ever-changing life here at Earth School. So our next technique can strengthen your very healthy process of identification.

- Assuming that you have had prior experience with accepting your humanity and enjoying it, the following technique will probably be easy for you to do. Enjoyable, too.

- What if you're not yet so very enamored of your human self? Know that you can develop more skill at accepting your humanity. The following technique is designed to help.

Technique: I LIKE

What does your human identity happen to like? Right now? Let's find out.

Whether you call it *taste* or *personal preferences*, whatever you like really does matter. Back when you were two years old, you had personal preferences. You have them still. (Or else you can reinstall them.)

Allowing yourself to like what you already happen to like... can intensify a health respect for Me-Me-Me.

Brave Empath, please know that personal preferences are permitted in life. Contrary to what you may have been told, good people do not blandly feel an identical liking for everyone and everything. Spiritually Enlightened people don't, for instance. Personal likes and dislikes are normal for every human being.

The "I Like" technique invites you to explore your preferences for material objects.

By recognizing some things that you personally like, indirectly you will strengthen your ability to like *yourself*... and trust your own first thought or feeling.

1. Sit or stand somewhere you can *be alone,* or at least uninterrupted, for a minute or two. (Actually, this technique is excellent for times like being stuck in a long line at the supermarket, provided that you do the following steps discretely.)

2. Look at your surroundings. Find a color you like a lot. Is it the blue upholstery on your chair? The bright pink lettering on a poster? A fascinating and colorful food stain on your shirt? Go for likability, pure and simple. Say why you like it out loud. "I like the color of the _____ because _____."

3. Now it's sound time. Close your eyes. Such a variety of sounds is audible wherever you are. Listen and then ask yourself, "What is a sound I like, here and now?" Choose a

favorite. Open your eyes and say why you like it out loud, "I like the sound of ____ because ____."

4. For the final round, close your eyes again. Seek out and touch different textures, such as the fabric of your clothing, the surface of the furniture near you. Take a couple of fingers and explore your near environment until you *find a texture that especially delights you.* Open your eyes and *say why you like it* out loud, "I like the way ____ feels because ____."

5. Think, "Technique over." Because it is. Open your eyes.

Q&A. I Like

Q. *That was fun, I suppose. But what did it mean?*

A. Doing the "I Like" technique did something important for Empath Empowerment. Temporarily you just turned all your empath gifts OFF.

That's because you were consciously paying attention to yourself, just yourself, that delightful human self with excellent taste. An individual who can sometimes, maybe, be a bit hard to please!

Q. *How could I possibly do this technique in public?*

A. To avoid feeling self-conscious about being seen talking to yourself in public, pull out your smartphone and pretend to be having a conversation, sometimes listening and sometimes talking.

Q. *What about the touching part?*

A. People fidget all the time. Just touch your sleeve, your hand, some of the merchandise in your shopping cart. You can find a way to do this technique and make it socially acceptable.

Q. *It was hard for me to do this exercise. Why?*

A. "I Like" is a technique of pure selfishness and sensuality. You cease looking out for other people. Instead you jump into your own here and now. Unless you're used to doing this, it can be hard in the beginning. Soon you'll enjoy it.

Q. *What if I keep thinking, "Who cares what I like? What does it matter?"*

A. It thrills your soul to find pleasure through your senses. That is true for any human being, empath or not.

If you have ever hungered for closer contact with your soul, guess what? It honors your soul to pay attention to what you, personally, like. So ignore any inner grumbles and keep on exploring.

Q. *Why? What did I just give my soul, supposedly?*

A. Beyond giving yourself a vacation *from* empath talent, you were giving *to* yourself. You reminded yourself that, at will, you can delight in your senses. Ask your Inner Child how it likes this technique. Probably it's jumping for joy.

Q. *How often would you recommend playing the "I Like" game?*

A. Do it three times a day for a week, at the minimum. You're right, it *is* a game. And the more often you play it (within reason), the more you will enjoy it.

Q. *What is the purpose of the "because" part of the game? Why isn't it enough to choose something I like?*

A. When you push yourself a bit to say out loud why you like something, you're challenged in several ways, all beneficial.

1. You stay right on the surface of life, positioning consciousness at subjective human reality.

   Especially since The Shift into this Age of Energy, people are more likely to slip-slide deeper into subjective experience, distancing themselves from reality, exploring at energy frequencies that are astral and subconscious in nature.

   Actually, empaths do this more often than others. So it's good to stay right on that surface level, positioning your consciousness quite effortlessly.

2. Every time you probe for words, you strengthen coordination between your conscious mind and your natural ability to speak up for yourself.

3. Reasons you find for liking something may sound very
   simple, such as "I like the purple color of my calendar
   because it makes me feel happy." Speaking with such
   simplicity is good practice for you.

   As an adult, you can definitely do this. Yet, from
   childhood, many of us have been trained to make
   ourselves sound grownup, educated, complex,
   sophisticated, important, logical. Nonetheless, our
   personal preferences often *are* childlike.

Q. *What if talking that way makes you feel uncomfortable? That's*
what happened to me.

A. After you say your answers out loud, you gain a chance to
practice non-judgment. *"I like the carpet because it's soft."*
Maybe that's not fancy. Well if it is true for you right now, then
it's true. That simple. (And no crime has been committed.)

"The sound of the wind in the trees feels dark brown and soothes
my forehead." Whatever words come out of your mouth, strive to
accept them without criticism.

Being human, you do like some things and dislike others, prefer
some colors over others, enjoy certain foods more than others.
Even true for a saint! It is so good for any empath, accepting
your humanity.

Q. *I happen to have a major challenge about making decisions. This*
sounds stupid, but what if it takes me a really long time to choose
anything to like?

A. Keep at it. Eventually you may also improve your trust at
decision-making, especially if you add one simple rule: When
you're hunting for a color, sound, or texture, say your very first
thought.

This workaround can help, too: Set a timer for one minute. Not
to pressure yourself. Just a reminder not to drift off into some
familiar process of giving yourself a hard time.

Brave Empath, with practice you will find it easy to just choose something, then say it out loud. Oooh, commitment!

Otherwise, when that time goes off, blurt something out, however ridiculous.

Also it may help to remember that this technique can be light-hearted and fun.

You're not on the witness stand in some murder trial.

Pick something. Anything. With repetition, you just might lighten up enough to enjoy "I Like"

Q. *What if I don't happen to have any strong likes or dislikes?*

A. Deep down you must. Watch any two-year old. Once upon a time, you were that willful. Until somebody taught you to be oh-so-polite. Well, phooey on that!

"I Like" will start your spontaneity flowing. So will our next technique.

CHAPTER 35

Breathe Yourself More Awake

Brave Empath, you are ready to explore a series of easy techniques that involve breathing. Each one makes you more resourceful for managing your special empath gifts.

Just so you know, another reason to learn all these skills is that some will serve as preparation for the "Coming Home" technique in Chapter 43. Mastering that big technique requires that you learn several smaller ones first.

Meanwhile, got your nose? Got consciousness, Brave Empath? How about a bit of time? That's all you need. Trust that you can excel, for one simple reason....

Your Background as a Breather? Superb

Long before you heard the word "Empath," you have been breathing. Probably you have not been particularly self-conscious about it, either. In and out through nose. Unless you had a cold. Then how fortunate you have been to also possess a mouth!

Not too tricky, usually: Routine breathing is a great example of how the autonomic nervous system, guided by your subconscious mind, handles so many functions of the mind-body-spirit system. Ordinarily this subconscious functioning leaves your conscious mind free for other topics of interest.

Yet sometimes you may have consciously paid attention to breathing.

~ Perhaps you have studied breathing techniques from yoga, an ancient tradition from India just loaded with *pranayamas.* Yoga would have taught you about the fascinating link between breath and consciousness. Yes, it is definitely possible to actively use breathing as a way to shift your awareness.

~ What other past experiences could have made you aware of breath? Unfortunately you might have encountered respiratory problems, not just colds but scarier problems like asthma. One indirect blessing is to stop taking breath for granted. Have you been forced to value this precious and essential form of bodily functioning? On the bright side, breathing skills can be parlayed into empath skills.

~ You may have learned how to pace respiration for the sake of an art form. Actors and dancers, singers and other musicians, learn to make the most of their air flow.

~ Some folks develop breathing skills to avoid full-out panic attacks. The same with chronic pain.

~ Olympic gold medals are not bestowed for excellent breathing. However, many an Olympic athlete has developed superb skills related to breath. Well, so can you.

Regardless of whether you consciously worked in the past in order to develop breathing skills, you're ready now. I'm going to teach what you need to know for this Program for Empath Empowerment.

~ If you have previously done breathwork (for any reason) this will give you an advantage for understanding what follows in this chapter.

~ What if you never paid much attention to breathing? Apart from doing what was needed to stay alive! Well, no worries. You can do great at what follows. Congratulations that you have no bad habits to break about forcing yourself to control breathing, putting effort into breath's natural flow, etc. There's a lot to be said for innocence.

So you see, Brave Empath, to learn the useful skills in this chapter, you have the perfect background, just superb.

Breath Holding During
Unskilled Empath Merge

Routine breathing can actually help you to turn empath gifts OFF.

Remember our previous discussion of Prolonged Unskilled Empath Merge? I noted that some of you Brave Empaths may have fallen into a habit of staring at the person with whom you were doing a semi-conscious, unskilled empath merge.

Very likely, at such times, you were also holding your breath.

Technique:
INSTALL AN AUTOMATIC
SUBCONSCIOUS ALERT

The following sequence will help you to break the habit of inter-mittent Prolonged Unskilled Empath Merge.

Please read the following paragraphs silently once, and then out loud three times in a row. This will provide a bit of subconscious programming for your mind-body-spirit system, helping your inner self to change something that ordinarily would not be noticed consciously.

First, from the waking state of consciousness, I am now speaking to the part of my subconscious mind responsible for **breathing**. *From now on, while I am awake, if I start holding my breath as part of an unskilled empath merge, please alert me.*

Second, from the waking state of consciousness, I am now speak-ing to the part of my subconscious mind responsible for **blinking my eyes**. *From now on, while I am awake, please alert me if I start staring at someone or something as part of an unskilled empath merge.*

What does that mean, "Alert me"? Subconscious mind, send me a quick thought or feeling, in a gentle way, that is instantly notice-able to my conscious mind. This instant inner message will go like this: "You have started doing unskilled empath merge. Come back to reality. Now."

This alert is comparable to inner notifications that I have already established for myself, like knowing when I need to use the toilet. A subconscious inner alert of this kind is no big deal, yet clear enough for my conscious mind to get the message.

Once I receive the conscious message, it will be easy for me to resume regularly paced breathing in and out. Automatically I will begin to pay attention in the here and now, whatever interests me in objective reality.

This new mechanism for self-awareness requires no effort from my conscious mind. Once installed, it works automatically. I install this mechanism now.

Q&A. Install an Automatic Subconscious Alert

Q. *Are you suggesting that I monitor my blinking and breathing all day long?*

A. Please, no. Becoming self-conscious like that would amount to a cure that is worse than the disease.

Actually, monitoring yourself all day long — about blinking or anything else — is a "cure" that would *worsen* the disease.

When skilled, an empath lives naturally. Not in a state of perpetual self-consciousness.

This one-time technique simply activates the power of your subconscious mind to give you spontaneous feedback. In our Program for Empath Empowerment, this is one of many techniques for turning empath gifts OFF.

Q. *I'm a scientist with strong interest in brain functioning. Some research indicates that people hold their breath while learning, sometimes up to 40 seconds at a time. You wouldn't want to tell empaths to stop learning, would you?*

A. Of course not. Notice the combination of factors involved in this Automatic Subconscious Alert.

1. You are paying attention to the object of your unintentional, semi-conscious, Prolonged Unskilled Empath Merge.
2. You are staring.
3. You are holding your breath.

Having all three factors present at the same time? I think you'll agree that is different from internal cognition of the type usually considered "Learning."

Q. *So long as we're being technical, is there anything else you can explain about this Automatic Subconscious Alert?*

A. This is a unique technique among all the others in the system of Empath Empowerment®. Automatic Subconscious Alert could be considered a form of post-hypnotic suggestion. Developing this technique, I drew on my background as a hypnotism instructor, certified by the National Guild of Hypnotists.

Here's another technical point, one that can make sense right away, without your having to become a professional hypnotist. If you reread the language created to install your Automatic Subconscious Alert, it explained that you would receive an alert only if you were doing unskilled empath merge. Not other random times of holding your breath, such as "Email apnea."

Q. *Whoa! What is email apnea?*

A. Imagine this. (And maybe you won't have to try very hard to imagine.) You open up email for the first time in a while. Loads of emails are cluttering up your in-box. So you begin sorting through them, pressured for time, very focused, utterly absorbed.

Might you start holding your breath? That's common, whether we consciously notice or not.

Unfortunately scientific research has demonstrated that this technology-related breath holding — EMAIL APNEA — contributes significantly to stress-related diseases.

Doesn't that make sense? Apart from times of learning, unintentionally holding breath is not especially beneficial. Certainly that is true for Prolonged Unskilled Empath Merges. They contribute significantly to Imported STUFF.

CHAPTER 36

Breathing to Raise Your Vibrations

Brave Empath, I'm so excited to introduce you to our next technique in this Program for Empath Empowerment. I love this technique so much, it's like one of my best friends.

This breathing pattern can serve you like a faithful companion, useful so often during your journey as a skilled empath.

Vibe-Raising Breaths will help you to turn empath gifts OFF (in *The Empowered Empath*) and also prove indispensable for turning empath gifts ON (in *The Master Empath*.)

This technique may not be human, but I will give "him" a nickname. On first meeting, you might be encouraged to use this technique's formal name "Mr. Vibrational-Raising Breaths." Okay, no "Mr." is really required (this being a breathing pattern, not a person). Usually I just call him "Vibe-Raising Breaths."

When I teach you this technique, Brave Empath, it will be sandwiched between a simple kind of before-and-after picture. Later, when I teach you more uses for the breathing pattern, it will be used without the extras before and after.

The Purpose of Vibe-Raising Breaths

Why would an empath wish to get so chummy with her or his own breathing?

When you do the following technique, it can help you to turn your empath gifts OFF.

Specifically, this technique shifts consciousness in a way that assists you to become more vividly interested in your life. So you could consider it a way to learn more about "Who am I"?

Brave Empath, taking a vigorous and healthy interest in your life in objective reality will *always* serve to turn your empath gifts OFF.

Some ways are more effective than others, this one being extremely effective.

Prepare to Move Your Consciousness

Speaking of breathing, you are already familiar with the standard human version, done in-and-out through your nose. This habit doesn't count as a technique, being more a requirement for survival.

If you have a cold, or you're panting after a hard run, you might use your mouth for breathing instead. Also useful at the time and not particularly a technique.

By contrast, the following technique uses both resources, sometimes your nose and sometimes your mouth.

Go through the sequence provided, step by step, and you will discover a very useful way to breathe that is just a bit different. Do only two cycles of Vibe-Raising Breaths in a row. Then return to normal breathing.

Of course, Brave Empath, let's include common sense in this context. Do not try the following technique when your nose is stopped up from a cold, nor while breathing hard after a run.

What else? As usual for any of our techniques, sit comfortably. Keep writing equipment nearby. I recommend simple, old-fashioned pen and paper. Although you could make a digital recording of your voice, text yourself, etc.

Technique:
INTRO TO VIBE-RAISING BREATHS

As we go through the latest technique in this Program for Empath Empowerment, I will provide our standard caution for the last time in this book: Either do a technique or don't. Skip ahead if you don't have time for now.

When you do aim to explore Vibe-Raising Breaths, hooray! Preview all the instructions that follow with a quick read-through before doing.

1. Sit comfortably. Close your eyes. Let this latest technique begin!

2. Gently pay attention to yourself. Be especially interested in your emotions right now. Name one or more. These have names like *happy, sad, scared, angry.*

3. Open your eyes. Write down this "Before Picture about Your Emotions." Close your eyes again.

4. Gently pay attention to your physical body. Notice how your right leg feels. Sure, this has names like *strong, sore, relaxed, fidgety, heavy.*

5. Open your eyes. Write down this "Before Picture about Your Physical Self." Close your eyes again.

6. Take one Vibe-Raising Breath. Breathe in through your nose, then out through your mouth, nice and slow and deep.

7. Take a second Vibe-Raising Breath. And then return to normal breathing.

8. Repeat steps 2-5, only this time you are writing down an "After Picture."

9. Think "Technique over." Open your eyes.

Look over what you wrote for your "Before-and-After Picture." Did anything change? That would count as an immediate result, wouldn't it?

Q&A. Intro to Vibe-Raising Breaths

Q. *How slow and deep is a Vibe-Raising Breath supposed to be? Should I count to a number like 10 seconds while doing it?*

A. Slowish. Deepish. Please don't count seconds or otherwise attempt to be precise. Simply direct the flow of air, taking one breath at a time: In through your nose, out through your mouth.

Q. *Why take only two of these breaths in a row? Why not do it all day long?*

A. Right, as if you really need another job to do all day long! Isn't your life complicated enough without adding fancy breathing tricks? Besides, Vibe-Raising Breaths are powerful. Two or three in a sequence is plenty.

Q. *Comparing my Before-and-After Picture, I found myself calmer, both emotionally and physically. Is this normal?*

A. Forget about normal. Please, tell me that you don't consider it the purpose of your life... persuading other people to call you "Normal."

Q. *OK, was I successful? Does the relaxation I felt afterwards mean that I achieved success with my Vibe-Raising Breaths?*

A. Relaxation is one way to tell you were successful. Sure, you can officially count this as a result. Well done!

Q. *My result was kind of the opposite. Comparing my Before-and-After Picture, I felt clearer, more alert. Even physically! Was that wrong?*

A. "Vibe-Raising Breaths" will gently alter consciousness to provide of what you need.

Using common sense, how could it be "wrong" to feel clearer and more alert, even better physically? Although I do appreciate your rigor in asking the teacher!

Q. *What I noticed was different from either of my classmates here. After the breathing, I felt more confident. It was subtle, but*

I'm pretty sure that's true. Could an outcome of Vibe-Raising Breaths be more confidence?

A. Certainly!

Q. *Now I'm really confused. Rose, please explain how one little technique could produce such a range of results? How could all these different outcomes be genuine results?*

A. Breathing techniques shift consciousness. Energetically, what happens in a Vibe-Raising Breath?

Eyes closed, while you are in technique, something a bit different happens from usual when you take that long, slow, deep inhalation.

Your Crown Chakra receives a bit more prana, life force energy, chi, etc. This can result in more clarity of experience.

To be really technical, every time you take a Vibe-Raising Breath, you are opening up your Crown Chakra a little, compared to how it had been before. Hence the name, "Vibe-Raising Breath." You are raising your spiritual vibrations, just a bit, for keeps.

Q. How about the exhale?

A. Remember the context first. You are in technique, eyes closed, while taking that out-through-mouth breath. This breath is done intentionally as part of a technique. So results are different from panting because you just had a really fabulous kiss or whatever.

In a Vibe-Raising Breath, the exhale allows some STUFF to be released from your aura and subconscious mind. Not your deepest frozen blocks of STUFF from other lifetimes, but small frozen blocks of energy that were cluttering up your energy field.

Consequently, after a Vibe-Raising Breath you might feel a bit of relief, whether physically or emotionally.

Q. *What determines whether a particular Vibe-Raising Breath will relax you or energize you?*

A. Depends on what your mind-body-spirit system needs at the time. On one occasion, you might notice both results. Other times, you might find one result more than the other. It's even possible that you were pretty darned awake and also relaxed before the technique, in which case you won't notice much change at all.

Either way, congratulations.

Q. *For this exercise, you had us do a Before-and-After Picture that was about emotions and the physical body. Does that mean that Vibe-Raising Breaths only affect us emotionally and physically?*

A. Good catch! The entire mind-body-spirit system benefits. I was simply giving you a quick way to sample results.

We will do the same kind of Before-and-After Picture with our next technique.

CHAPTER 37

More Physical
Self-Awareness, Yum!

Brave Empath, have you fallen in love with yourself even more, thanks to Vibe-Raising Breaths? Let's continue the trend, developing a healthy fascination with yourself and how you can use the power of breath to subtly move consciousness.

Our next technique is called "Grounding Breaths." This is another simple yet powerful breathing technique with many uses in this Program for Empath Empowerment.

Before doing the technique officially, with Q&A to follow, let's practice physical positioning.

Prepare Physically For Grounding Breaths

As you can appreciate, Brave Empath, there is a difference between doing a technique that shifts consciousness versus practicing a physical position to use for techniquing.

This is our first time practicing such a position. Couldn't happen to a nicer person — or a nicer technique!

1. Hold up one index finger several inches in front of your mouth. Now pretend it is a candle on your birthday cake. Yes, this is one of those (Funny? Obnoxious?) trick candles that won't blow out normally. Your practice will be to huff and puff to blow out that imaginary candle flame, using one quick little breath at a time.

2. For this position practice, I would like you to keep your eyes open, staring at that candle (or finger). For a few seconds, breathe in and out through your mouth.

3. Now alter the rhythm, making your inhales and exhales short and forceful; puffy little breaths as if trying to blow that candle out. Take 5-10 of those quick little breaths, emphasizing the exhale, mouth open for the whole time

Got it? Then you are prepared to do the technique of "Grounding Breaths." What will be different when doing the technique below? Your eyes will be closed. No uplifted finger. No associations required with obnoxious candles, either.

When not just practiced as a position — but done within a technique — "Grounding Breaths" move consciousness powerfully. In the instructions that follow, you will take just two of those fun little breaths, pausing for a second between them. Afterwards return to normal breathing.

What will this technique do for you Let's find out.

Technique:
INTRODUCTION TO GROUNDING BREATHS

1. Sit comfortably. Close your eyes. Let this latest technique begin!

2. Gently pay attention to yourself. Be especially interested in your emotions right now. Name one or more. Emotions have names like *happy, sad, scared, angry*.

3. Open your eyes. Write down this "Before Picture about Your Emotions." Close your eyes again.

4. Gently pay attention to your physical body. Notice how your left hand feels. Sure, this has names like *strong, sore, relaxed, fidgety, heavy.*

5. Open your eyes. Write down this "Before Picture about Your Physical Self." Close your eyes again.

6. Take two Grounding Breaths, pausing a second between each one. Breathe in and out through your mouth, rapidly,

as if blowing out a candle. Emphasis will be on the exhale. Take just two of these special, fancy breaths; then return to normal breathing.

7. Repeat steps 2-5, only this time you are writing down an "After Picture."

8. Think "Technique over." Open your eyes.

Look over what you wrote for your "Before-and-After Picture." Did anything change? That would count as an immediate result.

Q&A. Introduction to Grounding Breaths

Q. *This didn't feel like some deep technique to move consciousness. It felt pretty surfacey, frankly. Why would it count as a technique?*

A. Different techniques suit different purposes. Your question contains an important insight. Grounding Breaths help a person to "Shallow up." That is exactly the point.

Empath merges are deep, whether unskilled or skilled. As you progress in this Program for Empath Empowerment, you will learn a great deal about the value of shallow, surface, fun, objective reality.

Q. *Physically, this breathing pattern made me feel more in my body. I don't know how else to describe it. Subtle. But a shift was definitely noticeable to me. What if I don't like how that feels, being more present within my body?*

A. Get used to it. Many a talented empath floats around in consciousness, exploring other people, evincing more interest in others than one's own sweet self. A habit like this stinks.

At least it can be changed! I'm glad that you are taking advantage of pursuing this Program for Empath Empowerment!.

Fact is, unskilled empaths can have a pretty, tenuous connection to the physical body. Or to objective reality in general. Sadly, without having a clue.

Seems to me, you're just starting to change this, which definitely can feel a bit uncomfortable during the transition phase.

Keep going anyway. Pretty soon you will feel way more comfortable, effortlessly becoming more present to physical reality

Q. *But why bother? Ignorance is bliss, right?*

A. Practical benefits follow automatically, like more effectiveness in life. That is what makes it worthwhile to progress through a bit of transitional awkwardness.

Another reason to land in your physical body more securely? As with the rest of Empath Empowerment, you will learn to feel like yourself, only clearer and stronger.

Grounding Breaths aren't just a theory. No more than having your spiritual consciousness grounded in your physical body is just a point of view.

"Take it or leave it" doesn't really apply, not if you wish to have a quality life. And not if you aim to become a skilled empath.

For this, having consciousness habitually anchored in the physical body is required, not optional.

Some chapters back we considered Out-of-Body Experiences, which are quite dramatic. A less intense version can be commonplace. Many an empath lives in a chronic state of Out-of-Body Experience, as if the physical body were not real.

Grounding breaths can help, as well as the rest of this Program for Empath Empowerment.

Want even more motivation not to give up on improved body awareness as a way of life?

Becoming more embodied can help you to gain credibility with family members and people at work. Could help you to make more money. Might even improve your sex life.

Q. *But what if I don't like paying attention to my physical body? What if it seems gross to me?*

A. You might benefit from doing "Introduction to Grounding Breaths" once or twice a day until you start feeling more comfortable in your body.

Body awareness does not have horrible side effects, like taking away your sensitivity. This positioning of consciousness is good for you as an empath. Beyond that, becoming more present, physically, can accelerate your personal development in many other ways.

Q. *Isn't it possible that I will never really feel comfortable with Grounding Breaths?*

A. "Never" is too long to wait for good results. After a couple of weeks, if you're still *pretty* uncomfortable in your own skin, seek out the services of a healing professional in energy spirituality or energy psychology. If *extremely* uncomfortable, invest in an evaluation by a psychiatrist.

Q. *I love how this technique made me feel, more solid and sure of myself. Is there a way I could safely use Grounding Breaths to help me turn empath gifts OFF?*

A. So glad you asked!

CHAPTER 38

A Human Reality App

Brave Empath, you have been developing skills needed for Coming Home, our big, fancy technique to turn your empath gifts OFF. And you just learned basics for Grounding Breaths.

Now I'll teach you a new use for this breathing pattern. Consider it like an app, if you like. So handy if your lifestyle includes any kind of spiritual exercise. For example:

- ∾ Your lifestyle might include meditation, prayer, reading uplifting materials like scripture or your favorite blog.

- ∾ Self-hypnosis is popular, too, deservedly so. Many self-actualizing people regularly do that, or use techniques for creative visualization, listening to relaxing CDs, and so forth.

- ∾ Maybe you spend minutes at a time speaking out affirmations or asking "What Would Jesus Do?" or seeking wisdom from some other source that inspires you.

- ∾ You might participate in energy-based exercise, like yoga or tai chi.

What do practices like these have in common?

They position your consciousness away from regular human-level objective reality. Afterwards, it is common for empaths to become floaty.

And floaty means — you guessed it — doing more unskilled empath merges than ever. The following technique will protect you by smoothing the transition as you emerge from a spiritual practice.

Technique.
A HUMAN-REALITY APP FOR GROUNDING BREATHS

Do the following immediately after finishing your meditation, yoga asanas, or any other kind of spiritual exercise.

Take a moment to recognize that your spiritual technique is over for now. You're returning to life as a human being, with regular human interests. Then:

1. Sit comfortably. Close your eyes. Let this different kind of technique begin!

2. Gently pay attention to yourself, in an easy and casual way. Be especially interested in your emotions right now. Name one or more. Emotions have names like *happy, sad, scared, angry.*

3. Open your eyes. Write down this "Before Picture about Your Emotions." Close your eyes again.

4. Gently pay attention to your physical body. Notice how your left hand feels. Sure, this has names like *strong, sore, relaxed, fidgety, heavy.*

5. Open your eyes. Write down this "Before Picture about Your Physical Self." Close your eyes again.

6. Take two Grounding Breaths, pausing a second between each one. Breathe in and out through your mouth, rapidly, as if blowing out a candle. Emphasis will be on the exhale. Take just two of these special breaths; then return to normal breathing.

7. Repeat steps 2-5, only this time you are writing down an "After Picture."

8. Think "Technique over."

Open your eyes. Review what you wrote for your "Before-and-After Picture." Did anything change?

That would count as an immediate result. Now reinsert yourself into objective reality. Move around. Touch physical objects. Talk or sing or hum or yodel. Welcome back to human reality!

Q&A. A Human-Reality App for Grounding Breaths

Q. *But Rose, this technique is almost exactly identical to the last one, Introduction to Grounding Breaths. What's the point?*

A. Context is the point, transitioning out of a spiritual practice. This can be a vulnerable time for us empaths because consciousness was positioned so differently during that spiritual exercise.

We empaths don't need much encouragement to continue traveling around in consciousness, with random unskilled empath merges to follow.

Q. *My yoga teacher has us do a kind of spiritual cooldown. Why do you think that isn't enough? Frankly, how presumptuous of you! Don't you think that teachers of other spiritual practices have also addressed this need?*

A. Yes and no. I agree that professionals in any form of spiritual development are aware of the importance of transitioning properly before resuming regular activity. It's the responsible way to teach any powerful spiritual exercise.

However, these teachers are not necessarily empaths. Plus, even if they are empaths personally, they don't necessarily know much about empath skills.

The purpose of this Program for Empath Empowerment is not to reinvent fields like yoga or prayer. Instead I am helping you to get skills that supplement all your other interests, skills, and favorite activities.

Q. *What does this little bit of breathing have to do with consciousness? It's really just breathing, if you're honest.*

A. For 10,000 years or longer, wisdom traditions have linked breathing techniques to shifts in consciousness and changing a person's aura.

With today's energetic literacy, we can easily research what breathing techniques really accomplish. I'm one of the people who has done just that.

Returning from a really sweet prayer or other spiritual exercise, an afterglow is lovely. But spending the next few hours doing loads of unskilled empath merges? Not so lovely.

Personally, I would like to help you to do better.

What can happen, just because you take a few moments to use this "Human-Reality App for Grounding Breaths"? You are more likely to stay put at human frequencies of experience, empath gifts nicely turned OFF. At least, for a while.

Q. *I'm sorta convinced. But I'd like to do a shortcut. I can just add those two puffy breaths at the end of my usual practice. Won't that be okay?*

A. It may be okay, in the sense that a couple of random puffy breaths will not harm you. After all, you have probably survived blowing out trick candles on a birthday cake long before this Program for Empath Empowerment.

However, if you do not do the full "Human-Reality App for Grounding Breaths," you are wasting your time for the purpose intended.

Thank you for introducing the important topic of putting energy-based techniques into perspective so that you can get the desired results.

Self-Authority Versus Skills

For those best results, Brave Empath, do not overdo any technique from this Program for Empath Empowerment.

This caution extends to overdoing techniques just because you like how they feel. Overdoing for any reason, actually. Overdoing means overdoing.

For example, let's compare "Introduction to Grounding Breaths" to adding some salt to your food. Sprinkling on a little, by doing the technique once or twice in your *day*? Fine. Doing that same technique many times every *hour*? That's like eating enough salt to pickle yourself.

Over-using any technique in this Program for Empath Empowerment is like ingesting too much salt or any other healthy substance... where some is great... but too much adds up to a problem.

As for under-using, that can lead to problems too. With any technique that I teach you, please, either do the entire technique or don't bother.

Ever since publication of *Empowered by Empathy,* readers have come to me sheepishly, describing how they wrecked techniques for themselves.

Wrecked unintentionally, of course.

Of course, my students didn't literally put it that way. Jessica might complain, "Your technique doesn't work anymore."

Well, on inquiry it turned out that she had made up their own version of mix-and-match, like walking down the street while checking text messages and taking the occasional Vibe-Raising Breath.

Please, never! Never take one piece of a technique and use that separately, tossing away the rest of the technique sequence. No part of a technique is optional, at least not in this Program for Empath Empowerment.

Random experiments doesn't just disrespect your teacher and the enormous amount of research that goes into every technique I present to you. No, you would be disrespecting yourself. And simultaneously wrecking a technique's further effectiveness for helping you.

Doesn't Self-Authority Rule?

Self-authority can be tricky. It matters enormously for Empath Empowerment, as for every aspect of personal life.

Yet self-authority doesn't equate to knowledge, expertise, or skill. Creativity feels good. Yet good feelings alone don't automatically make us experts.

In this Program for Empath Empowerment, you are learning loads of practical, relevant skills. Not included, though: How to become a CONSCIOUSNESS ENGINEER, a spiritual teacher who specializes in designing effective techniques.

- If you're wise, you will use self-authority to evaluate skills being taught.

- Definitely use your self-authority to decide when and how to use various skills.

- Also, after giving any skill set a fair chance, self-authority is critical for evaluating what really works for you.

However, that's different from tinkering with the basic skills themselves.

Traveling into an Analogy

Here's an analogy to clarify the difference. Learning to drive a car is a skill. Once you develop that skill, you can use self-authority to decide when and where to drive a car.

By contrast, there are separate skill sets for learning how to design an automobile and how to repair it. Unless you learn these skills, here's a goofy example of what could happen.

Oliver has great skills as a driver, plus loads of self-authority. He can use this combination to choose the route he drives to work, find great parking spaces, even improvise a road trip.

But what if Oliver starts thinking like this? *Hey, I know how to drive. I deal with this car every day, and it moves slower than it used to. I ought to be able to fix that. Sure, I feel confident I can fix this problem. I own the car, don't I?*

So here's his solution, fueled by self-authority.

Oliver opens up the hood of his car to add a few missing ingredients. *I know how it feels to go fast. I've just got to figure out what would help my car feel the same way. How about one of my old skateboards? That ought to help. What, it's too big? I'll break it into a couple of pieces.*

After tossing that in, Oliver thinks, *Wait, going faster like that might be tricky for my engine. What else can I do? Of course! I'll add a padlock, to keep everything safe.*

Oliver feels so good about his improvements to the car, he wonders what more he might add.

Maybe that slow performance is an attitude problem. How can I get my car to know that my time is valuable? I guess the best way to do that is to throw in a sports watch.

Ooooookay. Finally, just to be on the safe side, Oliver hurls in a wire whisk from the kitchen.

My wife used to use that for cooking, but I can always get her another one. Now this old tool has a new job, teaching all the other car parts how to mix it up.

In you go, whisk. Help the old parts of my car to get along with all of these new improvements.

Then Oliver closes the hood, proud of his first foray into car mechanics. At his current skill level, everything he has done makes perfect sense to him. Self-authority galore!

Ridiculous example? Sure. Unfortunately, inexpertly designed techniques are common in real life. Results are not funny, either. I know because sometimes my job is to help clients to clean up the resulting mess.

Problems from poorly designed self-improvement techniques don't show obviously, like fictional Oliver playing around with his car right before it explodes.

Instead problems develop at their own pace in the subconscious mind, maybe not obvious to Oliver for 10 years, 30 years, or later. Finally he goes "OUCH!"

Delayed timing doesn't make such problems trivial.

Here's the practical point for now, about reality rather than fiction. Ultimately it is your responsibility what you do with this Program for Empath Empowerment. Be smart with your choices, Brave Empath. And don't confuse self-authority with skills.

Get real skills, then evaluate the results with your self-authority. That's the perfect combo.

Incidentally, what if you want to become a consciousness engineer? Get *those* skills. (I might be able to help you, one personal appointment at a time.) Meanwhile, let Empath Empowerment be your priority. You have accomplished a great deal. Now let's move forward.

CHAPTER 40

Explore Human Life, Divinely Protected

Learning to use the power of breath feels good, doesn't it? Vibe-Raising Breaths and Grounding Breaths are excellent skills for an empath.

Now that you're starting to manage your special gifts, maybe you're beginning to appreciate an idea that was there from the start in this Program for Empath Empowerment:

To turn your empath gifts OFF, use consciousness. Just like the breathing techniques you have learned, all our techniques from now on will involve your super-abstract, deeply personal consciousness.

And that use of your consciousness can be effortless. Concentrating, straining or otherwise trying hard will be counter-productive. Don't go there.

The Paradox of Effortlessness

For so many things you might want in life, the way to succeed is simple: To get more, try harder.

Well, Brave Empath, that won't work with techniques that involve consciousness. The harder you try to let go or relax? The worse your results. That's THE PARADOX OF EFFORTLESSNESS.

What are you going to do about it? Especially if you haven't felt terribly secure about paying attention to yourself, learning how *not to try* can be a very real problem.

Fortunately, there's an app for that. God can help. God, or whatever you call your Highest Power, your spiritual source.

To receive that help, faith won't be needed, nor some new kind of religion. Let's use a simple technique instead.

Brave Empath, this next technique will subtly expand your consciousness. I will teach you a way to connect your consciousness to a transpersonal source of huge joy, wisdom, and love. Ridiculously easy!

To prepare, find the usual tiny chunk of time when you will be uninterrupted. Also choose one name for God to use this time, for this particular exploration of the technique.

- You might choose the IMPERSONAL ASPECT of God, such as God, Allah, Holy Spirit, The Love That Rules the Universe, or The Intelligence That Rules the Universe.

- Or you might choose a PERSONAL ASPECT of the Divine, either an Ascended Master or an Archangel.

- ASCENDED MASTERS include Jesus, Krishna, Buddha, Kwan Yin, Athena, Isis.

- ARCHANGELS include Archangel Michael, Archangel Gabriel, Archangel Raphael.

Every time you use the following technique, pick one Divine Being to help you. Once you have made your choice, prepare for doing a technique as usual, including your quick read-through in advance.

Technique. GET BIG

Welcome to one of my all-time favorite techniques, Brave Empath.

1. Sit comfortably. Close your eyes. Let this latest technique begin!

2. Gently pay attention to yourself, in an easy and casual way. Be especially interested in your emotions right now. Name one or more. Sure, these have names like *happy, sad, scared, angry.*

3. Open your eyes. Write down this "Before Picture about Your Emotions." Close your eyes again.

4. Gently pay attention to your physical body. Notice how your upper back feels. Sure, this has names *like strong, sore, relaxed, fidgety, heavy.*

5. Open your eyes. Write down this "Before Picture about Your Physical Self." Close your eyes again.

6. Think, just once, the name you will use this time, doing Get Big. For example, you might think "The Love That Rules the Universe."

7. Immediately after, take two Vibe-Raising Breaths. Then return to normal breathing.

8. Repeat steps 2-5, only this time you are writing down an "After Picture."

9. Think "Technique over."

Open your eyes. Review what you wrote for your "Before-and-After Picture." Did anything change? That would count as an immediate result.

Q&A. Get Big

Q. *Does it always have to be the same choice of Divine Being?*

A. No. You're doing a technique, not getting a tattoo. Besides, Divine Beings don't get jealous.

Q. *What happens after you open your eyes at the end? Do you stay energetically Big?*

A. Gradually your conscious mind will shrink back to its usual identity, much like a rubber band that has been stretched beyond its ordinary limits.

This could take hours or minutes. For sure, the shift will be gentle and appropriate for your current level of consciousness.

Q. *Wouldn't it be great to do this all day long?*

A. Hardly! Overdoing is not recommended with this technique or any other part of this Program for Empath Empowerment. For jobs like driving to work, walking the dog, or cleaning the bathroom, we do fine with our everyday little minds.

I wouldn't recommend using "Get Big" as a way of life. This could space you out, the opposite of being an effective, skilled empath. Instead use this technique as recommended in our Program for Empath Empowerment.

Q. *Why use a name for the Divine. Isn't It smart enough to know what I mean without asking? Why can't I just ask the Universe?*

A. You can. Only you will not be doing the "Get Big" technique and cannot expect the same kind of protection for your explorations as an empath.

Q. *How about calling on your guardian angel or spirit guides?*

A. Same answer.

Q. *What if calling on anyone goes against your religion?*

A. Then don't think of this technique as religious. Think of it as convenience.

You might want to reread this short chapter. Will you find anything here about bowing down, graven images, worshipping in some other way, believing in anything?

Personally I find that "Get Big" is a pretty good deal, whether you believe in a religion or not. You ask for help in a particular way, no strings attached. Then you receive that help. Not too many people would do that for you but God will.

Q. *I was unprepared for what a powerful experience it was for me, doing "Get Big." What are some ways I can use this to become more skilled as an empath?*

A. Glad you asked....

Recommended Uses for "Get Big"

This little technique has innumerable uses because it is a super-easy way to co-create with the Divine. You will find loads of uses as part of other trademarked systems I teach; "Get Big" is included in many of my how-to books. For sure, Empath Empowerment depends upon using the awesome resource of your Divine connection.

Besides being so effortless, "Get Big" is flexible because belief is not needed, nor faith, nor belonging to any particular religious community.

You can even think of this resource as your own Higher Self. Just don't employ that name for Divine Being when doing "Get Big." As with 12-step programs, it is essential to have help *outside* yourself. (Incidentally, unlike 12-step programs, it won't be enough to use the term "Higher Power." Make that "Highest Power." You deserve that much.)

In the Program for Empath Empowerment, this tiny technique of "Get Big" is a component of more complex techniques that turn empath gifts OFF. (Coming soon.)

When you're ready to become a Master Empath, "Get Big" will also be used in *every* technique of Skilled Empath Merge.

CHAPTER 41

Wake Up Your Sense of Self

Brave Empath, being an unskilled empath can feel like a Catch 22. While unskilled, you are constantly picking up STUFF from others. So long as your aura is riddled with STUFF, it's hard to feel like yourself.

Until you strengthen that sense of self, what happens? Automatically, you keep picking up STUFF, like a random drip-drip-drip.

Such a vicious cycle, being an unskilled empath!

But hold on. That cycle has stopped spinning around quite so fast.

- By now, you understand that you really have gifts, not some nightmarish disability. Clarity has begun. Your *sense of self* can be understood as something different from *problems* formerly suffered due to lack of skill.

- You were given a model for understanding what has been happening to you energetically. Therefore you can stop "Blaming the victim." You're beginning to appreciate that you can also stop *being* a victim.

- You have learned techniques to break old habits of doing Prolonged Unskilled Empath Merges.

- In our last chapter, I taught you a no-frills way to co-create with the Divine. That can prove very helpful for breaking the vicious cycle where unskilled empath merges cause you to take on STUFF, resulting in random distortions to your sense of self. This, in turn, predisposes one to do even more unskilled empath merges.

Let's explore a powerful new technique that wakes up your sense of self by removing an empath's random STUFF. You will learn how to move out Imported STUFF that is in your aura right now, vanquisihing those globs and blobs of stuck energy that originally belonged to other people.

As you may squirmingly remember, taking on random STUFF is the inevitable consequence of doing unskilled empath merge.

No need to blame yourself; the whole process happened subconsciously. Consciously you are now learning how to stop that cycle, one technique at a time.

Technique: EMPATH'S FIRST AID

Heads up! Whenever you do "Empath's First Aid," it will include "Get Big." So decide which name you will choose this time around. Will your choice be an Ascended Master or Archangel? Perhaps you will prefer to use a name for the impersonal aspect of the Divine. Decide for this particular time.

In the steps that follow, I will use the name "God." Substitute your choice every time.

1. Sit comfortably and close your eyes.
2. Notice what it is like to be you, right now. No judging, please. Just pay attention as someone who is interested in you. Choose something about your current emotions or physical sensations in your body or anything at all that you notice about yourself. That's for your Before Picture.
3. Open your eyes just long enough to write something down. Then close your eyes.
4. Open your eyes long enough to read the following sequence of words, saying them out loud:
5. *God, remove from my aura whatever does not belong to me.*
6. *Remove from my aura whatever does not belong to me.*
7. *Remove from my aura whatever does not belong to me.*
8. *Fill me with new love, light, and power.*
9. Repeat Steps 2 and 3. This time it will be an After Picture.

10. End the technique. Think something like "Technique over" or "Thanks, God." Open your eyes.

Look at what you wrote down. Comparing your Before-and-After, do you notice anything different?

When to Use Empath's First Aid

Now that you have learned the technique, when is a good time to use it?

For the next week or so, use the technique routinely. Do it once around lunchtime and once after dinner.

Just that couple of times will get you accustomed to the contrast. Because unskilled empath merges do tend to sneak up on a person.

Count this as education. It's important to get a sense of being yourself, separate from taking on STUFF from others.

After a couple of weeks, use the technique only when you feel the need. That might amount to a couple of times a week. You see, "Empath's First Aid" is not the most important technique in this Program for Empath Empowerment. It is just one technique, a way to clean up Imported STUFF. Soon you will learn the "Coming Home" technique, designed to *prevent* Imported STUFF.

Q&A. Empath's First Aid

Q. *Strangely I do feel better, almost a sense of relief. But why?*

A. Subconscious experiences can be almost noticeable consciously, like the saying, "What I want to say is on the tip of my tongue."

Even though hidden in the subconscious mind, Imported STUFF can bother you enough to be vaguely noticed consciously. "Empath's First Aid" targets that STUFF and moves it right out. Then you receive PUT-IN with Divinely created love, light, and power. What's not to like?

Q. *But I didn't feel better. I felt grumpy before I started. Now I'm just as grumpy. Does that mean the "Empath's First Aid" didn't work?*

A. No, it just means that this particular technique was not
sufficient to heal other kinds of subconscious STUFF that are
bothering you now. "Empath's First Aid" will also fail to fix your
broken computer, restore your dog Fido to perfect health, and
remove all other causes of grumpiness.

If you own a measuring device for grumpiness, a Grumpy-O-
Meter perhaps, then you might find that some improvement did
register. Although a lesser degree of grumpiness might not satisfy
you, and rightly so.

Well, keep doing what you can. Aim to fix the human-level problems and also heal astral-level types of STUFF.

Personal development requires courage. It's a good sign that you
don't want to settle for feeling bad. Don't give up on improving
your life until you are feeling good.

Q. *I didn't particularly notice any result, either. Honestly, wasn't I
wasting my time?*

A. Learning a technique like this gives you a resource that can
bring you results. Of course, you may always prefer some
techniques to others. Give this one a chance. Use it for a week.
Twice daily. Then evaluate, okay?

By way of analogy, say that you are learning to drive. You started
Drivers Education because you want driving to be fun. Plus you
want the freedom to drive to exciting places wherever you want.

Now, suppose that you have just finished your first lesson, and all
you got to do was drive around the block. It wasn't especially fun;
you sure didn't go anywhere thrilling.

Well, that's the process of learning, right? Have patience with that
process. In order to succeed, and gain the benefits you desire, every
moment of education does not have to bring you ecstasy.

Q. *Look, I want my Empath Empowerment to be simple. I would
like to stop right here. Why not only use "Empath's First Aid"?
Couldn't that be all I need to turn my empath gifts OFF? Why
not just use this STUFF-removal technique once an hour?*

A. An ounce of prevention is worth a pound of cure. "Empath's First Aid" is for cure. Soon you will learn "Coming Home," which is for prevention.

The latter will powerfully turn OFF all your empath gifts, thereby preventing unskilled empath merges and taking on STUFF. Plus "Coming Home" will help with your emerging sense of identity.

Fix now, prevent soon. That's our strategy.

Q. *When I'm in a hurry, I can just use the words in "Empath's First Aid," right? Admit it. The rest of the sequence you just gave us — isn't that just padding?*

A. I respect all you empaths far too much to include padding. This is not done with any technique I design.

You know, in plenty of life situations, it's a matter of personal taste how thorough you are about doing things. Perhaps you never wish to have any conversation longer than a tweet. Someone else might feel terribly deprived that way, believing that genuine intimacy takes longer than a tweet. Up to you, though! With such choices, self-authority rules.

Remember the earlier discussion of self-authority not replacing skills, like Oliver as a car mechanic? "Empath's First Aid" will lose its full effectiveness for you by being changed, used out of context, or just sampled.

I appreciate that many of you readers are not interested in a detailed explanation of the construction process for "Empath's First Aid." So that will not be included in this book. However, if you are interested in the mechanics of any technique in this Program for Empath Empowerment, I would be delighted to provide a full explanation. Just take my workshop for Empath Empowerment. Or schedule a phone session for mentoring.

Meanwhile, want some simple advice? Consider yourself warned. Don't cut-and-paste portions of "Empath's First Aid." Do the full technique and enjoy the full results.

CHAPTER 42

Appreciate Your Multi-Level Humanity

Brave Empath, you can handle the ideas in this chapter. You can handle these ideas because you are both an empath and courageous.

Not that I'm calling other people cowards, necessarily. More like squeamish.

Human life is messy, humbling, complicated — whether we consciously admit that to ourselves or not.

Becoming skilled as an empath, you are going to learn much more about your human life than you knew previously, with fascinating insights about yourself in many contexts.

This chapter will complete our preparation for "Coming Home," the most important technique for turning empath gifts OFF in this Program for Empath Empowerment. If you can handle reading this entire chapter without throwing up, I'd say the odds are excellent that you can become a fully skilled empath.

Teasing! Every empath can become fully skilled. It just takes a willingness to show some adventurousness, take a bit of time, learn some skills. If you were to vomit, that wouldn't have to stop you.

Seriously, and fortunately, there is no instant way to prevent all pain as an empath and, instead, awaken the full potential of your empath gifts.

What's so fortunate about that? A deep learning about yourself is required to satisfactorily turn OFF empath gifts.

Automatically this can also help you to progress extra-fast on your path of personal development. Besides, getting to know yourself better can be such fun.

Celebrate Your Amazing Individuality

Unique in all the universe, and different from any incarnation you have had in the long history of your soul, wow! There really is nobody like you, nor will there ever be.

Part of the fun is that, since you're human, your individuality contains many levels. In that way, you're like Matroyshka dolls, those nesting dolls you have probably seen in gift shops. Only you are made of flesh and blood, quirks and consciousness.

At any given moment, each level of your individuality corresponds to a quality of consciousness. Well, Brave Empath, I'm going to teach you a technique for exploring that.

Exploring those distinctive qualities, you can anticipate fresh experiences of a delightful nature. It least, it will be delightful with practice.

Some empaths find this exploration delightful right from the start, but not necessarily. Regardless, it's productive for you as an empath every single time that you use the "Coming Home" technique. This is a step-by-step way to explore all five significant levels of your individuality.

What are these five different levels within? For clarity, let's start with....

Three Things You Are NOT

None of the following is a legitimate level to consider when probing for an empath's experience of who-you-be.

1. You are not your history

Instead, you *have* a history. Common sense suggests it would be limiting to define your present self (and future potential) in terms of what you have been through so far.

Yet isn't it tempting to label yourself, based on experiences from your past? For example:

- I'm successful in my career.
- I'm not successful in my career.
- I have a fulfilling love relationship.
- I can't seem to get my love life together.
- I own a fine, shiny automobile.
- My car is a pathetic old clunker.
- I am the product of a dysfunctional family.
- I am a recovering alcoholic.
- I have financial troubles.
- My spiritual teacher told me that I am saved/awake/chosen/psychically gifted.
- I am a great parent.

Could such versions of reality be true? And do you have the right to believe them as your only defining characteristic? Could any one of these statements distort your sense of who you are right now? Sure, sure, sure.

However, all of these are *ideas*, not *experiences* of how your consciousness functions in the here and now. Therefore none of these labels will be relevant for the "Coming Home" technique.

Beliefs like these will neither help nor hinder your becoming a skilled empath.

Why not? Brave Empath, you are a dynamically evolving being, loaded with empath talent. You're a vibrantly alive consciousness having a human experience.

Note the distinction: Not merely a human being, you are *consciousness* being human.

The particular flavor of your consciousness is what matters for Empath Empowerment. Every true level of human self will have its own, way-subjective, distinctive flavor of consciousness at any given time. For Empath Empowerment this matters far more than any life experiences you might have in objective reality.

2. You are not other people's reactions to you

Not unless you truly desire to drive yourself nuts.

One thing I will say in favor of basing self-concept on how other people treat you: It can be a very interesting experiment for all or part of an incarnation. Could be a game you have played for many past incarnations, actually.

What's the payoff? For one thing, drama galore.

However, skill as an empath requires no drama. And for you to position consciousness appropriately as an empath, it isn't relevant how other people treat you.

Until you develop an appropriate, nuanced appreciation for yourself as a person, other people's opinions of you will matter way too much for comfort.

Fortunately, nobody else is authorized to turn your sense of self ON, or to turn your empath gifts appropriately OFF during most of your waking hours.

You are hired. (If you want to be.)

3. You are not your lifestyle

Sure, your lifestyle *matters*. But changes to lifestyle help empaths only after becoming quite skilled. Lifestyle changes alone will never create a skilled empath.

It's not just a matter of putting the cart before the horse, or the trailer before the car engine. Each empath has a distinctive experience of consciousness. You, for instance, Brave Empath. In every social role, at every level of life, you have a way of being yourself. Normally this happens automatically, no need to pay attention in a self-conscious manner.

If you have done certain techniques for self-improvement, or been in therapy, you may have developed the habit of observing yourself rather than spontaneously being yourself, saying and doing whatever suits the occasion.

Has that sort of self-consciousness become a habit? Then let it go for a few weeks. I invite you to such an experiment, a quiet call to innocence.

Neither self-conscious monitoring of behavior nor consciously adjusting personal boundaries truly helps an empath. Because conscious-level analysis cannot touch the subconscious functioning at the five levels you will soon be exploring.

The "Coming Home" technique will give you an opportunity to taste this hidden aspect of life. You will spend a short time at each level of self, gently paying attention. Then you can experience directly how your consciousness flows at each vibrational level of your human personality.

Acceptance can result. Acceptance means experiencing yourself just the way you are right now: No forcing yourself to change or improve in any way.

What, notice yourself directly, without fixing a thing? This can wake you up as a soul, awaken you even more powerfully than the not-too-shabby technique you recently learned for "Empath's First Aid."

You Are Not Just One or Two Preferred Levels of Yourself, Either

And here is where many empaths get tripped up. Even if you are already savvy about consciousness, philosophical self-knowledge, psychological inquiry, financial planning, human history, animal husbandry, deep sea diving, whatever.

You are *every one* of the levels of you that will be discussed in the rest of this chapter. Not merely one, and definitely not only what you prefer. Every single level built into your human system really does count. Even if understandably you will always have some favorites.

By way of analogy, which do you like better, Brave Empath, your head or your left elbow?

So glad you don't have to choose! Both count as part of you, and you do get to keep them both. Meaning no disrespect to your noble head, it really is fine to continue owning your elbow. To understand your depth identity as a human, let's shift from this analogy to consider....

Five Different Levels of Your Sweet Self

Yes, let's take inventory of who you are now. In this chapter, we'll clarify the concepts. Next chapter, when you actually *do* the "Coming Home" technique, you will be invited to experience each of these levels in succession.

Every one of these brief experiences will involve a moment of gently paying attention. Afterwards, you will be invited to write down something quickly, as with the Before-and-After notes you took while doing techniques for "Intro to Vibe-Raising Breaths" and "Introduction to Grounding Breaths."

What exactly are these levels? Just because you *have* them subconsciously doesn't mean that you know about them consciously. So, yes, let's consider them individually.

Level One: Social

Brave Empath, you have a way of being yourself, here and now. This is true in genereal through all your waking hours, even if the social situation changes and, with it, your particular way of being yourself.

Where you are does not mean the same thing as *who* you are. Yet some environments make you feel more comfortable than others, right? In some situations you feel more resourceful, more clever or popular or attractive.

Within your own home, different rooms might likewise arouse different feelings about self-worth and your importance to others.

Wherever you happen to be while you do the "Coming Home" technique, that will be your current environment in objective reality.

- ➣ Are you alone at home with this book?
- ➣ Perhaps you are visiting a difficult relative and have captured some precious time for yourself, locked in the guest room for the express purpose of exploring yourself on your own terms.
- ➣ Alternatively you could be sitting with one favorite friend, enjoying this book together, eagerly preparing to do "Coming Home."
- ➣ Or you might be a graduate of this Program for Empath Empowerment, having gone through this book more than once. Now you're preparing to deepen your knowledge and experiences.

Wherever you are in objective reality, you have a related social self. Well, that is the first level you will explore.

However it feels to be you, in any way — while you're in technique that particular time — that is what you will be exploring at the level of your social self.

Level Two: Physical

Sometimes you might be more aware physically than at other times. Hey, for an entire *incarnation* you might be more aware physically, compared to other past lifetimes.

Just the opposite could be true as well. This lifetime, enthusiasm over your physicality might be like the saying attributed to Robert Maynard Hutchins, "Whenever I feel the need to exercise, I lie down until it goes away."

However interested you are in your body right now, it does count as one of your levels of self.

Gently paying attention there, while in technique, your self-confidence and intelligence and comfort could be entirely different from the Level One, The Social Level.

Usually we don't give a thought to which level of self is working well and which is not. We're too busy participating. Especially for the "Coming Home" technique, you will be bringing awareness to a direct experience of how you are being yourself at each one of the five levels. No wonder, these subtle experiences can become a quiet revelation.

Level Three: Mental

Thinking. That's the common denominator for your signature experience at this inner level. But what does it mean, having that abstract experience called "Thinking"? For you, Brave Empath, thinking could include:

- Words that you hear inwardly
- Images or cartoons that you see inwardly
- Abstract textures to your experience
- Strongly held opinions
- Thoughts about your thoughts
- How much you like learning, right now
- How comfortable and confident you feel about learning in general

The technique you'll learn here allows for all of this to count. At any given time, you will have some degree of comfort and confidence with your own thinking process. While exploring, your job will be to gently notice this... whatever.

Not to fix, not to heal, not to judge. Simply to notice.

Level Four: Emotional

Consciously, Brave Empath, you always have at least one underlying emotion. Happens automatically whenever you are awake.

But consciously *noticing* that you have an emotion? Now that's another story. Not every empath has had much experience at purposely noticing and naming emotions.

Emotions include happy, sad, scared, angry; so loads of variety is possible.

Emotions do not have to include big drama, like the degree of intensity we can expect from watching TV.

Emotions can be recognized as words that you hear in your head or an idea that crosses your mind. In the "Coming Home" technique, noticing your emotions does not have to be mushy-gushy and loaded with feelings. It's just info.

Also, emotions do not have to make intellectual sense; no need for emotions to fit together logically. It is absolutely human to feel conflicting emotions simultaneously, like:

- Both joyful and impatient
- Both proud of yourself and ashamed of yourself
- Both calm, curious, and anxious
- Both worried, secure, furious, and superior to others

When doing "Coming Home," at The Emotional Level, you will write down the series of emotions, whatever it is. Or the one emotion, whatever it is.

Or you might write down something about the *flow of emotions*, like "fascinated by my emotions, overwhelmed by all the feelings, emotionally numb."

Just write it down, not doing anything more complicated — such as trying to make intellectual sense of it all. That would be way too much work. (Besides, purposely analyzing would sabotage how this technique can help you.)

What else about the emotional level of your human identity?

It includes plenty of information about your *way of relating* to this level of self. Just like every other level of self!

When awareness goes to this level, experiences may not be especially emotional in nature. Any of the following would count and be worth writing down while exploring your current experience at the emotional level:

- Physically tense
- Hard to think
- Feeling uncertain, not trusting myself
- Noticing a lot of energy
- Time seems to move really slowly, and not in a comfortable way

In short, don't judge what happens at any level. Simply wrap words around it and write down your souvenir.

Level Five: Spiritual

Spiritual experience for you could be about silence. Or space. Or light. Or colors. Or shifting energy.

You might have an emotion, and that would count, too.

Perhaps you might sense a presence. Whatever! Please trust your self-authority enough to count whatever you experience. Count it enough to write it down.

Maybe you have heard this wonderful term, "The God of your understanding." That means your version. Isn't your version the only one that really counts?

Like that, everything about your experience of self at the spiritual level is personal. It's yours and yours alone. And it counts.

Therefore, for the purpose of the "Coming Home" technique, whatever you experience is just something to wrap up in a bit of language and write down.

Of course, just like any other level of self, you could have experiences about your way of relating to this level of yourself, comfortable or not.

Positive or negative, exalted or mundane, please remember that everything counts when exploring yourself. It is what it is, right now.

Also, any experience you have at this time could be completely different tomorrow.

Whenever you do the "Coming Home" technique, your goal is not to find patterns or evaluate yourself. You will simply notice whatever you happen to notice and then write down a quick summary.

Techniques to move consciousness, or turn OFF empath gifts, are not designed to meet other needs as well.

If you want to do religious studies, do them separately. If you seek entertainment, go to the movies.

Exploring yourself at the spiritual level can feel different from each of the other levels. Why wouldn't it? Each of these five levels is distinctive and important. That's right, Brave Empath. Each of your levels of self is both distinctive and important.

None of them matters more than the others, at least not for the sake of waking you up from the inside and, automatically, turning your empath gifts OFF for hours to come.

Shadow Self? Says Who?

Long as we're clarifying levels within you, it occurs to me that one more distinction really ought to be made.

Have you ever heard the expression "SHADOW SELF"?

The great Swiss psychiatrist Carl Jung, described it as dark aspects of the personality that can be made conscious only with concerted mental and moral effort.

Agreed, this concept is valuable. From a psychological perspective, it can be useful to consciously reclaim aspects of the personality that have been disowned. Yet emotional and spiritual healing have evolved a great deal since Jung completed his doctoral dissertation in 1902.

Living now, after The Shift — during this new Age of Energy — it has become relatively easy for people to develop energetic literacy. Just as today we can learn how to surf the net, something not available to Dr. Jung despite all his genius.

Living today, depth aura reading is an easy-to-learn skill set. With this ability to access information, it's a gross oversimplification to describe anyone as having a "Shadow Area." Instead, each person is hardwired in consciousness to have hundreds of CHAKRA DATABANKS or nadis, each one containing a gift of the soul. (Many of these chakra databanks are related to the Five Levels of Self that we have been exploring in this chapter.)

Each person's aura can contain STUFF as well. Depending on the amount and quality of STUFF in chakra databanks, one's sturdy sense of self can be diminished or distorted. Life experience can even go numb.

Psychologically normal people can have quirks like despising physical exercise or refusing to feel inconvenient emotions.

Before aura reading became readily available, back in Jung's day, it was a breakthrough to call a person's numbed-out components a

"Shadow Self." Psychological techniques and theories were developed for dealing with this repressed material.

Today's equivalent is the emerging field of energy spirituality. Dedicated sessions with a healing professional are required to address the sticky old problems related to STUFF. Now it is obsolete to call stuck astral energy a "Shadow Self." It may not be terribly productive to analyze patterns caused by having STUFF; this might even be considered a waste of time, fabricating notions of self from this mess.

Energetic, subconscious STUFF can always be healed... through appropriate skill sets. Furthermore, taking on additional STUFF can be prevented. One rather important example is what you are doing in this Program for Empath Empowerment, learning to prevent Imported STUFF. For this, "Coming Home" is an amazingly effective technique for turning your empath gifts OFF.

Okay, Just a Bit More Inside Info

Here you have been learning about Five Levels of the Self as preparation for a technique that is not touted as a technique for healing. "Coming Home" is designed to help you to wake up consciousness at each level of the self. It is the most powerful way I've found yet to turn empath gifts OFF, with results that last for many hours and, also, are cumulative.

But, okay, want to know a secret? A side effect of this technique is to gently move out a bit of STUFF at different levels, as needed. Also provided will be appropriate PUT-IN. This depth healing will happen automatically.

The type of STUFF being removed is not Imported STUFF. Instead, the type of STUFF that can be moved out is called "Frozen Blocks of Stuck Energy." Or, for short, FROZEN BLOCKS.

This term was coined by Dr. Coletta Long, a brilliant clinical psychologist who devoted her career to pioneering work in past-life regression and energy healing. Frozen blocks of energy get stuck in a person's aura due to overload experiences.

A number of healing techniques have been expressly designed for this sort of healing. "Coming Home" is not one of them, yet it turns out to be effective for moving out small-intensity Frozen Blocks.

That's a big deal because Frozen Blocks are a unique type of STUFF. Unlike Imported STUFF, cords of attachment, and other types of astral debris, Frozen Blocks can be carried forward from previous incarnations.

Brave Empath, any one of your Five Levels of Self could be limited right now because of Frozen Blocks you incurred while a caveman.

Bottom line: Healing minor Frozen Blocks is just a side effect of "Coming Home." The purpose of this technique is awakening each level of self, and doing this in a way that turns empath gifts OFF. If you happen to receive permanent energy healing as a result, great!

So now you know:

~ Frozen Blocks can spontaneously be released.

~ Immediately afterwards, the Divine Being who is helping you — your choice for the "Get Big" part of "Coming Home" — will make sure that you get appropriate PUT-IN energetically.

~ This combo, of STUFF removal and appropriate PUT-IN, will make that energetic healing permanent.

Although "Coming Home" Is Easy to Do, Many Component Skills Are Required

Guess what? Brave Empath, you have learned all those components. Besides knowing about your Five Levels of Self, you have mastered Vibe-Raising Breaths and Grounding Breaths; plus you have experienced the "Get Big" technique.

Other useful skills were built into techniques you have learned in this Program for Empath Empowerment.

For instance, when doing Before-and-After Pictures in previous chapters, you practiced how to open your eyes while in the midst of technique, then make some ridiculously sloppy notes. No read-and-reread, play-penmanship-practice for you!

Your quick SCRIBBLE NOTES will be great for evaluating what happened. Since you can turn to them *after* a technique is over. Which will certainly be ideal for all notes that you take during the "Coming Home" technique.

Brave Empath, you are so ripe, so ready. Now let's put those pieces together.

CHAPTER 43

"Coming Home," Our Most Important Technique

If you hadn't been prepared so systematically, you might find it tricky to do the "Coming Home" technique.

Now? It can be simple and effortless. Besides all the component parts, your other important prerequisite is effortlessness. Your effortlessness when doing techniques that involve consciousness — this has been developing beautifully, Brave Empath. You are thoroughly prepared to have a fresh experience every time that you use this technique.

And just to remind you, although each experience of "Coming Home" can be fascinating, having fun with it is not the purpose. Incidental healing of STUFF in the form of Frozen Blocks? That is not the purpose, either. Which is turning your empath gifts OFF, bringing about wonderful results in your everyday life.

Here's an overview of what we'll be doing. In the following sequence of technique steps, I will guide you through brief exploration of five essential layers within. You will experience each one in turn.

- Moving inwardly through progressively deeper levels, you will be propelled by taking just one Vibe-Raising Breath at the appropriate time.
- Outward bound, you will take one Grounding Breath as directed.

Overall, your job will be simple. Notice things without trying to change them. Then write a few scribble notes.

So get your writing equipment handy, Brave Empath. On that page, or computer document, write the following sequence of words. Leave space in-between for the scribble notes:

1. Social
2. Physical
3. Mental
4. Emotional
5. Spiritual

6. Emotional
7. Mental
8. Physical
9. Social

Technique: COMING HOME

So, you have prepared your note-taking equipment by listing all nine categories. And did you take reasonable precautions against being interrupted? Superb, you Brave Empath!

Read through the following and then you're good to go. Take it one step at a time. (Open one eye and peek at these steps, as needed). Allow 15-20 minutes the first few times you go through this "Coming Home" technique. With practice, you can do the sequence faster, as will be discussed later. For now, enjoy taking your time, getting to know you-know-who.

1. Sit comfortably and close your eyes. To help yourself wake up inwardly, Get Big. Then take one Vibe-Raising Breath. You are preparing to learn more about yourself.

2. Right now, Brave Empath, awareness is positioned at *your social self.* How does it feel to be you right now? What do you notice? Find some words and open your eyes long enough to write down a few scribble notes. Then close your eyes.

3. Although it is interesting to keep your consciousness positioned at this level, your consciousness is fluid and flexible. Effortlessly your awareness can shift to different positioning. In a moment, with eyes closed, take one Vibe-Raising Breath. Continue to sit with eyes closed, breathing normally. Automatically your awareness will travel to the

next level inward, which is your physical self. The shift in consciousness will be effortless. Take that breath now.

4. Right now, Brave Empath, awareness is positioned at *your physical self.* How does it feel to be you right now? What do you notice? Find some words and open your eyes long enough to write down a few scribble notes. Then close your eyes.

5. Although it is interesting to keep your consciousness positioned at this level, your consciousness is fluid and flexible. In a moment, with eyes closed, you will take one Vibe-Raising Breath. Continue to sit with eyes closed, breathing normally. Automatically your awareness will travel to the next level inward, which is your mental functioning, mind and intellect. Take that breath now.

6. So now, Brave Empath, awareness is positioned at *your mental level.* How does it feel to be you right now? What do you notice? Find some words and open your eyes long enough to write a few scribble notes. Then close your eyes.

7. Although it is interesting to keep your consciousness positioned at this level, your consciousness is fluid and flexible. You will find it effortless to travel in consciousness to the next level inward, which is your emotional self. In a moment, with eyes closed, take one Vibe-Raising Breath. Continue to sit with eyes closed, breathing normally. Automatically your awareness will be positioned at this level of yourself. Take that breath now.

8. How familiar, Brave Empath! Your awareness is positioned at *your emotional self.* How does it feel to be you right now? What do you notice? Find some words and open your eyes long enough to write a few scribble notes. Then close your eyes.

9. Although it is interesting to keep your consciousness positioned at this level, your consciousness is fluid and flexible. You can easily travel in consciousness to the next destination for awareness, the next level inward, which is your spiritual self — who you are right now energetically. In a moment, with eyes closed, take one Vibe-Raising

Breath. Continue to sit with eyes closed, breathing normally. Automatically your awareness will be positioned at this level of yourself. Take that breath now.

10. Yet another way of being yourself, Brave Empath! Awareness is positioned at *your spiritual self.* How does it feel to be you right now? What do you notice? Find some words and open your eyes long enough to write a few scribble notes. Then close your eyes. If you wish, linger at this level for a while. Then continue.

11. Now you can begin to travel outward in consciousness, one level at a time. Your next level to re-visit will be the one about your emotional self. In a moment, with eyes closed, take one Grounding Breath. Continue to sit with eyes closed, breathing normally. Automatically your awareness will be positioned at this level. Take that breath now.

12. Here you are, with awareness positioned at *your emotional self.* How does it feel to be you right now? What do you notice? Find some words and open your eyes long enough to write a few scribble notes. Then close your eyes.

13. Next to experience, moving in consciousness, is your mental self: In a moment, with eyes closed, take one Grounding Breath. Continue to sit with eyes closed, breathing normally. Automatically your awareness will be positioned at this level of yourself. Take that breath now.

14. Here you are, with awareness positioned at *your mental self.* How does it feel to be you right now? What do you notice? Find some words and open your eyes long enough to write a few scribble notes. Then close your eyes.

15. Which level will come next? The level of your physical self. In a moment, with eyes closed, take one Grounding Breath. Continue to sit with eyes closed, breathing normally. Automatically your awareness will be positioned at the level of your physical body. Take that breath now.

16. Here you are, Brave Empath. Your entire body has come back. Go from feet to head. Check out how your full body is there. Just the sort of thing that you are well positioned to notice with awareness at *your physical self.* How does it

feel to be you right now? What do you notice? Find some words and open your eyes long enough to write a few scribble notes. Then close your eyes.

17. The final level for experience in the sequence you're doing right now is your social self, what you are like at the level of the environment. In a moment, with eyes closed, take 11 Grounding Breaths. Pace yourself comfortably. Avoid taking these breaths too fast. Afterwards continue to sit with eyes closed, breathing normally. Automatically your awareness will shift outward and you will start noticing yourself where you are sitting right now. Take all 11 breaths.

18. Now awareness is positioned at *your social self*, Brave Empath. Isn't it fascinating how you can start to notice furniture and other things about your environment? That can happen easily, even with eyes closed, while awareness is positioned at objective life, human reality. How does it feel to be you right now? What do you notice? Find some words and open your eyes long enough to write a few scribble notes. Then close your eyes.

19. Think "Technique over." Maybe also, "Congratulations, I am definitely a Brave Empath." Open your eyes.

Look over your notes. What happened this time? No matter what you wrote down, so long as you followed all the steps of this technique, you did just fine.

Q&A. Coming Home

Q. *I love, love, love this technique. Except I didn't enjoy the body level. Or the mind level. Can I leave them out next time?*

A. Eventually you will love, love, love the experience of yourself at each one of these levels. At least that will be the overall pattern.

Every time you do "Coming Home," your experiences could be different. Each time, let your experience be what it is. To enjoy the benefits of the technique, experiencing each level is required.

Here I won't go into more detail about results, but will leave that topic for our next chapter. In this Q&A, let's continue to discuss doing the technique itself.

Q. *Was this supposed to be hard and give me a headache?*

A. No! When you're studying *any* technique in the Program for Empath Empowerment, take it easy. And keep breathing.

Q. *You may as well know, I'm a workaholic perfectionist. Any advice for people like me?*

A. Perfectionism can pay off when you do things in objective reality, where success is measured in physical terms like money. "We try harder" once helped bring mega-business to the Avis Rent A Car company. Maybe it's your slogan, too.

Here, though, we're concerned with your subjective reality, where something as physical as your body can be approached as a form of consciousness. Trying harder with how you use consciousness will never bring you extra success.

If anything, you will create "benefits" like a headache, a stiff neck, or a general sense of frustration. Luckily, you don't need to push. Ideally, "Coming Home" is as comfortable as taking off your tie, un-squeezing your feet from tight shoes, or plopping down into your favorite armchair with a refreshing drink.

Q. *What if all the time you're supposed to be Coming Home you keep thinking about other people?*

A. Many empaths do that habitually. But remember, you're in the process of switching your empath talent OFF. No matter which way your stream of consciousness drifts, eventually a choice will become available. In that instant, *you will realize that you're thinking about other people rather than yourself.*

Only then do you have a choice. Right then, choose to pay attention to the level of self being explored during that step of the "Coming Home" technique.

Returning to yourself, persistently but gently, will help train you to put yourself first instead of putting others first.

Keep persisting and soon your inner life will fascinate you. One way that I train empaths is with Book One of this Empath Empowerment Series. That how-to brings a perspective I call, "Become The Most Important Person in the Room." It can be especially helpful for learning to pay attention to yourself as a person. So you might consider that as a resource after you finish this book.

Q. *That three-ring circus was The Real Me? Scary.*

A. Going within can be a shock, especially if you haven't had much practice. So much can be happening.

Nonstop motion is an illusion, though. With more experience, you'll find that familiarity brings content.

Meanwhile, here's my advice. Whenever you have a choice, go back to the level of self in that technique step that you're officially exploring. For instance, being interested in your physical body.

Q. *Could I be a Brave Empath but also a klutz at being self-aware?*

A. A Brave Not-Completely-Skilled Empath? Sure. A Skilled Empath, no. Spontaneous awareness of yourself — naturally putting yourself first — is required for becoming skilled.

Therefore, count yourself successful every time you do the technique for "Coming Home." Regardless of your experience this time, the process will help you to accept yourself... at every level of who you are, consciously and also subconsciously.

Q. *My problem was just the opposite of his. I noticed myself just fine. It is sooooo boring. How can I keep from boring myself to death?*

A. Lightly pay attention during your self-survey. If boredom strikes, write that down. Just as you might write down:

∽ I hate this.

∽ Feeling insecure.

- ∿ Worrying that there is something wrong with me at this level.
- ∿ Seems like nothing is there. Blank. Zip. Zilch.
- ∿ Feeling angry or weird or sad or any other uncomfortable experience. (Hint: These feelings are related to having awareness positioned at that level of self. On this particular occasion.)

Small frozen blocks of STUFF are being dissolved at such times. By gently allowing awareness to stay at that level regardless, you allow a PUT-IN of consciousness. And, thanks to the "Get Big" part of your preparation process, Divine protection organizes that PUT-IN beautifully.

Remember? Removal of frozen blocks is how "Coming Home" can bring permanent emotional and spiritual healing.

Of course, another possibility is that what you call "boredom" is simply discomfort with being left alone all by yourself.

Q. *You got that right. I hate it in there. So?*

A. Ever see a romantic movie where the couple starts off sparring? Think of "Coming Home" as a kind of courtship between your awareness and the rest of you. This particular friendship is worth the winning.

Q. *What if I noticed something really weird, like the fact that my head didn't seem connected to my body?*

A. Very important point about this technique: For best results don't try to fix a thing. Simply pay attention and then write down your scribble notes.

Q. *I thought maybe if I sent myself a little healing energy....*

A. Then you'd be doing a different technique. The power of *this* technique consists in your doing nothing except for a sloppy sort of paying attention, then writing down some words.

Paying attention to yourself, *as you are*, can be a powerful form of self-acceptance. Every empath, every person, needs plenty of that.

Q. *How does your technique for "Coming Home" differ from cutting yourself off from people?*

A. Context makes the difference. What you are doing here is a specific technique, done for a limited amount of time.

Furthermore, you're doing this technique to help yourself become more skilled as an empath. Nothing about this technique involves trying to push people out. That would actually cause you to send some energy in their direction, due to the dynamics of resistance. Rather, temporarily, you are drawing awareness inward.

You see, the awareness that turns OFF your empath gifts is simultaneously turning ON your authentic, full, sense of identity. You can never get that same ownership of yourself by waiting for somebody else to give that to you. Only you can give it to you.

Q. *Parts of this technique remind me of other things I have done. What makes this different?*

A. This particular sequence of steps, done in this particular way, has a unique value for you. Here's a tip for you about comparing techniques: Don't.

Either do a particular technique, as taught, or don't do it.

In this Program for Empath Empowerment you are a student, a consumer. You are acquiring concepts and skills to move yourself forward as an empath. So keep it simple. Just do the program. Then notice the results.

Only after giving this full program a chance will you be in a position to compare Empath Empowerment with other things you have learned. This is different from intellectually analyzing a technique or system, which provides little more than an intellectual exercise.

Q. *I was asking because I have done other techniques where I noticed my body and my mind. So I felt like "Been there, done that." Can't I just substitute other techniques where I notice different parts of myself?*

A. Not if you're wise. Complete Step TWO of this program exactly as it is given to you. Only then evaluate. Or complete this Program for Empath Empowerment all the way through Step THREE (which is presented in *The Master Empath*). And then evaluate.

Why would it surprise you that a program for personal development refers to the same human components as other programs and techniques? That hardly makes them interchangeable.

If you study tennis, you use your hand in a certain way. Does that make tennis interchangeable with golf or calligraphy or painting or playing the guitar? Because they use that same hand, too.

You live at a time of abundant resources, with huge availability through the Internet and social networking. Many folks are experimenting with... becoming chronic dilettantes.

Will you choose to limit yourself to that sketchy attention span? Avoid the temptation, especially if you wish to gain skills as an empath.

Q. *I think it would be more fun to play background music while doing this technique. Is that okay?*

A. No, definitely not okay. By playing music, you are likely to turn the instructions into a process of hypnosis. Technically "Coming Home" is constructed as a form of meditation.

Meditation and hypnosis represent radically different approaches, good for different things. My background includes extensive professional training in both fields. If you would like to learn more about the difference between meditation and hypnosis, one convenient resource is my blog. Search under "Hypnosis OR Meditation."

However, I appreciate that having something to listen to might be helpful. You might wish to record this technique. No background music, though. Just use your wonderfully familiar voice.

Read aloud one step at a time. Leave the same amount of time between each step. That time could range between 10-90 seconds, depending on how much depth of immersion you wish to experience. Just be consistent.

How might your life change if you do "Coming Home" every day for the next month... or longer? Experience can supply the best answer.

However, our next chapter can give you a preview... plus other information vital for living with your empath gifts routinely, and effortlessly, turned OFF.

CHAPTER 44

Break out of the Amusement Park

THE AMUSEMENT PARK is my name for the lifestyle of an unskilled empath. A Disneyland for your consciousness, it's the opposite of staying home. Since you have 1 or more of the 15 empath gifts, you will find attractions galore at this fascinating playland.

Your amusement adventure happens in consciousness rather than physical reality, so you neither pay for tickets nor have to wait in line. However many other empaths might be in the crowd, your turn comes first every time. Instantly.

And the number of rides you can take is unlimited.

No wonder unskilled empaths routinely ride to the point of exhaustion.

Think about it: Free rides, all day, all night. So tempting to overdo!

To make matters worse, pleasure is associated with these rides. Split-Split-Second Empath Merges, one after another, yum! Prolonged Unskilled Empath Merges, even more alluring! Unfortunately all this subconscious intrigue does not protect you from the inevitable, inadvertent Imported STUFF.

For instance, your best friend Brody's emotional wavelength is not obvious like a clattering roller coaster. So you may never have noticed that your consciousness goes riding on it whenever the two of you visit. Regardless, each amusement park ride on Brody's energies will bring you consequences that last long after that friendly time together.

Will bring you, not *may*. You *will* definitely receive some new Imported STUFF from Brody... every single time.

The following awareness regimen will help you to break out of the amusement park so that you can return home at will. Live a more stable life, secure in your human identity.

By now, Brave Empath, you may appreciate more than ever why it is not responsible to learn Skilled Empath Merge until you have become very, very comfortable with keeping your empath gifts OFF.

With experience, you can adapt the "Coming Home" technique to work most quickly and conveniently. Here's how.

Adapt "Coming Home" in a Responsible Fashion

Phase 1. Orientation

For the next week or so, do "Coming Home" within 45 minutes of waking up. Do this before you check for messages or contact any friends.

Brave Empath, this will help you to establish a sense of self that does not depend your relationships with other people.

Take your time with the technique, allowing 90 seconds or more for each level. Be sure to write down your experiences.

After you come out of technique, read those notes. Then praise yourself for your courage as a skilled empath. Exploring your inner experience is so important during this phase of this Program for Empath Empowerment.

After completing "Coming Home" for that day, go forth and enjoy interacting with others.

In the back of your mind, remember, it is safe to be yourself. You are allowed to have your own thoughts, feelings, physical sensations, etc.

Basically, everything you used to do as an unskilled empath... you can do now... except for Split-Split-Second and Prolonged Empath Merges.

Phase 2. Familiarity with Yourself Grows

Over the next few weeks, or months, continue to do "Coming Home" every single day, preferably soon after waking up. It's helpful to get that going each day before you start talking to others.

This routine will help you grow more accustomed to being yourself, feeling comfortable that way. No extra pushiness or self-conscious attitude will be required beyond that simple routine. Automatically your sense of self will grow stronger.

In Phase 2, doing "Coming Home," you can shorten the amount of time you spend exploring most levels of self. With one important exception, it will be fine to spend just 30 seconds at each level: Social, Physical, Mental, Emotional, Spiritual.

That exception? Handle the timing a bit differently if you find one or more levels of self where you feel uncomfortable or go blank. Spend extra time there. Linger for a full 90 seconds or more.

As always, while doing "Coming Home," simply experience that level as you naturally do in the here-and-now. Don't try to pretty up your experiences or otherwise change a thing. Gently pay attention, then write something down.

What about a level of self that you don't happen to enjoy particularly? Scribble-write some words, as usual, e.g., "Grrrrrrr, this stinks."

In general, when making your scribble notes during technique, let them be as honest as ever. Whatever you notice, it is what it is. After ending the technique, read your latest notes in that spirit of interested self-acceptance.

During the rest of your waking hours, outside of technique, integration of your personality will continue rapidly.

Phase 3. Your Exploration Becomes Downright Enjoyable

Brave Empath, your next phase in using the technique is based on experience: This new phase will begin when, for several day in a row, you have enjoyed every level of yourself while doing "Coming Home."

Then you can cut the time for each level of "Coming Home" down to five seconds.

After you come out of technique, go about your day, more integrated than ever.

What's new at Phase 3, besides the shorter time spent at each level? You might start to add a few minutes of journaling to your daily routine.

Do that journaling before you go to sleep every night. Summarize positive little discoveries about your human life that you made today, things accomplished in objective reality plus:

- How you reacted in a particular situation
- Things you did well
- Any new textures or qualities that were part of your personal experience that day

Brave Empath, you can expect to find that more and more about everyday reality fascinates you. Trust that this is healthy, because it is.

Non-empaths who have basic mental health have *always* been living this way. Hello!

Phase 4. Exploration Accelerates

Is your sense of self growing stronger? Then you can start decreasing the amount of time you spend at each level, day by day. (Unless something happens on a particular occasion that is not enjoyable, in which case linger a while, exploring gently.)

After some days, you might spend just a second or two at each level of self. And writing down scribble notes is no longer needed. Simply grab information as usual; put it into words as if you were writing things down, only not opening your eyes to do that quick scribble-writing. Noticing is enough now.

Consider this a graduation of sorts!

With your journaling at the end of the day, continue to write only positive things. That contrasts with thinking-type notes that you might make *during* the technique, which could be positive or icky or anything, really.

Both "Coming Home" and journaling in Phase 4 will bring you an empath's version of adult education, ongoing learning about yourself as a human adult. Discover more every day about your quirky, individual sense of identity. Relish your varied experiences here at Earth School.

Phase 5. Graduate to the Eyes-Open Version of Coming Home

Brave Empath, advance to this phase of exploration only when you are feeling truly comfortable in your own skin. By now you are used to waking up and noticing *yourself* first, not other people or ways to clean up your home or rush to work. Yourself.

Not self-improvement or goals or religious obligations, either.

Overall, each new day here on earth is about you. Definitely allowed! Non-empaths have always lived that way. Now you can, too.

Given this balanced way of life, it is appropriate for you to move to the Phase 5 Version of "Coming Home."

Early in your day, speak aloud the following sequence of sentences, substituting your name for "Henrietta" (unless you really are named Henrietta). Change some of the language if it makes you more comfortable. Because not everyone feels comfortable lavishing praise on yourself to such an extent, while some others of you empaths might wish to say something even more appreciative:

> *Love and gratitude for you, my human identity as Henrietta.*
>
> *Love and gratitude for you, dear, precious body.*
>
> *Love and gratitude for you, dear, precious mind.*
>
> *Love and gratitude for you, dear, precious emotions.*
>
> *Love and gratitude for you, dear, precious spirit.*
>
> *I feel grateful that I am able to live this day as myself.*

What else, Brave Empath? About that end-of-day journaling... continue it only if you find the practice enjoyable.

Phase 6. Continuing to Deepen Your Experience Over the Years

Whenever you like, repeat the previous five phases of exploration with "Coming Home." How often, exactly?

- *Once a year might serve you. Or once every few years. Your choice. You, the person with self-authority.*
- *Sometimes you might go through rough patches on your journey through life. That could make it especially productive for you to repeat those five phases at a new level of personal growth.*
- *Or you might have a lovely spiritual awakening.*
- *Or you might even cross the threshold into Householder Enlightenment.*

Brave Empath, feel free to restart the previous five phases for any reason. Or for no reason in particular.

Now you have the great combination, Brave Empath. Self-authority and skills, both. That's the ticket!

It is healthy to focus on yourself in this lifetime. You, a person who now happens to be a skilled empath.

CHAPTER 45

Ten Rules for a Skilled Empath

For your emerging comfort as an empath, a handful of rules can make a big difference. Of course, these are not coping tips nor are they a substitute for all that has gone before in this Program for Empath Empowerment.

Each of the following rules makes sense only if you have already gone through our previous chapters. Brave Empath, this has helped you to develop finesse at positioning your consciousness appropriately.

Empath skills are mostly about how you use your amazing gift of spiritual awareness, or consciousness.

Based on that, it is appropriate to explore some simple rules to make your life better. I know you can read them with an appreciation of the consciousness factor.

Every born empath can live as a skilled empath if you will only do the following.

Skilled Empath's Rule 1.
Do the "Coming Home" technique early each day

Each day at Earth School provides a new beginning. You can start fresh, doing what you wish, helping and learning, becoming what you want to be. Set the tone appropriately by doing "Coming Home" within 45 minutes of waking up.

Automatically this will turn your empath gifts OFF, positioning consciousness appropriately for all that follows in this new day.

Even that Phase 5 "Eyes-Open" quickie will suffice, once your skill has developed enough for this phase to be appropriate.

Skilled Empath's Rule 2.
Use "Empath's First Aid" appropriately

Enjoy the comfort this little technique can bring you. Just use it sparingly, not as a substitute for the preventative help of "Coming Home."

"Empath's First Aid" will keep your energy field clear. It can also get you accustomed to feeling like yourself.

When is it a good time to use this technique? Out of nowhere, you notice a change in how it feels being you. And that change does not seem warranted by what has happened to you in objective reality. For example, no piano just fell from a window, missing you by inches. More likely examples follow:

- After hanging out with your friend Carlos, you literally feel a pain in the neck.

- While in a business meeting, you find it hard to know what you think. Other people's ideas and opinions seem overwhelming.

- Talking on the phone with your mother, you feel depressed. Before that conversation you felt just fine. And nothing your mother said was particularly depressing.

- At the gym, you start feeling as though your body is fat and blobby. (Regardless of the actual size and muscle tone of your physical body, which has not changed a great deal since you entered the gym.)

- One look at your neighbor Zeke and you feel like a victim, not your usual way of living or feeling. Not at all.

Changes like these can definitely result from Split-Split-Second Empath Merges. Don't stop to analyze, though. Soon as you can find a private moment, do the "Empath's First Aid."

If you feel better, you needed it. If nothing changes, you haven't sacrificed much time, have you? Consider those minutes an investment in your personal development.

You'll note however, Brave Empath, I have also recommended that you use Empath's First Aid sparingly. See our next rule to understand this more thoroughly.

Skilled Empath's Rule 3.
Engage in life, not incessant self-improvement

This Program for Empath Empowerment has given you many powerful techniques to turn your empath gifts OFF naturally, also ways to banish Imported STUFF.

Use these appropriately. Don't make them your life. Let your life be about your life.

In particular, do not overuse "Empath's First Aid." Once or twice a day is fine. More than that and you may be compensating for patterns of STUFF that have nothing to do with Skilled Empath Merge.

For example, what if you feel depressed many times in a day? Maybe something happening now in your life triggers that reaction. Appropriately. Because a problem in objective reality warrants concern. Every negative feeling you have is not inappropriate, necessarily.

The Serenity Prayer might apply to your situation: Change the things you can. Accept the rest. Develop skill at telling them apart, "the wisdom to know the difference."

 ⌒ Maybe one special person in your life is going through a patch of terrible difficulties. If that depresses you, it doesn't necessarily mean you are doing loads of unskilled empath merges. Life at Earth School is challenging. Do your reasonable best to be a good friend. Grieve privately when you must.

~ Maybe nothing is going wrong with your near ones and dear ones, and life externally seems to be fine. Despite that, you still might go through strong, negative feelings. Well, don't just keep doing "Empath's First Aid" all day long. And don't overuse other healing techniques either, like E.F.T. tapping sessions that you give yourself 20 times a day.

Instead, it might not hurt to get a medical checkup. Or sometimes a psychotherapist would be your best bet. Alternatively you might find a professional at mind-body-spirit healing whom you trust. Imported STUFF is not the only kind of energetic problem that could be limiting your life.

Skilled Empath's Rule 4.
Refuse to do boredom

Brave Empath, having less Imported STUFF makes it all the easier to vanquish boredom. You possess unique ways to accomplish, to learn, to serve others. An amazing life awaits.

One common cause of boredom is not using your self-authority. Do things your way. Now! (Just remember to get skills for your chosen activities that require skill, not confusing self-authority with mastering skills.)

Sorting out the difference between self-authority and skills will be all the easier for you now, given the clarity that results automatically from Empath Empowerment.

What can help you to live large and lively, rather than bored and brooding? Enjoy having your own natural, brilliant, amazing consciousness.

Throughout your long history as a soul, you may have had some pretty fabulous incarnations. But never have you been given another incarnation exactly like this one. Nor will that identical chance ever come again. In that sense, the popular saying is true. "You" only live once. Celebrate YOLO.

272 The Empowered Empath

One technique you have learned is especially helpful as a boredom buster. When you feel sooooo booooooooooooored and inwardly fidgety, do the "I Like" technique. Then find something else to do in objective reality.

"An idle mind is the Devil's workshop." So goes a pretty useful saying, even if (like me) you don't believe in a devil.

There has to be more to life than sitting around, by yourself or with others, waiting until you get the munchies.

Skilled Empath's Rule 5.
Avoid recreational chemicals

Another advantage of playing "I Like"? You can substitute that for mucking up your aura with big frozen blocks of STUFF, the inevitable result of taking recreational drugs like marijuana.

Sure, STUFF incurred from cannabis can always, always, always be healed. Still, life flows far better without recreational drugs messing up your consciousness and aura. Based on my work helping clients let go of those false (chemical) friends, here's my advice:

What can you do in a social situation with a choice between alcohol and pot, when you feel like you'll burst if you don't get high one way or another?

Choose the booze. Even a revolting episode of throw-up drinking, complete with horrible hangover the next day... has far less auric impact long-term compared to weed. Even a little fun with a reefer will put high-intensity frozen blocks into your energy field.

Granted, current social pressure (and sometimes even sanctimony) around smoking grass is so thick, it's almost enough to set off a smoke detector.

Mind-altering chemicals put STUFF into an aura in a way that alcohol doesn't. Sure, drinking kills brain cells; I don't particularly recommend it. Just saying, alcohol sure is preferable to the more subtle long-term effects on consciousness from psychoactive toys.

Incidentally, enjoying a glass of wine with your dinner will not counteract your authentic sense of identity, so important for continued growth as a skilled empath.

Skilled Empath's Rule 6.
Take a vigorous interest in your human life

Actively pursue relationships and hobbies, Brave Empath. Move forward in your work life, making it great.

Automatically you will spend less time thinking about other people and what's wrong with them, replaying past conversations and dwelling on emotional pain.

Skilled Empath's Rule 7.
Reach out daily. In person

When possible, choose to visit people in objective reality. Real-life visits will enrich your consciousness and build social skills.

Texting, tweeting, and social networking cannot compare. Aura reading research clearly demonstrates that people evolve faster by being present with others in energetic real time, whether in the room, by phone, or webcam.

By contrast, electronic interaction done at random intervals? This directs consciousness in shallow ways.

Admittedly, shallow experiences can supply a different kind of fun. At least these electronic conversation are still done in objective reality, through voice or keyboarding or other ways of interacting electronically.

Can you appreciate how different all that is from wishing, hoping, thinking, praying, fantasizing, or other endless journeys into subjective life?

Skilled Empath's Rule 8.
Whenever you have a choice, live in the present

However you enjoy connecting to people, Brave Empath, choose to do it with your conscious mind rather than old habits of slip-sliding into unskilled empath merge.

It is perfectly normal to get lost in thought. Eventually, though, you have a moment of choice.

Huh? You realize that you were just having an away moment. What to do then? Reinsert yourself into objective reality.

- ～ Say something.
- ～ Do something.
- ～ Move your body.
- ～ Use one or more of your senses.

Anything will do, so long as you engage with objective reality.

Automatically your consciousness will shift, positioned in a way that is the opposite of drip-drip-drip. That consciousness of yours will be living in the present.

Skilled Empath's Rule 9.
Downplay seeking grand purpose. Just for now

We empaths tend to be such idealists. We can long for something bigger than life's trivial little activities.

Unfortunately, this can make us susceptible to joining cults, taking drugs, and other dangerous ways to jazz up humdrum human reality.

A related vulnerability is disregarding your life due to a valiant search for some grand purpose.

Brave Empath, have you been tormenting yourself unintentionally, seeking a grander, mystical purpose?

Then consider this. Creating demand for "Find your purpose" happens to be a very big business. Follow the money. Then you'll appreciate how easy it is for unscrupulous people to capitalize on the human search for meaning.

Truth is, most adults never find a flashy grand purpose. Because there may not be one.

Evolving at Earth School, finding human satisfactions, fulfilling ideals the best you can, and being of service to others — for most of us, that's It. Purpose enough. A pretty sacred purpose, actually.

Your life can also gain meaning by how you use your free will. Use it to set goals, choose interests, make new friends, evaluate the friendships you have now. Doing all this is hard work, but there's no substitute if you really want to grow spiritually.

Finding a fancier special purpose will not let you off the hook. Nor will it keep life on earth from being frustrating, confusing; sometimes downright ugly, sometimes beautiful.

Here is a way to grow super-fast as an empath. For your first year as a skilled empath — maybe starting right now — stop seeking your purpose. Simply live your life.

You can still find plenty to keep you interested. Maybe more than if you have constantly been struggling to find some greater, higher, fancier purpose.

Your newfound identity as a more skilled empath? This will be strengthened by saying and doing things, grand purpose or not. Be willing to live that human life and see where it gets you.

Skilled Empath's Rule 10.
Enjoy your life

It really is the only one you've got. (For this incarnation, at least.)

Paying attention to your life as though it mattered? This can get easier.

Brave Empath, you can expect interest in your human life to grow. Now you are free to explore it as a skilled empath.

In recognition, I'm going to start calling you something new, EVOLVING EMPATH. (Short for "Rapidly Evolving Empath.)

You are growing so quickly now, moving forward more beautifully than ever along your path of personal development.

CHAPTER 46

Gifts Owned, Embraced, Managed, SKILLED!

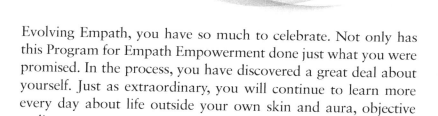

Evolving Empath, you have so much to celebrate. Not only has this Program for Empath Empowerment done just what you were promised. In the process, you have discovered a great deal about yourself. Just as extraordinary, you will continue to learn more every day about life outside your own skin and aura, objective reality.

When it comes to dealing with that objective reality...

> *Unskilled empaths are less effective than non-empaths.*
> *But skilled empaths are more effective than non-empaths.*

Why would that be? Consider what has been happening with you.

Techniques You Can Use for the Rest of Your Life

You've got skills now, not just talent. This Program for Empath Empowerment has taught you:

> How to use Vibe-Raising Breaths in everyday life. The technique called "Intro to Vibe-Raising Breaths" can release some of the Imported STUFF in your aura that has resulted from unskilled empath merge. (Just be sure to include this powerful technique sparingly. Don't sprinkle it throughout your day. Let your life continue to be about your human life.)

◦ The use of Grounding Breaths can help position your consciousness more appropriately in everyday life.

◦ Installing "An Automatic Subconscious Alert" has begun to break the pattern of Prolonged Unskilled Empath Merge.

◦ Teaming up with the Divine at will is so useful for techniques that involve consciousness (such as when you do "Get Big").

◦ The "Empath's First Aid" technique, also to be used sparingly, provides instant help for Imported STUFF from unskilled empath merges.

◦ "Coming Home" prevents the old drip-drip-drip.

◦ Conscious ownership of your gifts helps you to respect yourself.

◦ Embracing your magnificent sensitivity, you can rightly feel proud of being a Highly, Highly Sensitive Person, an empath.

◦ Intellectually you can now clearly distinguish skill versus self-authority, honoring the latter while you develop the former, and using both resources to strengthen your sense of self.

Evolving Empath, congratulations on completing Step TWO of this Program for Empath Empowerment.

Actively Engage an Empath's Greatest Resource

Evolving Empath, what is that superb resource you have learned to engage?

Your consciousness. You have begun using an effortless awareness of your own awareness. You have begun to purposely position awareness through conscious choice.

Not doing this often. Just doing it occasionally. And, at those Technique Times, doing it marvelously well.

Every one of the techniques you have learned works because of your magnificent consciousness, an empath's greatest resource.

Consciousness is abstract yet indispensable. Many of us living now, after The Shift that occurred in December 2012, are noticing energy more than ever. Humanity has moved into The Age of Energy — which brings us more interactions with astral-level energy than ever before in recorded history. By definition, astral (or psychic-level) experience is flashier than anything human.

By contrast, how about everyday, human frequencies? It takes a certain kind of humility to explore them. Yet living here at Earth School, your main job is being human.

Not only do you have the special assignment of being an empath. You are *human* while developing those empath skills.

Looking back at this Program for Empath Empowerment, you have learned how to use consciousness to help explore your humanity. Only the appropriate positioning of consciousness will turn empath gifts OFF: Positioning your consciousness at *human* frequencies!

Exploring flashy astral experiences or Divine-level sacred experiences? You have found an alternative. Explore human experiences first. Yours, not experiences belonging to random other people!

Spending time on non-human vibrational frequencies could be compared to eating chocolates. Fine for a treat, as part of a balanced diet. No substitute for a body's required nutrients.

Your sense of identity can grow strong only when you are willing to pay attention to human frequencies, to notice objective reality and solve problems through speech and action.

So why is it that skilled empaths are more effective than non-empaths, while unskilled empaths struggle through life with less effectiveness than the non-empaths?

Three reasons, seems to me.

#1. With Skills, You Prevent Imported STUFF

Evolving Empath, this is the first major way you have started to become more effective through this Program for Empath Empowerment.

All that Imported STUFF was subconscious, of course. Consciously you may not have noticed a big difference yet, having a new kind of energetic freedom from astral debris. Subconsciously, this change amounts to a very big deal. You have lessened the random STUFF entering your auric field multiple times each day.

Split-Split-Second Empath Merges weren't obvious to your conscious mind any more than the Imported STUFF that was deposited. Even Prolonged Unskilled Empath Merges weren't announced to your conscious awareness, as if trumpeted by a uniformed officer playing "Reveille."

Probably you didn't notice that drip-drip-drip entering your energy field, nor did you track all the accumulation, and its impact on daily life. Not consciously, anyway.

Over time you will consciously appreciate the significance. What can it mean, for everyday life, that from now on you will have way less Imported STUFF?

- ~ You can become more effective at work.
- ~ You can explore hobbies with more gusto.
- ~ You are free to engage in social relationships with a stronger sense of identity.

Over time, all this growth will continue in cumulative fashion.

#2. Your Skills Help Other People Respect You More

It's ironic, I know. Evolving Empath, you could even call it sad.

Doing all those unskilled empath merges, you used to help other people. Temporarily, it's true. And with icky consequences for your own aura. Still, you *were* helping people as a clueless kind of volunteer.

So it could be considered both sad and ironic that, previously, this caused problems for you. Clearly visible to everyone you have known, at a subconscious level. Uh-oh! Imported STUFF was clinging to your aura like dirt on a car's windshield.

Junked up with this subconscious kind of debris, you couldn't see others so clearly. Nor could they see the real you.

Having less STUFF makes you more attractive subconsciously. Others will automatically respond to you better, due to your improved auric modeling.

Just think about your relationships lately. Hasn't there been an upgrade? Non-empaths, in particular, will respect you more.

To them, you probably used to seem a bit spaced out. While now you seem to walk with your feet on the ground. Or call it "Driving through life with a way-cleaner windshield."

#3. With Skills, You Can Solve Problems Better

Evolving Empath, of course, you have always done your best to solve problems. But consider what I have learned from facilitating thousands of sessions with clients who are empaths.

Unskilled empaths try to solve problems with awareness.
Non-empaths use speech and action.
And so do skilled empaths.

For example, say that Frederick is your close friend. One time while you're talking together on the phone, he seems preoccupied, distant.

As an unskilled empath, most likely you would have done a sequence of unskilled empath merges. Trying to figure out what was bothering him, all that flying in spirit might have informed you in a vague, subconscious way. Throughout the conversation, you would have kept at it, multi-tasking rather than carrying out a normal conversation.

Now, being a skilled empath, you will not choose this way to solve problems. You're more likely to just ask the guy. *Hey, Frederick, you seem a little preoccupied. Is anything bothering you?*

You know, talking. Asking questions. Dealing with what the other person says in reply.

Mind reading? Needing to check out other people subconsciously? This is not how human life is designed to work best.

Which is why problem solving, for humans, becomes far more effective when you play by the rules. Skilled empaths are more effective at life than unskilled empaths. Our extreme sensitivity helps us when we stay right on the surface of life.

We really can be more effective than non-empaths. And that's not even counting what happens after learning techniques for Skilled Empath Merge. Hint: High-quality inside information, safely and appropriately made your own.

More About Adding Skilled Empath Merge

Evolving Empath, wait as long as you like before doing Step THREE of this Program for Empath Empowerment.

The Master Empath, the sequel to this book, will coach you. Why choose to be coached? That Step THREE is totally optional. You have done the far more essential Steps ONE and TWO in this Program for Empath Empowerment.

Only aren't you a bit curious about what empath gifts are for? Why did you incarnate with this kind of lifelong talent?

Empath talent doesn't help a person to solve human problems, particularly. As you now know, it's no substitute for normal human communication or taking appropriate action.

Yet that hardly makes it useless. Skilled Empath Merge is a form of deeper perception. Actually, it is the ultimate form of deeper perception.

Don't you continue to be curious about what makes other people tick? I have a hunch you are curious in that way, more curious than most — even though now you're much better adjusted to being human.

Still, that old drip-drip-drip in our analogy came from an extra faucet. Extra goodies!

Since birth you have had an amazing talent for reading people deep down. Well, what's with that?

When your first priority is — rightly — to be healthy and happy, how can you satisfy that lifelong curiosity to learn more about other people?

A Brief Survey of Deeper Perception

Let's survey different ways to read people deeper. Which of them have you explored so far?

Shallow perception

It's only reasonable to begin our survey with the opposite of deeper perception. Which would be paying attention to objective reality

Pretty darned important! Pretty informative, too!

What does a friend like Frederick really do? Maybe he delivers what he promises. Maybe not. Maybe he treats you with respect. Maybe you used to be far too busy with multi-tasking to notice.

Shallow perception can be tremendously useful. It is available to every normal human adult with average intelligence. Don't turn up your nose at it, Evolving Empath.

Could be that, now that you are a skilled empath, you will appreciate shallow perception more than ever. Without the distraction of unskilled empath merges, human speech and action can become far more interesting and informative.

Theories about what makes people tick

Belief systems galore can help you to deconstruct reality, torque it, analyze it, shred it, play with the surface of life to your heart's content.

Whether you compare baseball statistics or analyze human motivation, theories about life are available to non-empaths as well as to you. Techniques abound, based on theories about the surface level of reality: Techniques to win friends and manipulate people, slick ways to gain success and prosperity — you name it.

Your belief system about what makes people tick may change over time, of course. I mean no disrespect to beliefs by pointing out the obvious: Theories allow shallow perception to be treated in an elegant manner. Shallow perception it remains, however, being based on what people say and do in objective reality. Evolving Empath, you can outgrow mere theories.

Expression reading

Once you open the door to READING EXPRESSION and body language, it's hard to ever go back.

Right there, near the surface of life, those funny faces that people make actually *mean* something. Nonverbal communication indicates something deeper than the surface level of reality, and that can be quite a thrill to discover.

Maybe you still remember when you first learned how to read body language. What a huge thrill that tends to be for an empath.

For non-empaths, expression reading may be plenty deep enough, even seeming almost too far-fetched and impractical. By contrast, all Highly Sensitive Persons tend to love this kind of exploration. We're naturals at it, too.

As for Highly, Highly Sensitive Persons like you — sure you're great at this. But, honestly, does it satisfy you? You have talent for going so much deeper.

Face reading for character

A deeper way to read people is PHYSIOGNOMY. For at least 5,000 years, professional face readers have interpreted physical data like ear angles and cheek proportions.

If you think that face reading means reading expression... some delightful surprises await. Face reading for character is entirely different. It is a much deeper form of perception than expression reading. This study can reward you with greater success at work, improved personal relationships, more effective communication.

As with all the types of deeper perception that will be summarized in the rest of this chapter, it is important to know that gaining skill matters, and so does the system being used. I have trademarked one system in this field, Face Reading Secrets®. The purpose is to gain detailed and practical information about character. In the background, the system is designed to boost the face reader's self-esteem and also help open up greater compassion.

Other face reading systems aim differently, such as fortunetelling or diagnosing health problems or typing people. Ever notice how many types of automobile exist in the world? By comparison, the field of physiognomy includes way more variety. Each school of face reading produces consequences for the knower, so use your discernment before committing to any particular system.

For empaths, physiognomy can be an excellent form of deeper perception. The resulting insights will be very human. As a side effect, noticing physical face data can prevent unskilled empath merge. Just stay right on the surface of that face, checking out nostril shapes and lower eyelid curve.

Energy reading

Living now, in this Age of Energy, it is easier than ever to notice... energies. Highly Sensitive Persons (empaths particularly) have always had some awareness of energy, but now all humans are starting to notice it more.

Reading energy can include vibing out people, getting a gut feeling or intuitive hit, seeking inner guidance, seeing colors or lights around people, or simply knowing about somebody in a somewhat deeper way.

Does energy reading require doing empath merges, whether skilled or unskilled? Definitely not. READING ENERGY happens automatically when your consciousness is positioned at the astral and subconscious frequencies built into life.

Energy reading is especially effective when done as an intentional, attentional shift of consciousness. And done with skill.

Since The Shift into The Age of Energy, it has become easier than ever for anyone to move awareness in this subtler direction. However, this is not necessarily done with skill. As you know, skills are learned.

Skill at reading energy does not spring up automatically due to casual curiosity or a desire to be special. And self-authority about reading energy cannot substitute for skill.

For you, Awakening Empath, I recommend that you postpone energy reading until you have learned Skilled Empath Merge from *The Master Empath*. This part of the Program for Empath Empowerment will offer you a more stable life than randomly alternating between the surface level of reality and various energies.

With your level of skill now, as an empath, noticing energies can become a conscious choice. Because all you need to do is position awareness in the desired direction.

Say that you are talking with a new colleague at work, Jeanette. What if you want to figure out whether you can trust her or not? You could:

1.   Notice what she says and does. Surface-level human reality!

2.   Monitor her expression while she talks to you, a skill set that comes naturally to human beings. Expression reading!

3.   Quickly note an interesting facial characteristic. When experienced at physiognomy, you can rapidly interpret that face data. Not so experienced? Do your face reading in installments: Make a mental note of that one characteristic so you can look it up after returning home. Then re-engage in the conversation. (Maybe later you can find Jeanette's photo online and do a proper face reading along with your reference book, which could be even more useful.)

4.   Check out Jeanette's vibes while you are talking. This would be energy reading (for a non-empath) or (for you, probably) slipping into unskilled empath merge. Don't go there, Evolving Empath.

Why do I warn you to avoid random energy readings? It creates problems even if you are using a dedicated technique for Skilled Empath Merge, alternating that with regular interactions. In that case, you would be dividing attention, multi-tasking with your consciousness.

To be sure, your colleague Jeanette will notice — subconsciously and maybe consciously, as well. This will not win you points with her. More likely this multi-tasking of yours will arouse suspicion.

Jeanette may not be an empath, but any person of average intelligence can feel when somebody else is doing something thing extra, not simply talking in a natural way.

Subconsciously, and maybe consciously, too, Jeanette may well find "something about you" a little off-putting.

How can you bring yourself back to everyday ways of paying attention? A simple shift of attention is all that's needed to avoid weakening yourself in the relationship. Tell yourself "Later." Then resume your normal conversation.

Pay attention to that conversation — which just might, actually, teach you some interesting things about this person, Jeanette.

Fortunately, face reading and energy readings are not compulsions. They are skills.

As skills, they do not just happen to you. Evolving Empath, you can consciously choose whether or not to use deeper perception.

More sophisticated energy reading

After The Shift into this Age of Energy, everyone has become eligible to do some energy reading. How well you do it depends on whether or not you educate yourself about energy readings.

By way of analogy, everyone you know wears clothes in public, right? Outside of a nudist colony, anyway.

Some people wear whatever. Other folks pay a bit of attention to what they wear. Then there is Tim Gunn.

He's my favorite fashion expert. Okay, I skipped a category. Between paying a bit of attention to clothing, versus becoming a mega-fashionista like Tim Gunn, lies the relatively obtainable option of dressing well.

About energy reading, most folks are unsophisticated about what they're doing. I call this Stage One Energetic Literacy. With this kind of talent but lack of skill, the hunches are likely to be incorrect.

Sorry. But it's true. Self-authority about reading energy does not automatically equate to skill.

Developing genuine skill is required to progress at energy reading.

> ～ One direction for study is psychic reading, which brings benefits like flashy perception and the support of mainstream New Age culture, which emphasizes The Romance of the Astral.

～ A different direction for study is Energetic Literacy, which I teach to empaths and non-empaths alike. In my experience, everyone who desires to learn these skills for aura reading can be successful.

～ Each system for learning to read energy has consequences. So use your consumer smarts before you commit to one type of study rather than another.

The ultimate in deeper perception, Skilled Empath Merge

Available only to empaths, this is the very deepest perception for human beings. Even people who are spiritually Enlightened. (And yes, I have taught this skill to people in long-term, high states of consciousness.)

Evolving Empath, your entire life, you have been capable of learning Skilled Empath Merge.

You have been hardwired with soul-level gifts. These special gifts, now owned, embraced, and managed... can be used along with additional skills to reveal so much about what it is like, being another person.

Steps ONE and TWO have been accomplished now. This Program for Empath Empowerment has taught you skills for being safe, living vigorously and effectively.

Step THREE will include other skills, especially a variety of techniques for Skilled Empath Merge. When you are ready for that, meet me at the sequel to this book, *The Master Empath.* Meanwhile....

Celebrate What You Have Accomplished

At every level of perception, it shows. From the depths of your chakra databanks to the surface of your behavior, your degree of empath skills definitely shows.

Your new absence of Imported STUFF, the clarity as you talk and walk and engage in the surface of human life — yes, your skill level shows.

For those with the discernment to notice *consciously*, your empath skills show.

For every human being you meet, *subconsciously* your new skills show.

Most important, this achievement on your path of personal development shows clearly to God. And to you.

Congratulations on your persistence in learning. Among the millions of empaths in the world, you have proven yourself a leader.

- In objective reality, enjoy using your greater effectiveness.
- Subjectively, you are set for a sweet adventure as well. Every day can awaken a stronger sense of identity. Fulfilling human discoveries will illuminate your path of personal development.

Evolving Empath, you have learned to own, embrace, and manage your special gifts. You really do know how to live as a skilled empath.

CHAPTER 47

Ten Empaths, Empowered

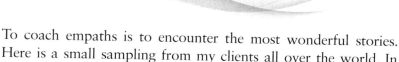

To coach empaths is to encounter the most wonderful stories. Here is a small sampling from my clients all over the world. In their own words, these 10 empaths will share what stands out for them, having developed Empath Empowerment.

1. An Australian Acupuncturist's Awakening

In retrospect it seems like my life was shaped in so many ways by being born an empath. I think of one major aspect and think, "That's the main one." Then another aspect of equal significance pops up.

I had actually read a fair bit of Rose's work for empaths, knew about it for a while. For a long time I was on the fence about whether it applied to me.

What settled the issue was beginning my practice as an acupuncturist.

One problem for me was those unskilled empath merges that are regularly performed until we become skilled. For me, in addition, this was complicated by doing my diagnostic process, which required close focus on my patients. I was doing LOTS of unskilled merges on some very sick people.

My health deteriorated with frightening speed, since I began experiencing all my patient's various ailments as if they were my own. I found myself with an unexpected new smoking habit, to boot.

This forced me to think seriously about whether or not I was an empath. As it turned out, I have most of the empath gifts a person can have, and many of them are very strong. While I appreciate them now, these many and powerful talents constituted a serious vulnerability for a new healer.

One incident sticks in my mind as my first really clear recognition of what it meant for me, being an unskilled empath.

After doing the "Empath's First Aid" technique for the first time, I was reveling in what felt like my first experience of just being me. Nobody else's weirdness rattling around inside. Just me. At this point, I knew how to divest myself of other people's STUFF, but I didn't yet know how to avoid taking it on in the first place.

I went to a pharmacy and overheard the end of a conversation. It sounded like the woman at the counter had been trying to convince the pharmacist to give her strong painkillers. Evidently she didn't have a prescription and the pharmacist, believing her to be an addict, refused.

This woman passed me on her way out.

Immediately I had a clear experience of merging with her. I felt the shocking contrast between my previous sense of self versus the desperate emotions seething inside an addict who has just been refused a fix. The physically ill feelings of a body suffering from drug abuse. The spiritual twistedness that drug abuse creates.

This overwhelming experience nearly made me vomit.

Worse still was the realization that quickly followed. *I had been doing exactly this with everyone I had ever met, my whole life.*

What was the only difference this time? My sense of contrast.

Since then I have increased in skill as an empath. Gradually my health has begun to return. The number of patients I can treat in a week is increasing as well. My work is no longer destroying my health. And I can be in public without suffering other people's traumas.

— Adam McIntosh, Acupuncturist, Canberra, Australia

2. A High-Powered Business Coach Discovers Inner Silence

Getting skills as an empath has dramatically altered the texture and feel of my everyday life. Before I even knew what an empath was, I was taking in all of this noisy information from the people around me.

It was a little like having my car stereo on SEARCH and having it go from channel to channel, tuning in and then switching, whenever I was with other people. I learned to ignore it, but like ignoring the radio in a small car, it was not so comfortable.

I had this dawning awareness that everyone in the world was not experiencing what I was experiencing, and I was surprised. We tend to assume that our gifts are not that interesting because everyone must have them. That turned out to be not true at all.

I embarked on a search of the Internet, trying to find out what the heck was going on with me. I got a lot of quacks, and some very bad advice, until I found Rose.

When I wrote her, to sign up for the Empath Empowerment Workshop, here is a little bit of what I said:

I found and read your book, "Empowered by Empathy," and the top of my head spun around and wobbled back on, slightly askew....

When I read your book I realized that in everything I have done I have used Intellectual Empath Ability and Emotional Oneness to guide my work. I just did not call it that.

I have also had some very ungrounded, scary experiences of going down the rabbit hole with other people's strong emotions that worked as a vortex into which I got sucked and had to fight my way out.

And then last year I realized that I had to get a handle on my feelings, as they were too much what other people felt. I needed to learn to only feel my own feelings. That sounded impossible to me until I read your book.

When I went to that Empath Empowerment Workshop, I had one of the happiest moments of my life. I felt internal silence for the first time in my memory.

When Rose taught us to turn the unskilled empath merges OFF, and I did this as part of an extra-intense group experience, it was as though peace descended into me and I was so incredibly grateful and happy.

The other remarkable thing was it was easy. Once Rose explained the steps of the "Coming Home" technique and made it very simple, it was just easier not to do those unskilled empath merges. Easier, quieter, happier, and more satisfying.

Now I can pay attention to my human everyday life. I am less clumsy, distracted, and less tired from trying to block out the noise all the time.

My friends and kids and husband notice that I am more present and happier, and they feel better about their relationships with me. Without my doing all those unskilled merges, they are able to tell me themselves all the things they want me to know. They can keep to themselves the things they don't. And they don't have the odd feeling that "Michelle knows everything and has invaded their space."

Having learned how to do Skilled Empath Merges, sometimes I will do them, with the very simple steps of a dedicated technique, and this has been beautiful and educational. I can do these empath merges on purpose, and it is serving me and the other person to do so, and I am in and out and then I am able to go back to human life with gratitude.

It has actually made my skill as an empath much stronger to have learned to turn OFF the unskilled merges and only do the skilled ones. So, if anyone is worried that to have the skill you must let it run away with you, it's patently not true. You actually get better and better as you use your empath gifts more and more consciously.

— Michelle Auerbach, Communications Consultant and Executive Coach, Boulder, Colorado

3. A Skilled Empath Relishes the Texture in Her Teeth

As an empath I have Physical Oneness, which is very strong. I also have Spiritual Oneness. Before developing skills, life's been full of anxiety except when I've minimized contact with people or lost myself in things like books, work, etc.

I bought Rose's book for empaths back in March, and yes, wow, I've really started to fall in love with myself and the world.

I will never again be able to say "I'm bOOOred." It seems impossible that I ever could have been bored.

I have surfaces to my skin and texture in my teeth, an amazingly available mind, ever-changing feelings and ideas, shoes that make interesting spaces around my feet, a much better idea of the things that entertain me, some divine friends, and even the beginnings of a handle on Relationships With Other People. (Big hurrah on that one!)

I've gone through the book three times now and it deepens every time. It's like having a fresh sharp shower in good common sense, and it's been the most accelerated process of personal transformation I've ever undergone. In February I felt fogged, dull and stuck. Now I feel like me again.

So all that's been fun and challenging and relaxing... but this weekend something really amazing happened. I spent the whole day just in my own skin. No effort required, I was just inside my own skin all day.

I didn›t know it was possible to feel such peace. Everything inside and around me was smooth, calm, and peaceful. It wasn't empty; I was getting on with everything and having a normal day — but in this encasement of my own skin. And this feeling of complete wonderful peace stretching out as far as I could sense. It was stunning.

Why settle for a thimble?

I remember that Rose wrote somewhere that if you're asking the Divine for water, you might as well ask for it ocean-sized, because too many people ask only for enough to fill a thimble. I had a Lottery approach to that one. I thought "Well, all right, I'll ask for the ocean — might as well." But my expectations were thimble-sized.

Imagine ordering the ocean from Amazon and expecting it to arrive in one of their brown cardboard packages. Well, that was me. And the delivery turned up, and I opened the front door and yes, there's the ocean, right on the doorstep.

One thing about the ocean — it's quite big, and impossible to mistake it for anything else.

I'm so excited because I know this will become normal. Because that was just me with my empath gifts turned OFF. Also I'm excited because from that place I can actually connect with other people — not as "an empath" but as me.

Rose told me once that for non-empaths that sense of peace is normal. What an incredible idea. To me it seems like the best present I ever got in my life!

If I can live like that as standard and travel by choice out into the "other" then, YES, being an empath could become fun rather than a burden. And I never thought I'd say that and mean it.

— *Amanda Flood, Tai Chi Instructor, Cambridge, England*

4. Not Fixing, Just Living Ridiculously Well Here in Norway

Getting empath skills changed my life from feeling like a leaf in the wind — where I kept being blown into an emotional gutter. Gradually I have become a man who knows who I am, what I want, and how I want it. For years I used to live in fixing mode, waiting to figure life out before I could begin living it. In this fixing mode, I read a huge number of books, attended so many workshops, and learned so many different techniques.

When I met Rose, finally I found what I had been searching for. Empath skills taught me how to protect myself, and without first needing to solve all the big questions in life.

What else didn't I need to do any more? Push people away. Isolate myself. Or constantly feel the need to fix myself.

Turns out, I can protect myself without needing to manipulate anything, just by positioning my consciousness a little bit differently. How awesome is that? No need to figure out everything else about life, but just reposition my focus!

After learning that I was an empath — which came as a huge shock — pieces started to fall into place. I'll admit, at first I didn't believe in the idea of being an empath. Sometimes I have trouble believing it still, and I'm not even absolutely certain which empath gifts I have. But in desperation, I tried Rose's Empath Empowerment techniques. Despite not believing, my life gradually shifted. How could I not notice that?

I noticed. As the months go by, I feel more and more like I understand the meaning of "Coming Home."

What do I believe now, definitely? My relationships have improved. I can visit people without feeling the old kind of emotional cramp, where I felt forced to turn away and protect myself.

Constant worrying and other problems that burdened me? They have been falling away, too. At times I feel so passionate and juicy about my life, it's ridiculous!

— Astrit Wold, Social Worker; Oslo, Norway

5. A Revelation Like No Other for a Teacher in Singapore

It was a revelation like no other: That I was an empath and had the habit of merging in consciousness with random people, lifting their STUFF and making it mine.

No wonder I had spent my life avoiding people, running quickly back to the sanctuary of home. And no wonder energy shields had limited impact for me.

Reading Rose's book, I slowly began to understand... and soon I caught myself in action. At a meeting, I was sitting completely still and fully focused on the speaker. My own existence was totally forgotten; only the speaker existed for me. Catching myself, I broke the focus and felt a sudden relief.

I feared that the real cause of this was my not having a strong sense of self, and that was why giving my full attention to others came naturally to me. But then how could I develop that strong sense of self, as someone doing all those unskilled empath merges?

Understanding more about Empath Empowerment now, I realize that my sense of self was basically fine all along. I just lacked skills for turning my empath gifts OFF. Besides, it didn't help my sense of self when I was taking on all the Imported STUFF.

No wonder I blamed myself, and also blamed other people for sapping my strength. For good reason, after being with those people for a while, all I wanted to do was to get away.

The reason wasn't really their being a problem. Similarly the reason for my feeling overwhelmed was not that something was wrong with me. Nothing was deficient in my sense of self. I just needed empath skills to support my true sense of identity.

Becoming skilled as an empath, there have been many benefits to my life. I take an interest in people now, initiate conversations, and am able to spend longer periods with friends without feeling spent.

Recently, after an outing with two friends, I was pleasantly surprised to find myself still full of life when I got home. The old me would have had to retire early for the night.

Now, when I do go to bed, I am able to fall into a deep and peaceful sleep the minute my head touches the pillow!

I work more efficiently too, and I don't do tedium.

What else do I notice? In general, there is far more clarity. This helps me to set personal goals. As a skilled empath, I have so much more awareness of my life — and how I can continue improving it.

— Jeya Devi, Primary School Teacher; Singapore

6. Other People's Problems? No Longer My Problem

As a skilled empath, what really sticks out for me is how differently I handle people now, especially those with big problems in their lives.

When I was an unskilled empath I had a colleague who was questioning whether or not she wanted a divorce. Back then, I went home from work in tears and prayed for God to help her. How great was the anguish I felt over *her* decision about divorce? Mine was nearly as strong as hers.

And mind, I had never met her husband. Nor been married myself. And my parents aren't divorced, either.

What changed after I became a skilled empath? Here's one example. My music teacher told me that she was getting divorced. I made sympathetic noises and commiserated but did not have a conversation about it (although I could kind of see she was angling for one).

Six months later, we went out to a jazz show together. We laughed and joked about her ex-husband and my ex-boyfriend, because it seemed they had some similarities, actually. We had some deep conversation too, about revelations we'd had and our current views about romantic deal breakers.

What else is remarkable about this conversation? Despite the subject matter I didn't go home that night with any emotional pain. I felt happy that I had made a closer friend of her; I felt glad that we related to each other on the topic of breakups.

As for the original colleague, whom I cried my eyes out for? We haven't spoken in years.

More former problems, no longer my problem....

Another thing is poignant for me about when I was unskilled. Back then I very clearly made some people uncomfortable. On some level they surely knew that I was experiencing their mostly subconscious emotions and discomforts. This made our relationships stifling for them, even when I didn't say much.

For example, I used to be friendly with both the sister and the mother of an ex-boyfriend. They were very social and gregarious creatures who could charm anyone, and they were lovely.

However around me they struggled to maintain the facade of "Everything is fabulous, Darling."

They resented me. Why? I was unable to pretend that I had no clue about their unhappiness (or latent alcoholism), finding myself completely unable to respond enthusiastically to statements they made that I felt to be untrue.

Another problem when I was unskilled? This one happened when others around me had a strong opinion and articulated it forcefully: I found it very hard to argue my case or present my own opinion.

When I was having this discussion through a medium such as emails, I would be fine. In person, though, I would be kind of stuck — seeing the argument from their point of view and knowing that I didn't agree with it, yet not able to put forward a coherent stream of my own thoughts.

In general, as an unskilled empath it was hard to be "myself" as I didn't really know who that was. I became so influenced by other people's dramas, with my ups and downs coming to match theirs.

It wasn't until I became skilled as an empath that my sense of self became stable day after day, and I woke up in the same spirit, and the inner barometer of how my life was going became consistent.

Finally, before my becoming a skilled empath, it was also very easy to become co-dependent in relationships. I did have to break up with a woman who had become friends with me, back when I was unskilled.

Here's what happened. She didn't really take to my becoming skilled. When we were together she desperately tried to engineer our relationship back to how it used to be, which just made it wearying and tiring to be around her. Such a contrast to the rest of my life now, as a skilled empath!

She didn't understand why I no longer enjoyed (or vicariously experienced) all the drama she was having.

Before, because I was unskilled, I was constantly picking up random bits of her emotional pain. When experiencing my friend's situation from how she experienced it, I was responding and reacting from that position. Now though, I could relate to her without that. What did I find?

She was happy to just go in circles. Actually she had never listened to anything I suggested. I realized I wasn't enjoying the friendship and decided to walk away!

— *Emily Turner, Psychology Student; London, England*

7. Engineering My Life, Based on Having It Be MY Life

Empath skills have changed my life in many positive ways. But it was the concept of **EMPATH**, as used by Rose, which has been most important, allowing me to achieve a better sense of who I am.

It was a complete shock to me, learning that it was possible to have a direct experience of someone else, both consciously and subconsciously. Sure, I was aware of the word "Empath." But my understanding was limited. I thought I was just vicariously experiencing someone else's experiences.

Actually, at those times, I was also having those experiences subconsciously, too, in a direct and personal way (what Rose now calls "Prolonged Empath Merges"). Plus there were so many Split-Split-Second Unskilled Empath Merges. Between these two types of empath merge, I didn't notice how often I reacted to situations based on energies and emotions that weren't really my own.

With skills as an empath, my relationships are improving because I am now responding to social situations spontaneously as myself, not just reacting to the other person's energies. For example, the other day a colleague was telling me a story that was very emotional. I could feel the emotional charge, recognize it for what it was, and not claim ownership. I effectively said no inwardly and kept my empath gifts turned OFF.

The "Coming Home" technique has been especially helpful for me. I do it in the morning and it provides me with a baseline for how I feel throughout the day.

For me, Empath Empowerment is about developing a clearer understanding of who I am. It's about being the most important person in the room!

— *Paul Romero, Electrical Engineer; Philadelphia, Pennsylvania*

8. Where Did All Those Needy People Go?

Living as a skilled empath has become a way of life. Seldom do I consider the contrast with all those struggles that once were quite standard for me. It's not as though I congratulate myself, how amazing it is that now I routinely keep my empath gifts OFF.

Earlier this year I was reminded. I'd embarked on a project to declutter my home. This included going through a huge pile of old journals that I had kept for years.

When I picked up a journal from ten years back, oh, the angst! Pages and pages were filled with worries, my thoughts about other people.

Such mental turmoil I went through back then. How I interpreted all this worry was that I had to work hard to extricate myself from the claws of needy people.

Somehow I couldn't get away from them. It seemed that one needy person after another demanded attention.

Consequently I sought refuge journaling. On a regular basis I would spend hours retreating and regrouping, trying with pen and paper to figure out better ways to deal with one "terribly needy" person after another.

Only when reading this particular journal did I realize — with great joy — how far I'd come. Today I am not thrown off balance by other people's emotions, moods, and needs.

What made the difference? I'm convinced that the change has been mine, not anyone else's.

Perhaps they hadn't been so terribly needy after all... especially since I'm no longer falling into unskilled empath merge on a regular basis. Certainly I don't have to work hard at figuring out elegant ways to cope with other people's (alleged) incessant demands and insatiable needs.

All my empath skills have been acquired from Rose's book on Empath Empowerment. The skills required are subtle, even simple. While learning, I wasn't even sure that anything was really changing.

Reading that journal made me appreciate just how much more energy and focus are available to me — now that I can be myself more fully. No more inhabiting the needs of other people. Now I fill my own space.

— Rachel Murdoch, Teacher; London, England

9. Empath? So That's What It Is.

Growing up, I discovered I was sensitive. For a boy that was considered a bad thing — a weakness, not a strength.

Avoidance was the most effective strategy I found, although that was hardly a good life skill. Later I was startled to read, in one of Rose's books, how empaths often learn to be invisible. That was the story of my youth!

However, until I went to a conference in my 50's, I was oblivious to being an empath. In one session, they had us do an empath quiz. I was surprised to get a high score. But when I read the speaker's material later, she only covered a couple of empath gifts and I couldn't relate to them. So I had some information but nothing I could work with. I certainly didn't gain any skills or insight.

Skip forward some years and I ran into Rose Rosetree's work. Her Book One in the Empath Empowerment Series brought me a series of personal revelations. I discovered that I have multiple empath gifts, and that some of them were on all the time.

Once I became more conscious of my empath gifts, I was taken aback to discover I was constantly "reading" others. Previously I had no idea I was doing this. I also had no idea how to dial it down, let alone OFF.

OFF was completely unfamiliar. In experience, I had no reference point for it.

Ironically, all this reading of others was largely subconscious, so it was not adding anything to my interpersonal skills. Since childhood, I subconsciously had my antenna up all the time, checking if others were OK or safe.

In retrospect I appreciate this didn't help anyone. Especially when I was concurrently trying to be invisible! Mostly the effect was stressing me out, as I soaked up anxiety and other energies of people around me.

While not recognizing I was doing this, I was very aware of some of the effects; things I largely attributed to personal deficiencies. Like how I adapted to work environments and became a different person on the job. Then how I struggled to not carry that home with me. I also see now how this affected many of my life choices.

Once I learned about the importance of empath skills, I was rather astonished that I had understood so little about my gifts. But thinking back on it, I recognize why.

I was born with those empath gifts and lived with them all along. Not having grown into those talents, I felt no shift that would have allowed me to recognize them. Life as an empath was just part of how I experienced my world from day one. Now I'm shifting from random reader to skilled empath, thanks to Rose. What a relief!

— *David Buckland, IT Consultant; Vancouver, Canada*

10. The Problem Was Never My Boundaries. It Was Talent

For most of my life... therapists, teachers, friends, so-called friends, tarot readers, psychics... kept telling me that I did not have good boundaries.

They all suggested things I could do to have better boundaries... so that I would not be adversely affected by other people, certain kinds of plants, grocery stores, airplane rides.

The list was extensive... parties, motel rooms, books, etc.

I spent thousands of dollars on spiritual candles, salt and soda baths, crystals, smudging practices.

I imagined all kinds of bubbles around me.

I used aromatherapy.

Oh, the list is endless.

Bottom line? Until I learned to be a skilled empath, my life consisted of mostly trying to stay away from people and things.

Rose's system of Empath Empowerment® has allowed me to have a more relaxed and comfortable life. And compared to all the other complex gyrations I went through in order to feel safe in the world? This is simple, straightforward, and permanent.

I now use my empath abilities to help others. Now I see being an empath as the gift it really is... instead of the curse that I used to think it was.

— Linda Stone, Rosetree Energy Spirituality Practitioner; Carlsbad, New Mexico

Acknowledgments

Enthusiasm from my students motivated me to write the first book for empaths, *Empowered by Empathy*. Even more enthusiasm led to this series of Empath Empowerment® books.

The pattern is simple: Students keep teaching this teacher.

As a teacher of personal development since 1970, I get it by now. The more I teach, the more I learn. Every success at helping readers furthers my resolve to help whenever and however I can, while maintaining integrity.

By now I'm convinced that, more than anything else I have been given to teach, empath skills help people to live with a deeper spiritual awareness. Amazing and humbling it has been for me, how well my students have done.

After one workshop, it took a week for me to recover from just how well they did. Since the techniques had been a real stretch for me to develop, I expected my students would struggle at least a little. As if! The learning came easily to them, a far cry from my earnest efforts to teach them.

It's as though I had been a mother bird pushing little ones out of the nest, anxiously hoping my fledglings wouldn't have too much trouble working their wings. Instead they stretched and sailed so easily, exploring like the birds they were born to be. And as we all flew together, I heard them chirp to each other, "That nest was okay but, hey, didn't it seem a little confining?"

So, who taught this teacher, who sometimes struggles and other times feels like a proud nest emptier?

Let's start with my husband, Mitch Weber. No other person has understood me so well, accepted me so thoroughly, supported me so generously. Any success I have as a teacher is really *our* success.

What else? The naming of deep experiences was required for me to bring forth this system. Until you dare to trust the outer reaches of your perception, naming cannot progress. So I honor Rev. AlixSandra Parness and the late Rev. Rich Bell, both of them instructors in Teaching of the Inner Christ (www.teachingoftheinnerchrist.com), for modeling spiritual trust. This led to my ability to name empath gifts, experiences, and techniques.

Around the same time that I studied with AlixSandra and Rich, in 1985, Susan Kingsley-Rowe facilitated my first past-life regression. I revisited being among the multitudes who heard The Sermon on the Mount. Or its equivalent... since the experience hardly came complete with a theater marquee.

The chiming presence of Jesus re-awoke in my consciousness. Under Susan's expert guidance, I remembered more about what I learned, privileged like so many of us back in the day, striving to honor what we were given from such a teacher.

Ever since, it has seemed to me that one of the ways Jesus used to help people was this: Connected to Spiritual Source, he would fly in spirit into the energies of those who asked for help. Joining fearlessly, joyously, fully, and fully supported. Empath merge of this kind was appropriate to the energies of that long-ago era, The Age of Faith.

A dozen years after exploring that past-life regression, I was inspired to write the first book for empaths. Many years after that was published, I listened again to the sound recording made by Susan Kingsley-Rowe.

Only then did I intellectually make the connection. Both empath gifts OFF and Skilled Empath Merge had been modelled for me way back then. With Susan's help, in depth hypnosis, I had remembered how such a thing could be done.

My hunch is that this long-ago learning was carried forward into this lifetime, dormant until the memory was awakened. This inspiration is what made it possible for me to develop a variation on empath skills that would be suitable for our Age of Energy: How to safely live as an empath and, as appropriate, facilitate Skilled Empath Merge.

Other acknowledgements are due. So many teachers, healers, and students — definitely from this lifetime — have helped me to develop the system of Empath Empowerment. Indirectly, every one of you has helped to refine my empath talent. Even if space here does not permit my acknowledging all of you by name, my soul bears the imprint of every one of you. It is my privilege to carry your legacies forward.

One among you just has to be singled out, though. It's my most amazing college professor, at Brandeis University in the 1960's: Dr. Allen Grossman. This highly regarded poet used to tell us about a poet's job. And what was that job? To find the special excellence of a person or a place, then to express it with a true name.

Naming as a sacred process? Definitely possible.

The search for true names has taken me through poetry and religion, healing and metaphysics, relationship after relationship, and into finding language to coach empaths.

Acknowledging this long journey brings joy and plenty of other emotions as well. Back when I wrote *Empowered by Empathy*, I flashed on a bitter memory.

For 22 years after college I followed an Indian mystic, placing him on such a pedestal that I believed he was my only guide to Enlightenment. As a disciple, my life was devoted to teaching at his meditation centers. Studying directly with him for extended retreats, I would wait outside his door for hours on end, seeking in vain for a personal audience.

In all those years he granted me exactly one. Just one conversation. It lasted less than four minutes. At the end, I asked about prayer.

"Please, teach me how to pray," I implored. My guru laughed long and hard. "Find it in a book" he said, turning away.

That memory burned for years because I heard contempt in his laughter. Hours of daily meditation, devoted service as a teacher, seven years of celibacy, work upon work and tears upon tears, despite all that — and in spite of all I had learned from my parents and teachers before him — would I always be such a fool that I didn't even know how to pray?

As I wrote my first book for empaths and sealed it with my thanks, I realized how my techniques to fly in spirit, through empath skills... how that could be considered a form of prayer. I heard my guru's laughter again. Only now I could hear the love in it. Could it be that he foresaw and, in a twinkling, fore-read *this book*?

Evolving Empath, I'm so glad I found it and you did, too.

— *Rose Rosetree, Sterling, Virginia, May 2014*

Continue Your
Empath's Adventures

The Master Empath can help you to take your skills further.

Preview a sample chapter at Rose Rosetree's website,
www.rose-rosetree.com.

At my website you'll also find
The Online Supplement to *this* book:

- ∿ *Glossary*
- ∿ *Recommended Reading*
- ∿ *Index*
- ∿ *Annotated Table of Contents*

Other goodies? Galore!

For starters, through Rose's website you can:

- ∿ *Sign up for a free monthly e-newsletter,*
  "Reading Life Deeper."
- ∿ *Join a lively informal online community*
  through Rose's blog
- ∿ *Comment and guest post at "Deeper*
  Perception Made Practical"
- ∿ *Get to know other skilled empaths. Enjoy!*

Share Your Experiences, Evolving Empaths

Easy to get and effortless — that's your new set of empath skills.

Hey, *do you know what can be hard to get?* Book reviews.

Here is where you can help, Evolving Empath. Please write a review of this book, then share it at Amazon.com, barnesandnoble.com, goodreads.com, and any other book review websites you know.

Even a couple of sentences can make such a difference for other empaths.

You'll also be giving back to this indie publisher, who strives to bring innovation to spiritual self-help... and do it with integrity.

What else? So many of you empaths have wonderful stories, like those you've read here. They might be perfect for my future books or at the blog "Deeper Perception Made Practical."

I would love to read your tales of triumph. Send them to Rose Rosetree, 116 Hillsdale Drive, Sterling, VA 20164. Email to rose@rose-rosetree.com

It is so exciting. You are among the pioneering empaths in the world to develop these powerful skills.

It has been my honor to guide you through this Program for Empath Empowerment.

Evolving Empath, I wish you such happiness!

Printed in Great Britain
by Amazon

27468839R00178